Spirit Unbroken

the two sides of love

奇跡

Rick & Alice Garlock

INKWATER
PRESS

PORTLAND • OREGON
INKWATERPRESS.COM

For more information visit http://www.rickandalicegarlock.com.

Edited by Nancy Anderson and Anne Friendly
Cover and interior design by Masha Shubin

Asian_Girl © 2008 Lorelyn Medina. Image from BigStockPhoto.com

Library of Congress Control Number: 2008924573

www.inkwaterpress.com

ISBN-13 978-1-59299-331-4
ISBN-10 1-59299-331-1

Publisher: Inkwater Press

Printed in the U.S.A.
All paper is acid free and meets all ANSI standards for archival quality paper.

~ DEDICATED ~

-to each other-

~ ACKNOWLEDGEMENTS ~

Thanks to Nancy Anderson,
Lindsay Burt and Anne Friendly
&
SPECIAL thanks to the Helen Steiner
Rice Foundation for permission to reprint
the poem "Ideals are Like Stars"

Table of Contents

The Daughter's First Dance with Daddy

Somewhere over the rainbow when my promised destination finally arrives, I will pass through the Portal into the misty clouds. My first obvious inclination will be to seek out my Daddy's eyes.

I will no longer need to run.

My father will approach and say, "Princess, would you like to dance?"

I will bow to him in deep respect as he directs my hand to his shoulder and slips his hand onto my waist; smiling in "God's Presence" with a quiet confidence. I will feel safe in his arms as we waltz among soft billowy clouds together.

I will no longer need to be afraid.

Should my weak ankle give out he will remove my high heels, the ones I so vainly wore and slip on satin Japanese slippers…so that his daughter may thoroughly enjoy the dance in complete comfort.

I will no longer need to cry.

As the music stops and the nearing evening brings the cool wind's chill, my Daddy will sacrifice his coat for my warmth and gently drape it across my shoulders, sheltering me from the elements. Again firmly placing his strong hand upon my waist, he sweeps me off my feet as the next dance begins.

I no longer need to dream of love, I am experiencing it.

And so I pray for that day, when I find closure to my desperate childhood needs. I anticipate the special moments we will share as my life finally knows total emotional satisfaction, free of sin and filled with true comprehension of a love between a father and a child, and a daughter and her father...

Isak Dinesen says, "All sorrows can be borne, if you put them in a story." ***My husband says, "All stories can be told, if you are able to bear the sorrow."***

I awoke to the sharp tearing of what sounded like clothing, followed immediately by a grunt and muffled scream. 'What the hell?' My racing mind was prone to swearing what my mouth was not allowed to speak. Then I realized that Kathy was not in her bed and my racing mind turned to panic.

My eyes were riveted open and my ears strained to hear every sound. I could see nothing, but I heard everything. It sounded like the springs when I sneak into Mommy and Daddy's bedroom and jump up and down on the bed. Like the heightening of a wave on the ocean, the noise would come and disappear and then begin all over again.

Like a snake, my diminutive Japanese body slithered out of bed and crept down the hallway following the painful noise. I was careful not to give my presence away by stepping over the squeaky fourth floor board. I followed the sounds like a homing beacon to my parent's bedroom. The muffled scream had turned to a forced whimper rising above the awful screeching of those bedsprings. Both pain and the squeaking were increasing in intensity and rhythm.

It was Kathy!

Someone was hurting Kathy! My panic turned into fear for her life! What could possibly be causing such anguish? Who was hurting her? I was faced with a moment of truth. I could run and hide, or I could try and save my sister. In a heartbeat I knew what I had to do. As a child I couldn't do much, but it was Kathy in there being hurt! My Kathy! My fear boiled over into desire to defend my sister. Like a volcano erupting, the quake in my hand and the fire in my mouth came spewing out.

"You leave my sister alone!" I shouted, pounding my fists on the bedroom door. Sweat was pouring profusely down my face and tears stung my eyes. It was as if my fear exploded and I had become a wild woman. I could feel my nostrils rising and falling with each sharp breath; my hands numbing with each pounding blow.

Whatever, whoever it was... it ignored me. The sounds of pain and hurt and disgust filled the air with no regard for me and my deaf pleas. I began to cry.

Then suddenly it stopped.

I held my breath, fearing someone had killed Kathy. I froze at the door not knowing what to do. Then to my relief, I heard Kathy's shaky voice.

"I'm all right Amy," she whimpered. "Please go to bed."

Moving like a zombie the last thing I heard as I turned the corner into my bedroom was the soft crying of my sister.

And it was deafening.....

ABOUT THE AUTHORSHIP

This book is a true story, and a total collaboration between husband and wife – memories full of tragedy and triumph, contributions of both in the "telling" and the letting of tears are equally shared in the penning.

But ultimately only one person can be the "teller," so even though the actual written words are a collaborative effort, this extraordinary experience of life and lessons are told as only this story can be, through my wife's eyes.

I must also add that those eyes generate three loves in me:

> 1/ my personal affection rooted in the privilege of having witnessed her life's victories after a childhood of defeats
> 2/ infinite love of our family – immediate and extended
> 3/ the embers she continually keeps glowing in me for my love of writing

Without all, I am incomplete. And in touching the pen to paper together, I realized another form of intimacy with my wife I never knew existed.

The events about to unfold are Alice's, of which I was but a "bit player." The miracles within are hers and arrive with uncommon regularity from her drive and desire to "never give up." In the end, this drive is the power that fuels her soul and finds triumphs in life I can only aspire to... she is truly "a spirit that cannot be broken."

Rick Garlock

PRELUDE

This is a psychological thriller but with no surprise ending – it begins with my mother, a Japanese Korean War bride; and her courage spawned out of culture shock, religious pressures, a rare hereditary disease and the not so rare disease of alcoholism. And somewhere lost in this story, but now found, is me. I did not use some of the real names of family and friends; it proven otherwise too difficult to relive. False names gave me the distance from the events I so desperately needed to complete the task. I would say that "the names have been changed to protect the innocent," but in this story there are no innocents; only victims, survivors and soldiers of life.

And so life marches on.

Lured to America with half-truths and exaggerated promises – okay, lies – my mother dreamt of an extravagant lifestyle, better than the one she was accustomed to in Japan. Deceiving Japanese girls to make an impression appeared to be entertainment to the military, but getting them to marry was deadly serious. In fact, my mother told me that Dad had actually convinced her that the wealth was so lucrative in America, streets radiated with the flash of gold!

Two years after marriage and one daughter later, a second bundle of life was now marked on the calendar for birth in eight weeks. With his military stint up, he was heading home and was working feverishly to bring his new family with him. All was right with the world as Mom made the not so difficult decision to walk those streets of gold. She had won the heart of a military knight in shining armor. Her adventure was about to begin....

as was my life.

My husband jokes to this day that I was "made in Japan." Something he reminds me of every time I have to go to the doctor to fix my broken Japanese parts. An analogy long lost in the '60s and '70s since Japan is a world leader in economy and quality in the 21st century.

My mother had endured many things in Japan: World War II that brought the death of her pregnant sister after being kicked in the stomach by a Chinese soldier, and the fight of her independent spirit which put her at odds with her family and with the subservient Japanese culture for women. Hardship in America surely would be pleasant compared to the murderous past and stifling culture she had been reared in.

Her first introduction to American life was two dozen stray cats of all sizes and colors straggling up the dirt pathway to her new in-laws' house. The cats' eyes were glued shut with infection as they bounced aimlessly around, so aimlessly that Mom became concerned she might trip in her delicate condition with a "baby on board." She next noticed broken steps to a broken porch, covered in dirty pie pans caked with dried milk, as matted in the pans as in the cats' eyes. Several disgusting bugs gathered on the milk crust, some of which also covered the screen door that stood ominously ahead.

Behind the door held my paternal grandmother. Short, plump and with rosy cheeks flushed from the harshness of farm work, she stood shy of five feet tall. She could not look at Mom as she gruffed a "nice to meet you," greeting. I can imagine the strain in Mom wanting to hug as is the Japanese tradition, but afraid to do so. Grandpa was in the barn. His grand entrance was complete with manure on the boots from his chores. The stench didn't bother seasoned farmers, but it was revolting to my mother. She watched in shock as he tracked into and through the house without so much as wiping his feet or removing his boots at the door, as is the custom in Japan. His only acknowledgement was to my father with a "just what do you plan on doing for money?" grunt.

It became sorely apparent from that first step in cow dung at that stark, lonely and dilapidated farm buried in the Midwest that she had been duped by the many false promises of my father. Somewhere between the cold spring of 1957 and sweltering heat and horseflies of the summer, she demanded to go home. With the language barrier, an infant and a toddler, she might as well have been spending her time talking to the cows. Lonely is not a strong enough word for the betrayal that saturated her soul.

My father surprisingly agreed to let her go back to Japan, but with one sinister stipulation. Her abandonment from America and her marriage must be complete, including her children.

Tears stained her cheeks when she recalled the story to me years later; her look of porcelain skin long consumed by the weather of time and ravaged with illness. Tears also ran down mine, as I envisioned the slow unpacking; piece by piece of her luggage....and her broken heart as she selflessly prepared to remain.

INTRODUCTION

"make believe," or "make <u>me</u> believe"

It's a rude awakening to be in your early twenties before realizing you had lived your childhood pretending to be someone else. I was so consumed with living a constant "out of body experience" that I actually fooled "outsiders." I played at acting happy; so much so it became easier and easier to "fake." In reality, only the "insiders" knew I was constantly depressed.

Translation – my life was a chilled empty wine glass waiting to be filled; having never tasted the richness of life. I realized my glass had been empty because I had never been offered the opportunity to fill it. My family succumbed to constant degrading and little nurturing. As children, we were isolated from the outside world not so unlike my father's childhood. Unable to count on the strength of my parents, (having been proven time and again to be lacking) eventually I decided to rely on myself. It was either live in "make believe," or it was time to "make me believe" I was capable of more.

I turned to therapy which slowly educated and reformed my ideas and low opinion of self-worth. I saw my frightening past for the first time in frightening reality. Then therapy began seeding the changes of my future. I slowly began my transformation into a whole person. Through steely resolve, passionate counseling and spiritual healing, I found the person my childhood had lost

And I wept.

No longer did people notice that I spoke of myself in the third person as had been my habit – detached from hurtful memories. I had always taken pride in being upfront and honest to a fault and at times, a hurtful fault. Then in therapy I had an epiphany – I was a liar, a cowardly liar…causing me to briefly hate myself again.

And I wept some more.

Sucking it up, I realized that a coward is weak, and I refused to admit I was weak. It's true I had been dishonest about my personal identity most of my life. I had been living behind what I call my "Mask of Pretense." I had refused (to the extreme) to become that sad, pathetic person my father had become. And in doing so, I found that in the absence of loving myself, I had falsely been seeking love and reassurance from others. I had become a sick, needy person – the kind even I would want to avoid.

And then it became clear.

I was needy beyond compare. Parents are never perfect and no family is without fault. My family was dysfunctional, but I didn't need to be looking for attention that was never going to come. There is no pot of gold at the end of the rainbow, but that shouldn't diminish the beauty of the rainbow. Thus, therapy began nurturing three simple rules of self-growth:

> Step 1 lower my impossible standards and expectations
> Step 2 stop play-acting and get real with my feelings
> Step 3 stop patronizing myself and others will stop patronizing me

In this growth process, I began to realize that family tragedy was only a part of my problem; a major part, but not the whole. Any contact with my Japanese family was severed in my formative years; but that didn't mean not having the joy of relatives to understand my needs had to be the end of the world. In childhood, my absent Japanese family persisted in my mind as strangers in a distant land. With separation from my school peers *because* of my Asian background, I had a hard time finding any understanding of my heritage in America beyond shame. And I did not have to go to therapy to know shame's author, or who caused my isolation.

My father had been in control of everything in the Wesson household before I was even born … He is dead now and I give him all the forgiveness I can muster.

And at times I still want to call him a son of a bitch.

SPIRIT UNBROKEN

the end of the beginning

I snapped to reality with the gentle touch of Rob's hand. I wasn't sure if it was the rain on the plane's window or the moisture welling in the corner of my eyes that caused my blurry vision as I looked down over Fukuoka City, Japan.

Rob had promised since marriage to make this trip someday – and suddenly 23 years later, someday was now. He was not negligent in keeping his promise even if his blond hair was receding; his mustache showed flecks of gray and his stomach had grown six inches since our marriage vows. A doting father, a hardworking businessman and a faithful husband, all 5'7" of his stubby frame was anything but negligent.

No, this was a dream of patience. For almost 50 years I had no connection with my maternal family. Mom tortured us with our lack of heritage – she never taught us Japanese, never instilled pride in our family roots and never took us to Japan to meet our relatives. I guess I should never say "never," because outside that window, never was now…

We had left Tokyo at dusk, and from the air a sunset never looked more new. As we skirted silently down toward Fukuoka, my heart never felt so refreshed. I was so ALIVE. I was about to touch the family that took so long to find. I was about to hold <u>my</u> blood in <u>my</u> hand and bond with <u>my</u> family.

I was about to complete the end of my journey, and I was scared.

Fears of early childhood rejections crept in and fed on a newfound fear of rejection again. Suddenly I was thrown back to that small town in rural Indiana where everybody knows the goings on of everyone else, especially the latest news of the arrest of Mr. Wesson for public intoxication.

But the alcoholic rages were only a small portion of the embarrassment that I carried. The realization that my own father actually planned the abuse of my sister and me was ingrained in our souls for a lifetime. The damage my father caused and the violation of the sanctity of our family forever weighted the plane down more than the five extra bags of luggage I had packed.

How ironic that I spent my formative years cowering from him, and now with the memory of the smell of his alcohol burning in my nostrils, he was present in my last thoughts before completing my journey.

As I crossed the Sea of Japan, a spirit unbroken; the two sides of love were very much present. One sitting beside me, and one whispering in the dark closet of my mind...

"Amy! Get out of bed right now!"

I was so sleepy! 'Daddy, just go away....PLEASE just go away. Don't get me up again,' I silently sobbed. I always wished he would go away but even at four years of age I knew better than to ignore his drunken roar. Stumbling barefoot into the kitchen, I was greeted with the foul stench of vodka in the air.

Daddy was flashing a shiny new pocketknife in front of my red-rubbed eyes. He stood there in all his foul smell of booze, his square frame outlining the rest of him. His light brown hair and weather-lined face betrayed his sly grin. My warning bells began to scream.

'I'm awake now' I thought, as fear gripped my shaking chest.

Seeing my body convulsing on the edge of tears, he commanded, "Take five steps back." I froze; wanting to move but the weight of fear holding me down. He laughed in a tone I did not understand.

"Amy, take five steps back right now. I need to practice with my new knife and if you don't do exactly as I say, then things could go badly for you…and then I would be forced to practice on someone else. You don't want that, do you? You don't want to bleed and then be the cause of someone else to bleed would you? Now, take FIVE steps back! Five giant damn steps!"

I hesitated, not knowing what to do while sucking in so much air my lungs felt like they were going to explode.

"NOW dammit!"

I did as I was told. All the fear in the world could not keep me from wanting to protect Mommy, Kathy and little baby Brock.

"That's better," he cooed at me.

'I have to be brave,' I thought, as we all knew the harder we cry the more Daddy hurt us.

"Shut the hell up. Now do not move," he cautioned sadistically. I wasn't sure what was going to happen, but I didn't like the tone of that last remark.

'What could he possibly do to me that he hasn't done before?' my mind screamed. But I kept quiet as I concentrated. I wanted to be brave…and I couldn't look at Daddy. I would just hate him more if I did that.

All my life I wanted him to love me.

'Daddy, why don't you love me?' my mind wandered, when suddenly I was snapped to attention, freezing my body rigid as the knife struck the floor between my feet. Shocked and then by reflex, I began to hop frantically up and down.

"Daddy, no," I sobbed, scared by what he had just done, and of what he might do next. "Please don't hurt me. Please Daddy, don't! Please don't! DON'T!" My hands were flopping at the ends of limp arms like a bird trying to escape a cage it knew it could not. Staggering forward he removed the knife stuck in the floorboard, accompanied with his awful twisted smile, which he stuck flush in my face. His shirt hung open, and I could smell the stink of his sweat.

"Pretty good, huh?" he gloated. "I told you this knife was a winner."

"That's a sick mother of bitch you have there, Ammieee," he snorted, slurring my name. "Ain't that pathetic that she's in bed, dead to the world on prescription drugs while your life is in my hands? Mother of a Bitch, ain't she? Hey that's pretty good, I guest that means either you or your sister will grow up to be bitches. What the hell, it will probably turn out to be the both of you." Then, turning calm, he said, "Well, I won't let you grow up like her. This will toughen you up."

Inches from my face, he rose from his squat by putting both hands on my shoulders and pressing down hard. The blade passed next to my left ear as he arose. Out of the corner of my eye I could see the coldness of its steel as I continued to whimper.

"Stop that crying. I'm doing this for your own good, you sniveling snot. Now, I want you to take one giant, giant step backward for me."

As the pressure of his weight slowly lifted from my shoulders I wanted to run. I wanted to hold Mommy, and I was so angry I wanted to hurt Daddy. But my fear was stronger than my anger. I took a step back, but only a baby step instead of a giant one.

This time I watched Daddy through my stinging tears. I was afraid, but I was determined not to show it anymore. He raised his muscular arm slowly. I counted the seconds with each pounding of my heart. Then, in a flashy blur, the hunk of ivory and silver came hurling at me again. This time I jumped in the air with a blood-curdling scream just as the knife landed right where my left foot had been. I rolled over backwards in dead fear. Scrambling to my saved feet, I turned and ran down the darkened hallway in my dirty tee shirt and soiled underpants, screaming for all I was worth.

Somewhere in the distance I heard Daddy yell, "Good reflexes kid," and then he broke into a drunken haughty laugh.

Later, I crept along the cold linoleum floor holding my breath. It was scary dark, but I inched along more determined than any four year old should have to be that I would steal that knife. It took hours, or at least it seemed like hours before Daddy had fallen asleep… and it took a couple more hours for me to find the courage to slide out from under the sheets and begin my plan.

Daddy had collapsed in a rumpled heap next to Mommy in bed, apparently satisfied with his night's work.

'If Daddy hears me he could get me up and do something worse,' I thought silently. But Daddy did not wake up.

I calmed myself with the thought of Mommy protecting me as she does when she tucks the tattered covers under my chin and kisses my forehead each night before waddling off in the dark.

My plan was simple. I had to get the pain away. I had to get that knife. I had to feel safe again. I had to protect Mommy and Kathy and Brock. I shivered as I slid out of bed and with determination, inched near Mommy and Daddy's bedroom.

I knew in the dark when I had reached the bedroom door by the smell…that stinky, stinky smell of sweat and booze. It made me stop crawling long enough to hold the gag in my throat back with both hands over my mouth. In a few seconds I gained control of my stomach. No problem. Over time I had become a master at holding back vomit.

I hated eggs. Especially the way Dad cooked them…if you could call them cooked. The more I complained that they were slimy, the more he would undercook them; yellow goo in a slimier white pool of more goo. One morning I cried while gagging on my eggs and threw up. Immediately Daddy made me lean over my plate and lap up my own vomit like a dog. I threw up three more times and three more times I ate my own puke. On the fourth time, I kept it down long enough to get up and run to the bathroom, choking and crying in convulsions. I learned shortly after to control my stomach by mentally shutting down about what I was eating. I had to because it was now a game with Daddy. The more disgusting he could cook something, the more he enjoyed watching me eat it.

I became very good at hiding food I didn't want to eat. A hiding practice I was about to put to the test with Daddy's new knife.

Breathing only when my lungs felt like a balloon ready to pop, I felt in the dark for Daddy's pants on the floor. He never hung them up. He just dropped them where he lay; it didn't matter what room in the house.

Suddenly the snoring stopped. I froze, desperately trying to blend into the background of the speckled linoleum.

'Be very, very still,' I heard my mind say in the back of my head. 'He'll kill you if he finds you. He will.' My chest hurt from my heart pounding. Thoughts of 'Mommy, please help make it stop. Make Daddy go back to sleep cuz I can't...' led my soul's battle cry against my panic

My legs began to cramp just as the snoring began again. Letting the toxic air out of my lungs, I slowly began breathing. The tension began to leave my tiny body as I began moving myself forward. There, half under the bed was Daddy's crumpled smelly pants. I groped the musky jeans in the dark for the knife. There it is! I felt the cold handle in the right pocket. Got it! Grabbing the knife ever so gently, I slipped out of the bedroom. I continued my exit crawling halfway down the hallway for fear the sound of my bare feet running would wake the monster in Daddy again. I pattered into the kitchen and with a stroke of ingenuity slid the knife under the refrigerator, then reached up and placed it forever on a rusty metal edge underneath.

Satisfied with my hiding place, I thought, 'Mommy never cleans under there. We'll be safe now....'

I jumped up and scampered to my bed before anyone could catch me, but I was haunted by one last thought as I pulled the tattered covers up over my head.

'Safe until the next time. God, please, don't let there be a next time.'

The next day Daddy went to work without so much as a word to Mom or me. But he fawned over my older sister – his *angel* is what I always thought. Still, I was glad. Not talking to him is much preferable in my already abused mind.

Evening however, brought not only darkness, but another dark cloud over our house.

A large set of faded black mahogany double doors separated our kid's bedroom from the living room. On each door hung yellow stained opaque curtains covering the small paned glass in the doors.

Through the corner of the pane Kathy, Brock and I watched Mommy and Daddy in our usual church-mouse silence. They had begun to argue as soon as Daddy had barreled home through the front door, leaving it standing wide open. The anger was like watching the ocean water rising and then falling at evening tide. I never knew who won, the earth or the sea, so I guess it's always a tie. I only hoped Mommy and Daddy's fighting would end in a tie too.

Suddenly, in horror our eyes jumped and then froze wide open. Daddy grabbed Mommy and flung her through the air as if she were a thief that had just broken into our house. But it was Mommy's house too! I screamed at the same time Mommy did as she landed in the television screen, glass shattering and invading her body; her cries of agony shattering my ears. Without thinking, I ran through the mahogany doors to protect my protector. Kathy and Brock stayed put. But halfway there, I wished I had stayed put too.

As I approached I could see that her knees were embedded through the glass, and that glass now lay everywhere on the floor. Whimpering, Mommy stopped me with her extended trembling arm and begged me not to step in it with my bare feet. When I stopped, unsure of what to do, Mommy hoarsely whispered in broken English to bring her a towel. I saw why. Blood was everywhere; on her legs, on the TV and all over the floor.

I backed up slowly and watched in shock as Mommy tried to escape the grip the glass had on her body. I whimpered as she screamed in pain. I had to help! I just had to! I ran and got a towel out of the bathroom, returning in time to see the flesh tear on her leg as she tried again in vain to escape. She stopped when she saw me, and with a faint smile, she took my offering of the towel and began to soak the blood from her legs. Almost calm now, I was spellbound in amazement as Mommy suddenly took a deep breath and then forced herself to stand by yanking her body backward, ripping her knees as the embedded glass broke off in her legs.

Free at last, she pulled out two pieces of broken glass and then placed the towel over the gaping wounds. I ran to Mommy and wrapped my arms around her neck holding on to her for all I was worth. In the background, I heard Daddy scream a distant string of swear words then watched his hulking body fade as he stormed out the open front door in a fit of rage. He was not the least bit sorry for the pain he caused Mommy. He was upset because he couldn't break her like he broke other things around the house; like he just broke the TV.

But Mommy's spirit was too strong. I held her for several minutes as she dabbed her wounds with my towel, and I could feel her determination in life as I continued to clutch her tightly around the neck.

Secretly I was hoping some of Mommy's courage was passing to me...

Chapter 2

out of the darkness comes light

We were sooo relieved not to miss connections in Tokyo. Rob, the "ever ready" traveler was sooo concerned. We had departed from Chicago late and had less than 50 minutes to deplane, clear immigration, get our luggage, clear customs, transfer to another terminal, check in, check bags, clear security and board – all in a foreign airport, in a foreign country, and one that Rob had not frequented. The consummate traveler that was my husband never liked to be late…and showed it.

His concern was genuine. Should we miss connections, it would be after midnight before we could catch another flight to Fukuoka. In the meantime, our relatives would be stranded, with no way of contacting them. We did not know if they had left home yet or if they even had a cell phone. And perchance if we could call, the language barrier was still an ever-looming problem. True to my word to Rob, I had purchased Japanese CDs and had studied fever-ishly the weeks before departure. However great my skills were in repeating phrases on the CD, common communication was circling somewhere in the great unknown. The trip was actually scheduled with the help of a friend and Japanese native from our home town. We were told and assumed my Japanese cousin would be at the airport, but in fact we were in the dark – flying blind and fueled by faith.

My Japanese friend Soshi was a miracle. My father had forbidden mother to teach any of the children Japanese. Her expression of her heritage and Japanese culture came and went like the seasons. If Dad was lenient, a phrase, a song, an oriental dish sprang up in our house. But should the wrath of Dad fall, the Japanese culture was buried in hibernation until the next thaw and only then would our heritage crop up in our lives again. Unfortunately, the attitude of winter lasted much longer than the other seasons of our lives.

Communication was severed early in my life with our family in Japan, in part due to the expense of phone and travel, but mostly due to the fact that Dad was a control freak. Mom's family represented something that threatened that control.

Later, after Mom's death, I had given up all hope of finding my Japanese family. The time lost and distance seemed insurmountable. My sister and I had searched periodically throughout our adulthood, only to get discouraged when we could not locate anyone.

Initially when Mom died, our hope of finding the Suzakis was ironically renewed at her passing. Feeling obligated to try to notify family in Japan of her death, we incorporated the aid of a fraternity of some of the best detectives in the world – funeral directors.

The funeral director sent a certified letter to a last known address of twenty years ago, alas with no results. We assumed they had moved, it was lost in the Japanese mail or they couldn't read it. There was also the real possibility that they simply didn't want anything to do with what we were sure they considered "the bastard children of a renegade sister." Reluctantly, we gave up for the next several years.

Then, thirteen long years after Mom's death, a series of miracles began to happen, slowly at first and then cascading in a domino effect.

First, Rob changed jobs. The winters of Indiana were traded for the warm summers of North Carolina. I was not intending to work when we moved, but soon boredom set in, and I took a job at a Woman's Health Clinic. At the death of my father, yes, my father – the clinic gave me a gift certificate to a local masseuse named Soshi. Anyone who knows me knows I like to talk, so somewhere between my shoulder blades and neck, Soshi heard the story of my lost family.

In her broken English, she encouraged me to bring her anything of Mom's to look at and perhaps help unravel the mystery of my missing Japanese family.

'Yeah, right,' I thought, having been down this path before. Almost in a blind trance, I went home and found virtually everything that remained of my mother's life. Except for a few pictures, her remaining evidence of existence had been relegated to a dilapidated shoebox that contained a few meager letters and some Japanese scribbles on torn corners of paper. I returned to Soshi a couple of weeks later, more out of a conditioned routine to the many failed searches than with any hope of success.

Soshi had moved to the United States with her American husband twenty years ago. Her husband passed away at the tragically young age of 43. Soshi saw to it that her two sons were raised as patriotic Americans. Still, she did something my mother had not. She proudly taught her customs to her children, and made sure they traveled every few years to Japan to keep the heritage embers burning in their lives.

The next miracle happened when Soshi stopped in shock as she rifled through Mom's tattered remnants. In a trance, she slowly raised a particularly worn envelope then abruptly began shaking it for all she was worth.

Her excitement got me excited as I frantically asked, "What is it? What IS IT?!"

She said, "This address…" then pausing for effect, "this address is my old neighborhood!" I turned pale with a combination of excitement and fear. I wasn't sure that it meant anything. After all these years…

And then, another miracle found its way into my life. Soshi was returning to Japan in two months! It was not practical for me to go with her at that time, but Soshi took it upon herself to go find my family on her trip. She introduced herself as my friend wanting to help establish contact. In the end, my two aunts whom we had spent years trying to locate were oddly reserved and Soshi recommended not making contact, but my uncle's family (we came to find out he had died shortly after Mom) was excited to hear from me through Soshi.

The last miracle was that Rob was given a new assignment at work, requiring him to travel to Japan. After that, there were no more miracles to be had in finding my long lost dream. Only hard work remained over the next year to make it happen.

I smiled to myself as I continued to look out the airplane on final approach and recalled our harried connection in Tokyo. I had no fear of making connections. God would not have taken me halfway around the world only to be late. As if a prayer had been answered when we had landed at Tokyo Narita Airport, we were immediately greeted with the efficiency of the Japanese and their ever-constant drive not to "lose face." They simply were not going to allow us to miss our connecting flight.

An attendant from the airline met us at the plane instructing us to go to the end of the hall, all the while assuring us that we WOULD make our connection. We were slightly puzzled at their confidence in our being able to navigate in a new airport in a foreign country, and unable to speak the language. Our answer greeted us at the end of the hallway – another attendant was there holding a sign with our name on it. Identifying ourselves, we were directed to go down the escalator to immigration. After clearing immigration in record time, another attendant greeted us with a polite bow and instructions on claiming our luggage and clearing customs. Again in record time we were through customs and yes, greeted by another attendant who not only escorted us to the terminal transfer bus but loaded our luggage as well.

All along the way we were being issued a departure time countdown, ensuring us that we would make our connecting flight. But in the new terminal Rob didn't know whether to smile because he was going to be proven right and miss the flight, or cry because it looked like we were definitely going to miss the flight. At the check-in counter was a herd of passengers a country mile long. But then in a country minute, as if spotted adrift in this ocean of humanity – you got it – an airline attendant greeted us with assurance and promptly escorted us to the front of the line. Clearing security was a breeze and we found ourselves boarding the plane with five minutes to spare. Rob was wrong and I was right and that doesn't happen often. If I smoked, I would have lit up a cigar just to celebrate!

I was shaking when we landed. Me, not the plane. I looked a mess. I had been traveling for twenty hours and crying inwardly and outwardly for the last ten minutes. It was truly a miracle. I was finally landing in Fukuoka City, Japan. JAPAN! Overwhelmed with joy and driven to put my best impression forward, I made Rob promise to let me visit the restroom and put on "my face" before greeting my newfound family.

What could he say; it's the Japanese in me! My mother would have been proud.

―――――――――

Mommy was beautiful. I was lucky to have such a pretty Japanese Mommy. No other Mommies looked like mine. That made her special. But tonight while Mommy was soaking in the bathtub as was part of her daily ritual in turning beautiful, Daddy came bursting through the front door with lunch pail still in hand, demanding to know where she was.

Visibly shaken, Kathy answered in a timid voice, "Mommy's in the bathroom." Without so much as looking at Brock or me, Daddy made a beeline for the bathroom door only to be stopped by the doorlock. We held our breaths as we feared the worst. In one step back and then a flashing burst forward, the door lock splintered under the brute force of Daddy's shoulder. Kathy, Brock and I ran and cowered around the corner of the couch. We heard raised voices. Japanese words were being shouted in the air. I never knew how Daddy could be so smart to learn Japanese and act so dumb. Arguing in a foreign language was a game to Daddy. It showed Mommy he was superior, and it showed us kids, we were inferior too. That was all right with me. I did not want to be superior if I had to be like Daddy.

Slowly I inched forward in a half-bent crouch to better see what was happening. Kathy grabbed at me to keep me from getting involved, but I reached back and slapped her hand away. It frustrated me not being able to understand Japanese, and all that yelling made me want to see what was going on.

As I reached the bathroom door, the yelling abruptly stopped. His eyes and face were burning red in a fit of rage as he slowly walked toward the bathroom sink. Then without warning, his Hulk-like strength ripped the bathroom sink right out of the wall! My eyes saw a hole where the sink used to be. Water spewed in the air and was soaking the floor! I stood there paralyzed, my mind not believing what I had just seen.

Then, as if Daddy did this everyday, he tossed the sink onto

Mommy's naked body in the bathtub. It seemed light as a feather as it flew through the air then bounced off the wall and landed with a sickening thud on her. Water splashed out of the tub and up the wall, adding to the mess I was already standing in. The thud came from Mommy's lap as the sink landed on her, followed by the slow escape of air from her lungs from its sheer weight. Almost as if giving in to pain would be giving in to Daddy, Mommy sat naked and stone-faced, not looking at Daddy but looking at me. Her eyes were bottomless pools of pain.

Not getting the reaction he wanted, Daddy reached for his water-soaked lunch pail and pulled out a carton of orange juice and a bag of sugar. He held the carton over Mommy's head and poured the orange juice all over her. When the orange juice was gone, he opened the bag of sugar and dumped its contents on top of the orange juice that now soaked Mommy's hair and face.

I could see Mommy's chest heave up and down as she huffed bravely, fighting the pain and humiliation. I stood frozen in time not knowing what to do, when I realized that Kathy and Brock were standing beside me too. We were so scared none of us could move as Daddy tried to make his way out of the bathroom. Not to be stopped by a bunch of snotty nosed kids, he gave us a mean shove and pushed his way past our trembling bodies. As soon as he cleared us, we bolted to Mommy to help remove the sink. Once free, we held her in comfort. We didn't care if she was naked, and we didn't care if she was sticky from the orange juice and sugar. She was all we had, and we never wanted to lose her. Never.

"Okay, it okay," she cooed, trying to reassure us. "He crazy man. He crazy. But I protect you. No worry about me. I protect you." I looked up and saw the tears staining a trail in the sugar on her face. And her hair, her beautiful shiny black hair - I thought it must surely be ruined. We were clinging to both of her naked shaking legs, getting soaked by the shower of water spewing from the broken pipes that jetted from the hole in the wall, and we didn't care.

"We love you Mommy," we all whimpered over and over. "We love you."

Under my breath I seethed, 'I hate you Daddy. And I hate you enough for Mommy too.'

• • • •

I watched Mommy apply makeup every morning and on special nights, and tonight was special. She was going to call *her* Mommy in Japan. She always dressed up to call Japan, almost as if they could see her. I didn't understand how that could be, but I knew dressing up always makes her feel better. After the horror of the bathroom sink, I was sure Mommy needed to cover both her black bruises on the outside and her crimson shame on the inside. And when Mommy was pretty, I felt pretty.

So I crossed my legs and straightened my skirt as lady-like as possible as I settled onto her bed, observing every stroke of her preparation. She brushed her black glossy hair, and then carefully teased it into a French twist. Next was the lipstick. Mommy's ivory skin needed no makeup and Daddy always said we couldn't afford it, but Mommy always put on lipstick every day, whether she went out or not.

The vanity she was sitting at was older and more broken down than our house. I was sure it was left there when the house was abandoned years ago; before we ever moved in.

'Victorian,' I heard Daddy call it, 'and damn lucky to have it.' Daddy damned a lot of stuff.

The reflection was all distorted when I looked at myself in the vanity mirror. I always looked funny. Mommy's reflection was always different though. She appeared to me as a painting – cool, smooth and soothing to my eyes. I wanted to freeze her reflection today and hide it away in my bedroom where only I could gaze on her beauty… and wish to be like her someday.

Looking clean and neat, and obviously pleased with herself, Mommy got up and paraded happily to the phone on the kitchen wall. I could tell she was in a gay mood as I tagged along skipping close behind. I was worried for her though. Before calling Japan Mommy was always happy, but afterward she was outwardly depressed; sometimes for days. She also would cry a lot. Daddy couldn't do anything with her when she got like that. She didn't ignore us kids but most times after calling Japan, she looked like a zombie from Saturday morning cartoons

I don't know what made today special, but it seemed to Mommy that it was.

It must have been special to Daddy too; *evil special* - because right in the middle of Mommy's call and with me sitting in the kitchen trying desperately to understand the funny sounds of Japanese clucking, Daddy burst in from the living room like the Looney Tunes Tasmanian Devil.

"I told you for the last time!" he shouted. Then, with monster-like strength he grabbed the phone box...ripped it out of the wall and tossed it in the trash. Disgusted, he stomped past me as I sat as a mouse in my chair. Mommy was in shock. But this time she didn't take it. She suddenly ran after Daddy crying and pounding on his back with doubled fists. I couldn't believe my eyes. Mommy was going to get herself 'kilt,' and I was gonna have to watch! But for the first time ever, Daddy didn't respond to Mommy's violence directed at him. He surprised me as he continued to walk out the front door to the car with Mommy wailing on him the whole time. She was screaming and pounding all the way until he got in the car and drove away.

Mommy slumped to the ground sobbing until she ran out of tears as the neighbors came to their front porches to see what all the commotion was about. But as Daddy drove away, not one of them came to help Mommy. I didn't understand why, and I don't understand why losing the phone hurt Mommy so. She had been beaten and abused much worse before. After all, it was only a phone.

Maybe mental abuse hurts sometimes more than a good beating. All I know is that Mommy won't be calling Japan for a long time... maybe years...maybe never...

• • • •

EDITOR'S NOTE: Years later Amy's father confessed to her that everything he did was cold, calculating and planned. He was training his wife with his version of military tactics – to incite complete obedience by breaking the spirit. And as the father, he was about to commence training on his children...

• • • •

I hate the night.

Most bad things in my life so far have happened at night. I lie awake at night frozen in the dark, expecting something evil to grab me from under the bed. The shadows play on the wall as I watch them. They form scary shapes and I am certain they will grab me at any moment. At times I whimper, and then the same as the countless times before, Kathy comes to my rescue cuddling me and making me feel safe and warm. Never complaining, it seems she comforts me in ways Mommy and Daddy can't.

This night was different though. I didn't have time to go to sleep before Daddy got us out of the bed to "play a game" with us. This was a rare treat. Daddy in a playful mood was not normal, so my guard was up. Games are supposed to be fun, and his voice was very playful too. Maybe this time it would be different. Maybe I'll enjoy this...maybe Daddy is changing...maybe....

Maybe not.

"Kiddoes, why don't we play soldiers? I want you to get in a straight line and march around the house!"

Brock and Kathy were at attention before I could even get out of bed. They were just excited that Daddy was speaking to them, and in a tone of voice that was spiked with excitement.

"Why do you always have to give me such a hard time?" Daddy chastised as he gave me a stern look for joining "formation" late. Kathy raised her eyebrow in disapproval as if to say, 'don't mess up a good thing.' She was always much better at understanding how things worked than me, so I decided to toe the line.

Kathy's look made me begin to feel guilty thinking so poorly of Daddy's motives. Out of fear of being left out, I sprang to the back of the single file line of three, and began following his rapid commands.

"Turn left! Turn right! Halt! About face!" he barked.

We giggled as we bumped into each other clumsily. Then we giggled again, just to be silly.

"Quiet in the ranks!" Daddy bellowed. "Are you stupid? Can't you follow a simple order? Keep a straight face or you'll be sorry. I'll drive you till you drop!"

We marched around the house. In and out of every room, we marched.

"One, two, three, four!" he snapped. "Straighten that line boy!" he yelled at Brock. "Get your lazy butt up there with private Brock, Amy!" Brock was only three; two years my junior, but he was big for his age. My little legs could not keep up with him so I constantly lagged behind. Besides, we were not soldiers. What was he thinking?

After what seemed like hours my feet began to hurt. I didn't know about my brother and sister, but I wasn't having fun anymore. It seemed like the only one having fun was Daddy.

"We will quit when I say we quit!" he railed, sensing our exhaustion. He began barking orders faster and faster. We all knew by the stern look on his face that we had better do it perfectly, or we would be here all night.

When his "game" finally ended, we were all on the brink of crying. In bed we did not speak to each other for fear Daddy would be listening, and in anger, start the game all over again.

I stuck my head under my pillow and silently cried in the dark. Why did Daddy have to be so mean? Then out of the dark came my shining light. Out of the dark, I felt the gentle hand of Mommy touching my shoulder under the sheet. I sprang upright and hugged her for all I was worth. Then, positioning herself between Kathy and me at the end of the bed, she gently began rubbing our sore and exhausted feet. I forgot all that Daddy had put us through, and was so glad to have Mommy...

Then for the briefest moment, I was something I wasn't very often. I was happy...

Chapter 3

two halves make a whole

Rob waited outside the ladies room of Fukuoka City Airport.

All I could think of was how important it was that I make a good first impression. And so true to his word he allowed me the luxury of making myself up as he paced somewhat impatiently outside the airport restroom. We were practically the first ones off the plane, but I needed as much time as possible to remove the tear streaks and hide two tired pouty eyes, as I put on my "new face."

In the middle of applying makeup to my bottom lip, I heard Rob's patience start to finally wane. "Come on, honey. Everyone has claimed their luggage and left. We're the last two people here. I'm worried that if we go through security too late, your family would have given us up for not being on the plane."

"Okay," I responded back through the doorless entry to the restroom. I continued on with my lipstick. I wasn't sure if it needed that much attention, or if I was like a bride at the altar experiencing self-doubt.

"We are in a foreign country, don't speak the language, and don't have any other place lined up to stay. What are your plans if we miss meeting your family?" Rob howled, now openly frustrated with my subconscious procrastination.

Good point.

I emerged with a new sense of urgency, grabbing onto Rob's arm and hustling the bags through airport security and into the unknown. I was concerned that in a Japanese crowd I could be standing beside my relatives and not even know it was them. We had exchanged pictures by email but...

I had given this concern some forethought and had decided to take a picture with me they could easily recognize. The picture I took was of our grandson in a Japanese outfit (previously mailed to us by my cousin Hidetoshi). His wife Miyuki had made the furry kimono-type jacket for their son Uuto. It would be an easy spot for them... As I glanced over at Rob, it was a good thing I brought it. His blonde hair and very American features would have stood out... if only you could find him. He was buried under a cart filled with eight bags of luggage, desperately trying to navigate something that had a mind of its own. If I hadn't been so tired and nervous, I would have laughed.

As we walked through the glass doors into the open forum, I scanned throughout the scattered crowd with darting, anxious eyes, clutching my grandson's picture. Then to my surprise, I spotted a huddled family to the right, clutching a picture of me!

I wanted to cry, but couldn't. A million emotions pulsed through my veins. I was tired and spent. I was both reserved and wary of what they would think of me, and I was filled with joy beyond description. But through all these emotions I knew one thing...As I rushed to hug my Aunt Iseko, I knew I had a maternal family for the rest of my life.

The embrace was quick but firm, and then I was passed to Miyuki and Hidetoshi, my cousin – Uncle Ilatto and Aunt Iseko's son. Any fear of acceptance faded into oblivion as I was bear-hugged with affection, and I think somewhat with respect – As I was to find out later, I had completed a journey for them too. In the middle of Hidetoshi's bear grip I felt a gentle tugging on my legs. Glancing down I spied Uuto and Ai, my cousin's children, each grabbing a leg and my waist respectively. Ai was a beautiful eleven-year-old girl and Uuto was devilishly handsome four-year-old boy.

Standing in the background was Rob, peering between the mountains of luggage. I didn't see him, but he told me later he was filled with a profound humility for helping make this possible. Then politely, not wanting to interrupt the moment, he slowly moved out from behind his hiding place and took *his turn in line, exchanging heartfelt hugs from all except the children. It was clear they hadn't seen many blonde men before and weren't quite sure what to make of him.*

I had feared this crossing of sorts; the ocean represented a sea of calm on the surface with constantly churning turmoil underneath. I had feared the daunting task of crossing it and facing all it represented connecting two worlds. But now I knew that all my years of wanting to build a bridge to my family were fruitless labor. The journey was done in God's time, and now the bridge building would happen on faith and the joyous labor of getting to know my family; MY FAMILY!

New friends could be made, and families could become whole again. A lesson I learned at an early age, and had totally forgotten...

Sometimes it seemed like Daddy's only family and friends were animals. He must have given me that kind of love because he didn't give me any other kind.

He always said he was bred, born and raised on an Indiana farm by an iron-fisted father who showed little love and held no remorse for its absence. Milking the cows, cleaning up after them and escaping the wrath of Grandpa was considered a successful day.

Daddy turned to animals for love, especially birds. He told stories of when he was a kid, not much older than me, raising carrier pigeons. He would send messages to his one and only true friend in the world. Back and forth, back and forth, saying nothing all his childhood – at least nothing that he could remember of any importance. It was just an escape from a lousy home life. Maybe Daddy and I weren't so different after all.

He loved doggies too. But like his children, he didn't know how to raise them right. We always had too many puppies – big breed dogs that Mommy wouldn't let in the house.

"The cat enough," she said.

I love all animals, but particularly cats. Daddy did not like the cats. They watched the birds darting in and out of the unkempt yard in a strange way that made him nervous, given his fondness for creatures with feathers. However, kitties – so warm, soft and cuddly bundles of cotton-like fur, were irresistible to me when they were born.

Late one night, a terrible scream came from the back porch where the newest litter of kitties and their momma cat slept. Only they were not sleeping now! Screeches of fear from panicked kittens pierced the cool spring night air, and as I sprang out of bed, I could hear the awful racket of boxes of stored junk crashing to the back porch floor. The noise made me involuntarily cover my ears to deaden the piercing of my eardrums.

Running through the house with my hands like earmuffs covering my ears, I expected to find an all-out-war on whatever the intruder was, but when I reached the back porch door, all I found was everyone standing around like wooden soldiers, frozen in time and unable to move.

'Someone's got to help those kitties!' I thought as I joined the wooden soldier ranks. I hesitated… and then, because no one else was moving, I suddenly knew what I had to do. The fierce battle screams of the defenseless kitties were joined by me as I began to jab out at the door as hard as my short little leg could kick; wailing with all my might, again, and again! My third strike was joined with as terrifying scream as I could muster, when suddenly I stopped cold in mid-kick. The terror outside had stopped, and all that could be heard was the chirping of crickets; the night as calm as it was cool.

Slowly, Mommy opened the door. A trail of blood began oozing on the linoleum floor under the door into the house. There must have been gallons of it! Following the spidery fingers of blood, I came upon the first sickening kitty. Daddy said it musta been a bobcat after the kitties. He got that crazy mad look in his eye, and donning his jacket, he headed through the back porch to chase it out of the yard. I followed silently in my bare feet and nightgown. After all, if Daddy was chasing the bobcat, someone has to gather up the scattered kitties!

But I was too late. The bobcat had exhibited her feline superiority. I moved from one trail of blood to the next, and then the next, and the next, and then the next…. all ending with mangled kittens;

all with dead cold eyes staring at me, their tongues hanging out. The furry bodies were split open like a melon with things I did not know the name of twisted in every direction. Some had legs missing. My swollen sense of pride for saving them left with the wild bobcat skulking somewhere in the woods. I sat down in my nightgown in the middle of the dew soaked lawn and began to cry. My furry little friends gone; all gone…

Then under the side opening of the lawn mower parked by the porch, I saw a glimpse of movement. I peered slowly under the mower fearing another bobcat. But instead, my heart leapt for joy as I recognized the flickering eyes of the fifth and final kitty.

I quickly exchanged false pride in my good deed for love of the kitty, as he let me gently pull it out from under the mower and clutch it to my chest. Instinct was mistaken for bravery as Kathy and Brock rushed to touch the frightened kitty and slap me on the back with praise for saving its life. Apparently, I was a hero!

Maybe so, I don't know. They told me that Mommy, fearing for my life, was screaming at me for all she was worth when I bolted on my rescue mission. I don't know about that either. All I know is that I had to save the kitties!

The next day was Sunday, and at breakfast Kathy and Brock were still singing the praises of my heroics the night before. That is when they told me that Daddy had been all scratched up chasing the bobcat into the woods.

His only praise at breakfast was a muffled, "damn stupid kid."

Sundays is when he spends his "alone time" while we are at church. He despised the church ever since they had called on Mommy and convinced her to start going. She was curious she said, but I think she just wants to get away from Daddy sometimes.

That next morning was a bright and sunny Sunday. The little country church was only a short distance from our house and on bright sunny days, we walked. When we went, we always went with Mommy; rarely with Daddy. Today, as we made our trek to church, I was attracted to a darting rodent that speared through the tall grass before me. Long separated from Brock, Kathy, and Mommy by my incessant lagging behind, I made my way hunched over through the spindly grass toward the old broken down barn, exactly opposite the direction of the church. Not that it mattered to me.

There! In a quick flash, I saw a varmint sporting a stripe running down its back. It was about the size of a rat but more colorful. It must be a chipmunk! My thoughts raced, 'if it could be caught, it could be tamed. I'm sure of it!' I cautiously approached the barn. Nestled in the worn and withered brown grass was a small dirt trail of tiny footprints scampering toward the open barn door.

Entering slowly, I found my untamed friend darting back and forth against a wall between stalls inside the barn. He danced to and fro looking for an opening but found none. I approached as close as I dared. Pausing, I took a deep breath, and then when I thought the time was just right, I jumped toward him with open arms.

I missed! But he had now backed into a corner with the only escape through me, and that was not going to happen! A stick cracked under my Sunday shoes as I gathered myself for another attempt. Poor Chippy; he was frozen in fear. His eyes constantly moving, his nose frantically waving in the air. He suddenly made his move for the opening between my feet just as I plunged forward.

I got him!

His quick movement almost let him escape, and instead of grabbing his body, I had him by the tail. Then in horror, I watched as with a sickening snap, the tail broke in two from his violent wiggling and my determined death grip not to let him go. Chippy was in pain, and it was my fault! I felt sick as he immediately stopped resisting me. I gathered him in my tiny palms, stroking him, apologizing and begging for all the forgiveness God could muster. Not that Chippy could care…

I held the still warm body and broken tail against my shaking chest, and turning, I ran toward the house.

"Mommy, Mommy, please come quick!" I shouted down the road. I caught her out of the corner of my eye, pivoting and then running like the wind toward me. We reached the porch door at the same time. With my heart breaking, I reached up and handed her the panting ball of brown and black. "Help Chippy, Mommy. I think I may have killed him!"

Moments later my sister and brother came crashing back into the house having heard my screams too.

"What happened Amy? Are you hurt?" Kathy gasped as she doubled over at the waist and leaned on her kneecaps.

I couldn't speak. I just held up the broken tail, exposing its jagged raw edge. Kathy and Brock recoiled away from me. Then glancing at Mommy, they saw the hurt chipmunk in her hands. Gently she caressed it and walked over to the kitchen cupboard; she opened some peanut butter and offered it to Chippy. To our amazement, he immediately began to nibble.

He was alive! Oh, I hoped he was going to be all right! Anything that could still eat after being broken had to live! Mommy diluted some milk with warm water and added a pinch of sugar. Using my dolly's bottle, we took turns feeding it while it lay on its back, suckling away. It liked me best; I could tell because I always got it to eat more than Kathy and Brock. Gradually over time, we introduced it to seeds and such from the woods.

This is one time that Daddy didn't mind having company in the house. He allowed Chippy to stay, warning that it would get wilder as it grew. I didn't care. I loved and cherished every playful moment that Chippy sat on my shoulder, or nibbled my collar or pawed my hair.

At least until he got so big that his claws actually started cutting me. I knew then, it was time to let him go.

We all decided to make a nice afternoon of his release by packing a picnic lunch and finding a nice secluded area in the orchard to release Chippy. As if free for the first time in his life, he practically danced his way from tree to tree after I reluctantly let him go. Then settling on one, up the trunk he scampered. For the rest of the summer I would go out and call him, sometimes finding him, but most often not. Then on our last chance meeting, I saw not one Chippy, but two! Chippy had a girlfriend! He had found a friend of his own and soon would be raising a family. I was saddened with the thought that he must have re-located deeper into the woods to protect his children from me. When I broke his tail, I accidentally made him into two parts. Over time I realized that he was once alone, and now he had new friends and family. I guess that maybe something broken can be made whole again.

What a joyous thing if that should happen to me someday.

> *Respect cannot be taught – only earned. To "teach"*
> *a child respect is the fastest way to lose it*

Chapter 4

dream castles do exist

My newfound family drove us to their home in Kitakyūshū City, about an hour drive from the airport in a new Toyota Estima (only made in Japan). To fill the void of missing words due to the language barrier, Rob and I were ceremoniously entertained with a movie. Hidetoshi tuned in the <u>Gladiator</u>, in English no less. In fact, the Estima was loaded with many extras, GPS, satellite TV, car phone and rear bumper cameras for backing up to the curb. Even Ai had her own camera phone; no car attached.

We were impressed and beginning to see why Japan is considered such an electronic culture.

Upon arrival at their home, we found ourselves jetting up an elevator to the eighth floor of a colorless gray apartment building. With shoes left at the door, we entered into a world that was neat, clean and different. The apartment housing this family of four was less than 700 square feet total. It was comprised of three closet-small bedrooms, a bathroom with the tub separate in a tiny cubical and the toilet in a closet, and a combined living, dining and kitchen area. Everything was functional and organized for maximum efficiency. It was the true definition of cozy – to the level that could never be experienced in America. Though tiny, we immediately felt at home there.

It had been 23.5 hours getting here; even Rob needed toothpicks for his eyes to stay awake. We unpacked quickly and then spreading out the sleeping mats on the guest room floor, expected to be able to undress and collapse in a sleepy stupor.

Wrong.

We got our first lesson in Japanese cleanliness when instructed to take a bath before bed, an announcement that repeated itself every day we were there. Entering the electronic culture once again, we were greeted with a heated toilet seat, and a thermostat on the bathtub water temperature. I'm not sure how hot 42 degrees Celsius is, but I do know it's "just right." Bathed and bedded down, Rob and I were finally allowed to pass out from our exhausting travel.

The next morning became a lesson in servitude, respect and more cleanliness. It seemed in our years of marriage we were always greeted each day with the laughter of darting children or the blare of a television, but we found neither of these at morning rise in Japan. Instead, Miyuki and her mother-in-law Iseko were busy in the kitchen area scurrying to prepare our breakfast, with the children respectfully quiet as they played a game on the coffee table. Still, I'm sure the children were relieved to confirm the strange visitors were not a dream. "Ohayoo gozaimas!" meaning "good morning," jumped off Ai and Uuto's lips as they politely greeted us with reserved smiles.

Seated at the table before us was our choice of brown tea, green tea, orange juice, bottled water or cohee (coffee). Rob and I both dove for the cohee. Hidetoshi joined us at the table to watch us eat, but the children remained patiently in the background as an endless parade of food marched before our eyes from the caring hands of Miyuki and Aunt Iseko.

Japanese food is nothing like Japanese-American food. For example, we had salad for breakfast! Soup and rice and fish were staples with every meal. And every meal included a half dozen dishes that Rob said looked like Klingon food – piles of wormy looking stuff and blood pie; which of course they were not – and contrary to his poor analogies, they were delicious. Every new dish caused our palates to burst with flavor, the first bite always accompanied with "you like?" from Hidetoshi. We ate our fill and still could not finish what they sat in front of us. When we were done, then and only then, did my Japanese family eat.

This very first morning was to be sightseeing. That was to accommodate Rob who only had the weekend to spend with me. He was then going to abandon me to my family for the week, while he journeyed to Tokyo on business. The first stop of the day – downtown Kitakyūshū City.

The city is on an inlet from the Sea of Japan. It is ancient in heritage but extremely artistic in the way the historic sites were woven within today's modern buildings, blending the two Japanese lifestyles of past and present.

The morning air was filled with the sounds of a street band playing wood-wind instruments under clear skies and refreshingly fresh sea air. We paused to admire the ethnic sound and stayed long enough to humor my clapping hands and dancing feet. Time seemed to slow as we soaked in the culture. We spent the remainder of the morning lost in the indulgences of a rickshaw ride and shopping. Lunch was pleasing to the eye in a traditional Japanese restaurant, complete with the difficulties of chopsticks and squatting on the floor to sit at two-foot tall tables. Curry and broth were followed by hibachi style fish-kabobs. We did not order dessert for good reason; it would have been a waste of money as we overate on the kabobs. Afterward we spent some time leisurely window-shopping at the open fish market and finger tasting salmon, tuna, octopus, squid and a type of mackerel. Tuna was the choice for supper, to be accompanied with oshinko and yasi, two Japanese vegetables – and you guessed it, rice.

Shopping done and bellies full, Hidetoshi artfully navigated the unruly Japanese traffic to the local castle (doesn't every Japanese city have one?). It was our first touch of how Japan lived in the feudal system for centuries. The ruling family had at its disposal in this region a beautiful white stone castle countless stories high, surrounded by a surreal moat at the bottom and breathtaking mountains flanking its turrets in every direction.

Foreboding to the enemy outside and magnificent in grandeur inside, the Kokura Castle made me wonder how such a home must have felt to the occupying ruler. Surely it was their "dream castle" as it was safe, secure, and built to endure their lifetime and beyond; with only two reasons to be parted from your castle home - death or conquest.

A novel idea to me since my childhood was full of moving, beatings and evictions.

===

Mr. Shew is a bad man.

He also is our landlord. He always growls at me when Mommy and Daddy are not around. I hate the way he looks at us, as if we were dirty. We learned not to look at him, saving myself in part from embarrassment and in part from shame because of Daddy. We are always behind in rent, and Daddy believes it is everyone else's fault. Mr. Shew doesn't want to hear of Brock's illness and mounting hospital bills. He just blames Daddy. It always seems like he is torturing us to move.

Mr. Shew's apartment is just another dumpy place for us to live after losing our dumpy old house. Mommy said it was because of money spent on Brock's illness. Daddy said it was them "somsa bitchin'" bankers. The apartment wasn't much to look at, but we were all together. I told Daddy that had to count for something, even if the "somsa bitchin'" bankers can't count money.

Mr. Shew turned off our electricity so long ago I can't remember the last time we watched T.V. No electricity also means there isn't any hot water, at least not coming out of the faucet where I daily tried to find some by turning the tap on and off and on again. Sighing with ultimate defeat, I shuffle aimlessly to the kitchen stove every night. At first, I thought the boiling of water on the gas stove for baths was like taking a "good old adventure." Now it is just old. It takes all evening for the three of us to finish bathing. We all volunteered to skip some, but Mommy won't let us. However, I don't see Daddy bathing every day. Maybe he did, or maybe Mr. Shew was right to look at us as if we were a dirty family.

It doesn't help that it is November. I don't know much, but I do know that November in Indiana is cold. I also know that it will get colder. Mommy always starts the kerosene space heater before we bath to keep the "chill" off. It also is our only source of heat while sleeping – that and lots of blankets. It helps that it is a one-bedroom apartment. That way we all sleep together. All of us in one bed is something I don't like, but Brock and Kathy are okay with it so I make do. I also made sure that I never sleep next to Daddy. Instead Kathy and I slept next to each other so we could wrap our bodies around each other to keep warm. Our feet and noses get really cold to the touch. On the really, really cold winter nights we burrow down into the mountain of blankets Mommy piles on - like bears in a cave, sleeping with our coats on. I think someday one of us is going to suffocate but Kathy says "no." I only worry about it when she sleeps on top of me, but I like her warmth so I don't complain. However, if I wake up dead someday, I'm going to sock her a good one.

Days aren't any better than the hardship of nights. November in Indiana is gloomy and gray and all the pretty flowers and leaves have long withered away. It's some warmer during the day, but since we aren't under the warmth of the blankets like at night, I'm always colder. Daddy also doesn't want to burn the kerosene during the day. Better to save it for night he says; that, and "go put on more clothes and stop whining or I'll knock the shit out of you." He says that a lot lately, too.

The apartment is connected to Mr. Shew's apartment through an inside stairway door that connects through his hallway. He always knows when we are coming and going. Right now we are living off of ring baloney and stale chips because it's about all the food available at the corner gas station. We don't go to a regular store much. Daddy says it's too far and if someone were not always here, Mr. Shew would lock us out. Kathy says its 'cuz we got no money. I think it's because Mr. Shew must be related to some of them bankers too.

Lately Mr. Shew has been trying to drive us away with very, very loud music, which I say is stupid. It seems to me that if it's loud for us, it's even louder for him and his family, but he doesn't seem to care. He props up humongous speakers at night against a bedroom door in his apartment that leads to our bedroom and blares rock and roll music all night. Then yesterday, he started leaving it on all day too. I think he must have been picking on Mommy because of her being Japanese since she and Brock are the only ones home during the day. Kathy and I go to school and Daddy goes to work, or so he says. All I know is Mr. Shew's two girls won't stand with us at the bus stop, so he's turned them against us too. Somsa bitch.

Mommy never complains about getting us ready for school in the candlelight.

"It's too dark to get dressed, Mommy," I whined this morning.

"Besides, we need to save the candles for night when we really, really, really need them. Okay?"

"No. No okay. You go school. You get smart; you no have to live like this. Lichard (that must be how Richard is pronounced in Japanese) is *bakatare* – dumb. He make us live like dirt. I think he likes making landlord mad. I think he dumber than *bakatare*. I think him stupid."

It didn't take a first grader to figure *that* out!

Daddy *did* seem to like getting Mr. Shew's goat. I pondered this while I crawled out of the bed of blankets and began undressing from my pajamas to get ready for school one day. And it's true that even with all of Mommy's nagging; Daddy didn't seem to do ANYTHING about it. It reminded me of one of his Army games, only with Mr. Shew now. Poor Mr. Shew. Daddy always wins at his Army games.

Daddy said Mr. Shew owns other apartments, and has to leave home once in awhile on business, and today is one of those days. It ought to be a fun "play Army" day for Daddy. He promised to fool Mr. Shew by finally taking Mommy to a real grocery store while he was gone. Our cupboards are bare as Old Mother Hubbard's waiting on Mr. Shew not to be home. I think he just gets bored bothering us and then has to go and bother someone else for awhile.

That afternoon I felt funny when I jumped down from the school bus. Mommy and Daddy were standing outside of Mr. Shew's. Mommy was holding Brock, swaying back and forth and bouncing up and down rapidly. Daddy was clenching a piece of paper in his raised right hand. Even from the street curb, I recognized that clenched jaw and that scary boom of Daddy's voice. Brock was bouncy happy in Mommy's arms, even though at four years of age, he was too big to be there. Kathy standing at the curb beside me didn't feel any better about this than I did. I could tell she was nervous when she reached over and grabbed my hand so we would slowly approach together.

"You can't evict us! You snake! You waited until we were starving and left to get food then changed the locks behind us. It's winter, you son of a bitch. Women and children on the street! How can we live like that? Maybe we'll just sleep on the sidewalk until the cops come by! How would you like that.... you son of a bitch!"

"Lichard, Lichard. We go. We go Social Security. They know what do, how help. Please Lichard! Look, girls home. We go now!"

Mommy scooped us around her as we arrived at the door and immediately began walking away, leaving Daddy to charge the door and pound it with his clenched fist for good measure as Mr. Shew disappeared inside. Mommy knew Daddy wouldn't call the police and wouldn't wait for them either. The police know Daddy from his drinking binges.

I wondered what would happen to our stuff as we were walking away with nothing but the clothes on our backs. I didn't much care if I lost the tattered clothes and broken toys we were leaving behind, but the blankets were still in the apartment. The cold air stung my eyes and cut into my lungs.

"How will we ever keep warm tonight?" I found myself wondering out loud.

We left Daddy still pounding on Mr. Shew's door after he had slammed it shut in our faces. The sting of Daddy's curse words vibrated in the crisp cool air burning my ears in shame as Mommy, Kathy, Brock and I crossed the street and headed for the Social Security office.

Thank God for Mommy.

• • • •

'This was all right' I thought to myself as I tickled Kathy. The "new" home was a house in the country and it was a dump, but a new dump to us…and better than the old dump because it was quiet. Except for my giggles.

"Shut up and go to sleep, you two! Amy, how can I sleep if you're giggling in there?" Daddy snapped from down the hall.

We held our breath, hoping he wouldn't hear us… and then here it came. It was a bubbly little volcano building in my throat. I knew I was not going to be able to hold back. A chortled snort erupted against all restraint and I went into a giggly jag again. I was somewhat famous for my piggy snort laugh.

Showing better control than me, Kathy began telling me to be quiet. She was afraid of getting in trouble. We hadn't been out of that old apartment that long, and Daddy still wasn't all that happy. I think it's because he lost his Army game with Mr. Shew.

The only thing that seemed to make him calm at night was when he came into our bedroom to say good night with what he called an "erection." I don't know what it's good for, but he says every man has one and told us not to be afraid if it – it was natural and so to repeatedly prove it, he would coax Kathy into touching it.

I always used to make her laugh, but by school age she had become more and more quiet. Sometimes she was so withdrawn I couldn't crack her up no matter how hard I tried. She means so much to me and in many ways fills a void of motherhood Mommy can't, with her being Japanese and all. But Kathy is always there. And we always *used to have* such great fun whispering in bed. Besides, this is no time to worry about getting into trouble. This is my sister - who I love more than any person on earth, and more importantly, who I loved to make laugh!

"Kathy, Kathy Alabama boo! Outchy, gotchy, domanotchy, out goes you!" I tried hard not to snort, but you might as well have tried to stop the wind. Out it came, and this time Kathy started giggling too. Sometimes I just can't help myself.

Suddenly, "I told you two to stop that crap right now!" screamed Daddy as he burst into the bedroom. He grabbed me and started to shake me as if determined to get every snort out of my body forever. The stench of alcohol made me just as sick as the violent shaking. Mommy, who knows when Daddy is going to explode, had followed him into the bedroom and began pounding on his back. He dropped me like a hot potato just long enough to send Mommy flying through the air with a ferocious backhand. I came crashing down in a heap on top of Kathy and Brock, who were screaming with the covers pulled up to their chins.

Daddy turned and stalked toward Mommy like an angry bear after its wounded prey with what looked to be a belt in his hand. Without thinking, I sprang up and tried to stop Daddy from attacking Mommy again. In a lighting blur, I was swept up in his arms, his drool splashing on my face and his bloodshot pulsing eyes burning a hole in me.

"I'll teach you to interfere with me!" and instead of beating Mommy, he greeted me with a powerful rip of my pajamas. Instantly I was stripped bare naked. He grabbed me and tossed me over face down on the bed and began whipping me violently with the buckle end of his belt.

"Agh, ugh, ahhh!" I screamed. The belt buckle ripped through my skin leaving what must have been bloody stripes on my back. I could feel the bruises begin to rise and stretch my skin like a hardboiled eggs trying to get out. Through everyone's nightmarish screams, I could periodically hear a click of the belt as if it had struck a bone. Like eating my puke, I shut down. I became calm, accepting my fate. Already with each succeeding blow, the pain had begun to lessen. I sensed Mommy trying to pull him off of me as I listened to Kathy and Brock's cries become more distant in the background. Or are they lying next to me? I'm not sure where they are as my vision begins to fade and blur from both the beating and tears. The last thing I remember was Daddy saying "and one for good measure…"

After what seemed like forever, I awoke and looked around dazed. The first thing I saw was Kathy and Brock on their knees, with frightened eyes as big as half dollars peering over the edge of the bed at me. Kathy took hold of my hand gently and not letting it go, began to weep.

"I was sure he had killed you," she cried.

"I'm okay, Kathy. Where is Mommy? Is she all right?" I whispered.

"Mommy went to get a doctor," she said as her cries turned to sobs.

"Why'd she do that? Who's hurt?" I inquired, totally puzzled and confused. My back was numb, but I really didn't feel any pain. Daddy must have hurt someone else.

Kathy pointed to blood on the sheets but couldn't speak. I somehow sensed the blood was mine. I tried to turn my head to look over my shoulder and see the carnage on my back inflicted by Daddy, but I was unable to move. Mommy had wrapped me like a cocoon in the sheet to help stop the bleeding. She had asked Kathy and Brock to watch over me while she was gone.

Daddy was nowhere in sight when the doctor arrived and took me to the hospital.

That was okay with me. Mommy said I had defended my home and my family and that my Japanese ancestors were proud of me. I went to sleep feeling loved by Mommy, Kathy, Brock and even my ancestors.

Daddy never entered my mind.

Chapter 5

christmas in the spring

The next day was Rob's last in Kitakyūshū City. He would be flying on for a week of business meetings, leaving me stranded and helpless with my new family. An event that frankly, I initially found a little scary. The language barrier still loomed large for one. All my studying had been invaluable, and I actually could blurt out a phrase or two when appropriate. However, I had to admit that my Japanese family was equally as bad at communicating as I was. Out of necessity, translation dictionaries had soon found their way into everyone's pocket or purse. Even then communication was difficult and lengthy. It would have to improve when Rob left; who seemed to enjoy getting by with a smile and a nod of the head. I don't think he knew what he was doing half the time, but I'm not sure he cared. Much more the seasoned traveler, he seemed to be soaking in the experience and didn't burden himself with my anxieties.

Fear of non-acceptance by other family members crept out of my subconscious, something I thought I had overcome. Instead, that feeling of being the bastard child of that traitorous Keiko from America began to hang over me again. Why couldn't I shake that feeling? The first day had been a resounding success, full of color and sights and life – a whole new beginning. But here I was, about to climb into the van and make for Aunt Yoko's house, Aunt Iseko's sister, and I was as nervous as when I arrived yesterday.

Aunt Yoko lived about 30 minutes away in the old part of the city that actually had houses instead of towering apartment buildings. The house was at the bottom of a raised road that appeared to be built on the edge of an old canal. The house itself was at least 50-60 years old. The yard didn't have much space but at least there was some green grass, a refreshing site to offset the gloomy gray skies and bland skyscraper apartment buildings. It was a quaint two-story house but not like conventional two stories. It was more like a tall ranch with what surely had been a loft for the second story rather than the full floor with bedrooms, bathrooms and spacious hallways we were so accustomed to back home. Still, the front porch with its hanging plants and wooden chairs gave it a cozy feeling. As I stepped up to deposit my shoes at the doorway, I began to relax a little.

Aunt Yoko greeted us at the door as if she knew we were coming, even though I do not recall ever seeing Hidetoshi call her to grant fair warning. Ai and Uuto bound in with the familiarity I wish I had. Aunt Yoko politely greeted each member of her Japanese family as she waited patiently for Rob and me to appear from the back of the line.

The gentle hug she garnished me with was perhaps the most loving I have ever felt. It was a warm embrace of kindred spirits; I could tell. Later, I was to discover her many talents as she let her life unfold for me. She was a singer, something I always admired but never had the nerve to do in public myself. She also was a photographer and a darn good one, too. Photography was something I had developed a talent for as an amateur, long before my heart was invaded by Rob and his two loving boys. Aunt Yoko gave me two photographs of Japanese sceneries capturing colorful fall foliage that are simply breathtaking. Both pictures proudly adorn my home today, always catching the eye of visitors; and a daily reminder to me of Aunt Yoko's kindred spirit with mine.

Ushered through the small hallway that served as a kitchen, we were greeted by Uncle Tekeshi, his son Hirokazu and Hirokazu's baby, Rena. In the center of what we would call a living room sat a floor-level table with a cover over it. We were instructed by hand signals to place our folded legs under the cover of the table as we sat on the floor. With such a dreary day outside, we were pleasantly greeted with warm cascading air on our legs and torso when we nestled down to the table. The warm breeze was being generated from a space heater hidden under the blanket that adorned the table top. Uncle Tekeshi was the only other one who was cozied up to the table with us. Rather than stand to greet us, he just nodded and smiled. He reminded me of the television stereotyped Native American Indian sitting at the tribe meeting; always ready to take charge and giving that air of commander and chief without ever having to say a word.

Immediately I saw why no one else sat when we took our place at the elf-size table. No sooner were we seated than an unexpected procession began. An endless parade of people and a mountain of gifts soon formed on the table and at our feet. I was speechless at first but by the time the last gift was stacked on top, I was overwhelmed – Rob just nodded and smiled. At first I thought they were showing me my Japanese heritage, but as I tried to pass back the set of ornate dishes, they were shoved right back at me followed by something in Japanese that translated into "you keep." After the dishes came a tea set, and chopsticks with soup bowls for eating noodles and rice. And then, the two most precious gifts of all.

As if in a ritual ceremony, Aunt Yoko walked in, arms extended with a major sized box. I felt like it was Christmas as everyone gathered around, anxious to watch me unwrap THE GIFT. The children caught my eye – Ai could have been my sister Kathy, Uuto could have been Brock and Rena could have been my baby brother Martin who died before the age of one of a birth defect. Japanese eyes were as big as the saucers they had just given me as I popped the lid off of the box. Inside was the most beautiful yellow kimono, complete with obi, the traditional wrap around the waist. We were told it was 50 years old; a family heirloom and in perfect condition. Tears streamed down my cheeks almost dripping on my new prized possession as I realized this kimono was new when Mom had left Japan.

And then, as if the topping needed put on the Christmas pudding, Aunt Yoko reappeared with a small envelope in her hand. With a Japanese smile that betrayed her emotions, she reverently handed me the envelope. I opened it carefully, unsure of its contents and was shocked to see pictures – not just any pictures, but pictures of me and my parents and siblings – pictures of my childhood I had never seen! Mom must have been proud enough of us to send them to Japan over the years. There weren't many pictures and most were *when we were small; perhaps preschool. But they were precious. It brought back some of the few happy memories I had of my childhood. Again I tried to return their pictures to them, but they insisted I keep them. They could tell by my reaction that I had never seen them before, making them the most treasured gift of all.*

Immediately, Rob and I pulled out some pictures we had brought including the picture of the graves at the cemetery where Mom and Brock and Martin were all buried. Now it was their turn to be shocked. In spite of all the efforts Kathy, I and the funeral director made to contact them when both Mom and Brock had died; they appeared to not know they were dead. Mom had died at the age of 62 and Brock at the tender age of 23, succumbing to the same genetic defect that had taken my baby brother Martin.

The sharing of this news was indeed sad. They didn't even know Martin had ever been born. But the sharing of my family's deaths instantly brought our being there to new heights of importance. It was indeed Christmas to them for us to be visiting since everyone they ever knew from my family, save my sister, had died. Our presence was as precious to them as the gift of pictures of my family was to me.

Even in sadness I was overwhelmed with this Christmas atmosphere and the universal joy we shared. After all, I had been disappointed at Christmas so many times during my childhood –

Christmas Day!

Every kid in school was bounding down the stairs with joy in their hearts and a twinkle in their eyes, running toward their stuffed stockings and Santa's presents under every other tree in town. Every boy and girl in the whole wide world except Kathy and Brock and me, I suppose. None of us had any stockings to be stuffed, and Kathy and I both know what sits under the tree for us... because we picked our presents out ourselves.

I know Mommy wanted us to have something for Christmas so I should be happy. As I lay in bed I thought about the nice fat lady at the Salvation Army who said I could pick out any dolly I wanted. She had taken us into a dark, dimly lit back room and showed Kathy and me a shelf with a giant pile of dirty old dolls. I felt so small digging through used toys, looking for something I could call my own and not feel ashamed every time I played with it.

I wondered as I plowed through the heap if I would find a Barbie doll? As long as I have been born Barbies have been popular. Every year in school after Christmas, Barbies filled the classroom - and my face. Every year beautiful pink carrying cases adorned most all desktops, save mine. At recess and after school, girls would line the sidewalks playing and exchanging the many new outfits for their Barbies. Most girls had more than one Barbie and many of them had Ken. Why couldn't I have just one? Either one. Even a used Ken would do…

I hadn't found a Barbie in the pile at the Salvation Army; not even a dirty broken one; not even a Ken. Resigned to failure, I chose a small but sweet fat-faced dolly. Do you know why? Because it was clean. I'll bet I was the only girl in class who based her Christmas present on hygiene. I still gave her a good cleaning when I got her home. I wanted her to look like new when I opened her up on Christmas morning. I somehow sensed I would feel better at school when I faced the invasion of the Barbies if I convinced myself my fat-faced sweetie doll was new.

I rolled over and looked at Kathy for a long time. She was still asleep. Kathy sleeps in a lot. She says it's because she always falls asleep after I do – something to do with age, her being older and all – so she says. I thought about her doll too. She picked out the absolute worst doll she could find. Its mop-top hair was all matted down and scraggly. When she brought it home, she shampooed the hair and then combed it for hours, crying mysteriously most of the time. She wanted to take something really, really dirty and unclean, and make it sooo beautiful, fresh and new again. I think that's because she doesn't feel beautiful herself, even though she is. She is very beautiful, on the outside – it's the inside that I can't see I worry about. With Brock in the hospital most of the time, I don't know what I would do without Kathy. She continues to protect me from Daddy when my mouth doesn't.

I felt a twinge of guilt being Christmas and all, remembering how Mommy had been depressed lately. I had been distracting Kathy from her daily chores and then would do hers *and* mine, telling Mommy that Kathy was too lazy to do them. My ploy worked as it heaped praise and what I thought was much needed attention on me, but I now wondered on this snowy-clean Christmas morning if the guilt didn't outweigh the praise.

Oh well, that was water under the bridge and a subject more suited for a New Year's resolution to fix than to worry about it on Christmas morning. This Christmas was about the best present I could have asked for and it wasn't my stinky old dolly.

Brock was home!

That was the present I had hoped for. Brock was home and more importantly, most days he seems to be feeling better. He has been so pale and frail ever since he was a baby. My first recollection was straining to see him in the bassinet. He always seemed to be sleeping, but he was beautiful; peach-colored and sooo tiny. What a contrast from now. After a couple of months of enjoying just being a baby, his health had begun to falter. The doctors said it was the same type of disease that killed my other brother, Martin. He had been born before Brock, so I only remember pictures of him. He died early; less than a year. Mommy says that at age eight, Brock is still just as fragile as Martin was, so I always worry.

I smiled to myself this bright Christmas morning as I lingered in bed; lingering on the image of Brock's funny twisted face when he binge eats, cramming bags of potato chips in his mouth and washing it down with soy sauce. The doctors say he craves salt due to his constant fevers and dehydration. I always laugh to help Brock think of the lighter side of things sometimes, instead of dwelling on his disease. But secretly I worry every time he binges on something new. Yesterday it was pickles and sauerkraut. I cringe to think of what it might be next week. Even so, I felt a smile creep on my face recalling the smell of that odd combination and seeing his smiling face, laughing with noodles of sauerkraut hanging out his mouth.

I hopped out of bed determined to get the Christmas formalities out of the way and vowed to try and make it as happy as possible for Kathy and Brock.

"Come on Kathy, get up," I cooed, leaning over her side of the bed, her back to me. "It's Christmas," I tried to say with some meaning. Suddenly, I froze in my tracks as I heard Brock beginning to sob and gasp for air in the next room. 'All better my foot!' I scoffed as I rushed to his bedside in a flash.

"Brock, Brock you're having a bad dream! Wake up! Wake up!" I pleaded as I gently shook his shoulder. I could see and smell the remains of vomit and diarrhea in his bed.

"Amy, make it go away! It keeps looking at me!" His whimpers turning into a full-fledged cry. I touched his forehead, and he was burning with fever. Brock didn't have nightmares when he got a fever, he had full-blown Technicolor hallucinations!

"It's the fever, Brock. It's not real. It's Amy, Brock. I'm here for you," I said. Gagging back the sickening smell, I exchanged my shaking repulsion for a big bear hug. His body was convulsing in fear that made me feel like I was riding a bucking horse. Relinquishing my hold on him, I leaned back upright and began brushing the hair back off his forehead with short gentle strokes. "Do you want a cool rag for your head?" I asked, wanting desperately to do *something* that would make him feel better.

"Get it off me! I can't breathe, I can't move! Kill it, please! KILL IT!" As I looked closer, he looked like something was smashing his face. It was actually contorting to appear flatter in his gripping fear. His eyes were wild, and his breathing was coming in short explosive bursts. There was no use getting Mommy or Daddy. I had seen him in similar states before…just not this hysterical.

"It's the fever, Brock. It's not real." I paused for some sign of recognition of me, but it didn't come. "It's Amy, Brock. I'm here for you," I said, as reassuringly as my nerves would allow. I could not understand why God had done this to Brock, and now on Christmas morning! I wrapped my arms around his skeleton of a body and exchanged my useless stroking of his hair for a bigger bear hug of love.

He was still convulsing in fear making my body rise and fall a second time in harmony with each tortured breath. Then another course of action hit me. Instead of comforting him, I decided that the best thing to do was to play along.

"Okay, Brock. I see it now. Let me help you." I bent over and with greatly exaggerated strain, I pretended to gradually be lifting the fake attacker. Then with all the flare and determination I could muster, I slammed the dreaded beast to the floor.

"Go away! In the name of Jesus, go away!" I had heard that at church and thought it wouldn't hurt to have Jesus on Brock's side too. I gave the invader one last imaginary kick for good measure.

"He's skulking away, Brock. We got him good. Boy, look at him scurry away!" Gently I sat at the edge of the bed and watched Brock's reaction. In a minute, he began to slow his breathing and finally out of exhaustion, he found a peaceful calm and fell back to sleep. I recommenced stroking his forehead for several minutes, just to make sure the demon was out of his head too. 'It was going to be some Christmas,' I thought as I slowly backed out of the bedroom. Before going to get Mommy to clean him up, I paused at Brock's door and drank in his plight, silently wishing it was me instead of him that was so sick. Maybe not forever; I wasn't brave enough for that, but for awhile. Just so Brock could run and jump and play like a normal boy should; off chasing bandits on his imaginary white horse, or playing superhero with other boys his age.

Poor Brock.

By age five, he had spent more time in the hospital than at home. Desperately wanting a little brother I could play with, I kept running out of patience for him to get better. When he was at home he was the center of joy, yet often that center was wrapped around the terrifying moments of his disease and drugs.

We often thought that he was a child prodigy. I recalled the one time he sat at the piano, and stretching his fingers like a professional, solemnly began to play The Flight of the Bumblebee. When he had finished we all were amazed; no one amazed more than Brock. Mommy said she was the same way with her guitar at that age.

We were told by heathen doctors that Brock would not live more than a couple three years, if that long. In the early years of his life, the disease went undetected, causing severe damage to his entire body. Then when something was determined to be wrong, he started spending most of his time in hospital after hospital, as if most doctors were on a scavenger hunt for the disease. The other young kids in the hospitals became his adopted family, and over time Kathy and I became jealous. We were not allowed to visit his room since we were considered a risk to bring normal diseases to abnormal kids. Occasionally, we got to see him in a wheelchair in the lobby. Periodically, he would get so depressed from constantly seeing so many other deformed and dying kids, the doctors would ask Mommy and Daddy to bring Kathy and me to the hospital just to cheer him up. Brock felt the pain of each and every one in the hospital he came in contact with. It didn't help that he made friends easily. Then inevitably he was struck with grief for days when one of them died.

No matter how much I prepared myself, Brock was always hard to look at when he came home from one of his "extended vacations." He was gaunt with yellowish skin and the contours of his bones stuck out everywhere. With his shirt off, his proportions seemed all wrong. The disease he had screwed up his body's control of growth. To me he was as beautiful as Kathy on the outside, and probably more so inside due to his immense suffering without much complaint, but to the world he was a kind of freak of nature.

I had Daddy write Brock's disease down for me and I practiced saying it until I had it memorized. If people were going to stare, they were going to understand it wasn't Brock's fault. The doctors called it Adrenal Hyperplasia with Hypogonadism, which involved something called a Dax One Gene Mutation. The doctors said it had to do with being born without a pituitary gland, or a lazy one that fails later. I don't know what the entire gland does but pretty much had already figured out it affected growth when Brock was taller than me at age two.

The doctors showed us pictures of gross, abnormally large and small people to make us understand how rare and difficult a disease Brock was fighting. They must have thought this "shock therapy" was needed to get the message across. At first I thought their method was cruel since I was so grossed out by the pictures. But as I thought back they probably were right – one hillbilly Dad, one Japanese Mom (with poor language skills) and two scrawny half-breed girls probably gave them the impression that we needed "special communication" on the seriousness of Brock's illness.

Brock has been on medication all of his life. It was supposed to help control his growth (with a warning it could have serious side effects). I can vouch for the side effects part. And even with medication, the doctors could not guarantee his future or really more to the point, any future. Although he was proving them wrong by not being dead yet, they were still sure that he would never see adulthood.

'Well, we will see about that won't we, Brock?' I whispered out loud with resolve. I turned to make my way toward Mommy to give her the rude Christmas awakening that she needed to tend to Brock and clean up his multi-soiled bed.

'Die before adulthood? If that's the case,' I thought, 'I hope I never grow up either.' A world without Brock or Kathy is a world I don't want to be a part of...

> *Since you cannot take your life back,*
> *why not give it to others.*

Chapter 6

ding dong, *buddha's dead*

I bound out of bed excited. Really excited. REALLY excited! Today was going to be a very special day. Today we were going to a real Buddhist Temple. Why special? Because my mother was a Buddhist teacher until she married my Dad and departed for the United States at the age of 30.

Then, somewhere between frosty lip gloss and hide-the-wrinkle eye shadow it hit me - Rob was leaving for Tokyo today. He had a jillion business meetings set up - the real driver of this trip. Of course he would have been considered scum on top of a cesspool if he had not taken me to Japan with him. At least that's what I told my friends, and neighbors, and his family, and our two dogs, which were <u>completely</u> on my side.

I thought briefly of Snuggles, a mutt golden retriever that got her name from her endless need for comforting all the time; and Skyler, a pure German Shepherd female that patrolled our yard like the assassin police. They were a perfect match for each other, romping and playing when they weren't intimidating visitors. And since all the kids have left the nest, they offer me companionship and security when Rob is traveling on business.

I pondered a little longer at the mirror as I realized how much I miss them.

Their odd combination of breed, yet playful affection for each other reminded me of Rob's family. A hodgepodge of cultures, it represented a mini-United Nations. Of course he was married to me, Japanese, but he also had one brother who was married to a distant descendant of Native American Indian, and another brother to a full blooded Korean. Our three sons seemed to follow suit with Rob's siblings. One is married to a Puerto Rican, another dating an Argentinean, and our youngest son, being from North of the Mason-Dixon Line, we kiddingly say, married a Southerner. Rob recalls with pride the first time he was sharing his family tree with some coworkers shortly after moving to his new job in North Carolina. The immediate quip back was "what's the matter? Made in America not good enough for your family?!"

Last but certainly not least, is a wonderful young lady in our lives named Thalia whose family is from the Dominican Republic. We had started mentoring in a program at a local school several years ago, having lunch with select children. Thalia, being from a single parent family, was assigned to us. We have since fallen in love with her and have over the years included her and her mom, brother and sister in many of our activities.

'Yes, my Japanese family was going to be a welcome extension to my multi-species, multi-cultural family,' I thought with silent pride as I staggered through the bedroom door and headed toward my first cup of cohee...and my first day alone with just my heritage family.

Our first planned stop that morning was at an electronics department store. Hidetoshi could not resist showing off Japanese gadgets and I suspect with some pride, the Japanese perception of superiority in the electronics field. And he would be right – high definition television was already common years before it was in America, with such clarity you felt as if you could step in the screen. There were video games, movies, and DVDs, all in colorfully bold packaging. However, our favorite was the vibrating chair before they ever became popular in airports. It pulsed, it squeezed, it "shaked and baked" every joint in the body – all for only $4,000 US Dollars. Hidetoshi considered it a bargain. Rob and I thought the price outrageous, but we took a dive into a trial model anyway, finding it deliciously delirious. It brought new definition to the word "relax."

Then, just as I was getting comfortable and Rob was dozing off in our free trial chairs, it hit. An earthquake! At first we thought it was the vibration of the chair – until it got bigger and louder and wouldn't stop. Jumping out of my chair, I immediately grabbed Uuto who was within sight, while Hidetoshi was scrambling to locate Ai. Overhead hanging banners, signs and lights swayed in uneven rhythm as the earthquake refused to stop. I saw Rob out of the corner of my eye following Hidetoshi while I covered Uuto with my hunched over body in case anything would fall from the ceiling. In the background I could hear some uncontrolled screams, probably from mothers who could not locate their children.

It seemed like forever, but in reality the quake lasted less than 30 seconds. It didn't matter. We hustled out of the building as quickly as possible. We were parked in the basement parking lot, and you could tell Hidetoshi was concerned about aftershocks. None of us wanted to be in a car in the basement of a concrete multi-storied mall when any aftershocks hit. We escaped at Olympic speed, and in a matter of minutes were home at Hidetoshi's. We had left Aunt Iseko there…and returned to find her quietly sobbing as she went about picking up broken dishes and ornaments that had fallen from shelves and walls.

We found out that this was Kitakyūshū's first earthquake in 50 years and the first one that Hidetoshi's family had ever experienced. We found this surprising for all of Japan's reputation of quakes, but later discovered that most took place on the Pacific Ocean side of Japan, not the Sea of Japan on the west. The quake epicenter was on an island 70 miles at sea, registering 7.0 on the Richter Scale. It registered a 6.0 where we were. The island was devastated, but there was surprisingly minimal damage in Kitakyūshū City.

This was also the first earthquake for Rob and me. We found it ironic that two split families for the last 50 years would experience their first earthquake together. It seemed fittingly symbolic that the last one in the area was before my mother left Japan, and the next one wasn't until my return. It was almost a roaring sign of "welcome back," or perhaps an ominous "warning…"

With everything apparently no worse for the wear, we piled the family into the van with Rob and his luggage and headed for Fukuoka City. We were concerned that the airport might be affected by the earthquake, possibly interfering with Rob's flight. Our fear was for naught and later that afternoon we deposited him safely at the airport.

The trip back to the airport seemed longer than the ride in when we had arrived. Perhaps it was because my emotions were on a roller coaster ride.

First the earthquake, then being separated from Rob, and (love aside for my husband) I was in a big hurry to begin my next adventure. We all have been excited and nervous at the same time; you know that feeling of an emotional cocktail. I was having pangs of guilt so I suspected that the suspense of seeing my first Buddhist Temple was actually more the driver of my mixed emotions than parting with Rob.

Sorry, Rob.

He was wonderful at the airport, with his Terminator 'hasta la vista baby!' good-bye and a gargantuan hug for little Uuto, who had already fallen into the habit of following Rob like a puppy. I think the king-sized hug was in response to the wrap around squeeze Uuto was always giving to Rob's leg the last two days. That smiling and nodding he had employed seemed to break the language barrier with Uuto without ever having to say a word. Rob seems to have a way with little boys, probably since we raised three of our own.

Wishing me happiness and me wishing him good luck on his business trip, Rob disappeared through the security check of the airport. I would not see him again until the next weekend when we were to rendezvous in Tokyo for the return home. We stayed at the airport to watch Rob's flight depart, which was rather anti-climatic. I could not tell which plane was his, but Hidetoshi seemed sure he knew. At least the kids enjoyed watching the planes take off and land. Me, I wanted to get moving.

The ride to the temple flew by in stark contrast to the ride to the airport. On the way we picked up Maki, a close friend and co-worker of Miyuki. She had studied for two years at UCLA and was semi-fluent in English. I couldn't wait to meet then abuse her in bridging the language gap.

As we approached the temple, it appeared much smaller than my movie-sized imagination. It took the form of a castle; very ornate, with detailed crafts-manship that looked as if it had withstood a thousand years of the elements. But it was also foreboding. The front door was weathered and worn, looking like the entrance to Dracula's castle. It was then we noticed, perched at the base of the door a very tiny lady was taking very tiny steps, attempting to close the door on us before we ever had a chance to breech its threshold.

Maki ran inside the temple as we parked. She wanted to talk to someone before the temple closed, aborting any attempt for us to get in. She reappeared in a moment with a broad Japanese smile across her beautiful delicate face. With a petite figure and pearl skinned face, she radiated everything I had imagined Japanese women to be, or at least wanted to be. We exited the car in reverent silence and bowed to the tiny caretaker who had stopped her attempts to close the door and bowed in return as we passed. We proceeded in single file to a square trough with running water in it that stood just outside the ominous temple door. In turn, we took a long handled cup and after dipping it into the water, poured its contents out letting its mystical powers cascade over our hands. Maki explained that this was to cleanse our impure thoughts before entering the holy Temple.

Inside, the ceilings were extremely tall with gigantic beams holding the weight of the structure over our heads. Everything appeared focused toward the altar at the end of the corridor. Benches with elaborate cushions ran down two single files on each side of the hallway. At the far end was a kneeling bench in front of a simple table holding burnt ashes and a vase of tall matches. The smell of incense filled the slightly damp air.

In the back of the altar but one step higher was a black onyx shiny floor. On the floor was the Buddha figure, surrounded by flowers and bathed in soft light from wrought iron chandeliers hanging above.

Maki gently grabbed my trembling hand and slowly led me to the kneeling bench. I watched as she picked up one incense and broke it in two. Then withdrawing a match from the long vase, she struck it and lit the incense. It sent up a magical whirl of smoke that encircled her head and then gently wafted into thin air. Clasping her hands in prayer, she closed her eyes and bowed her head in silence.

I followed suit, bowing my head as the smoke filled my nostrils with its enchanting aroma. But instead of praying to Buddha, I prayed to God with thanks for making the "Crossing the Sea of Japan," my dream miracle trip, a reality for me. I ended my prayer by thanking him for saving my mother. Then turning to Maki, I broke the silence by asking if I could get a closer look at the Buddha figure. She said that she believed the step up was only for the priest; outsiders were not allowed. At my urging, Maki asked anyway. After much conversation and much to our surprise, the petite elderly lady invited us up onto the step for a closer look.

I asked what sex Buddha was supposed to be as I admired the figurine God of my mother's childhood. Maki translated. The response was "whatever your mind sees it as." I gazed upon the Buddha trying to feel the attraction my mother must have felt. Up close, everything was so elaborate. I now saw *streams of gold woven in the Buddha in a very intricate pattern, making it appear gaudy to the extreme. It was making my eyes hurt to continue looking at it and still, I did not feel the attraction...*

I waited patiently as Maki engaged in Japanese conversation with the elderly caretaker for several minutes. When done, she explained that we were afforded such an honor because of the great distance I had traveled in search of my mother's culture, as she had become a sacred Buddhist teacher. I remember wondering what they would think if they knew my mother had turned Christian, and that I had just prayed to my God in the presence of Buddha. Yet she was exactly right; I was here to find what had been previously hidden from me; my family and my heritage. With that thought in mind, I asked through Maki if there were any teachings of Buddha in English at the temple. Without a response but in complete obedience, the smallish figure disappeared. In a few moments, she reappeared with a small book in hand.

Finally, I would be able to discover what my mother had believed in and taught for the first half of her life. As I closed my eyes, I thought of Mom and her conversion away from Buddha to Christianity. It was her shining moment in her life, and an inspiration to all.

It all began with a tongue lashing to Mom from a woman she had never met...

I peered in on Mom after finishing my bowl of Cheerios. I did not let the daylight shining through the cracks between the wood floorboards in her bedroom bother me as I reminded her, "Sally is coming over after school today."

Mom never moved. She was in the middle of her Buddhist chant, something she did religiously morning and night, praying to the one thing on earth that gave her strength. Perched on the makeup vanity was the chubby temple she called God. Surrounded in silk in its careful packing to America, Buddha was busy answering Mom's prayers, although you couldn't prove it by me.

"Oh well, I warned you," I said as I abruptly (and excitedly) exited the bedroom.

My plan was to "win a friend" with Sally since I didn't have any. Kathy had become more and more distant and my desire for companionship was full time. My hope was that Sally would find my cultural background interesting. I left for school with a tingle of excitement. I was sure that Mom's chanting to Buddha would be something interesting that Sally had never seen before.

School came and went with its usual blur. Sally and I met at the east corner of the school and skipped off innocently enough to my house, laughing and giggling. But as we approached the house now in plain view, my newfound friend became quieter with each passing step. She appeared subdued as she took notice of how neglected our yard was. Panning around as if seeing it for the first time, I suddenly realized she was right. The grass was long past due for mowing and weeds stuck out through the base of the rotting fence.

The screen door squealed in pain as we pushed it open. Sally was dead silent now. You could scarcely see her breathe. I had long accepted the house; a dilapidated two-story structure that stood out like the haunted mansion of the neighborhood. The sides had huge curled up strips of paint, as if they had been poured over with acid. Beneath the paint you could see rusty old nails poking out the weathered wood. The front window pane was held in place by a jagged piece of tape. The house actually was one of the better ones in a countless succession of evictions or "just moving ons" as Dad would say. Still it didn't matter; to me it was home.

To Sally, it was a nightmare. Sensing her trepidation, I took her hand and led her through the kitchen door into the living room.

"It's okay, really it is," I said with as much comfort as I could muster.

We stopped at my bedroom. Sally looked up and then froze in a stare at the cloth rags that were crammed into the cracks and crevices of the ceiling to keep the weather out. Just as she was soaking in the everyday hardships I had long since accepted, she was jolted at a strange sound coming from down the hall.

"Don't worry, that's just Mom praying to her Buddha god. She does it all the time. Come on, I'll show you," I said proudly. 'At last!

Something interesting to take Sally's mind (and my growing discomfort) off of the sad condition of the house,' I thought.

Wrong! It didn't matter. Mom's chanting was not only not interesting to Sally, it was intimidating! She turned to stare at me with haunting eyes, and then as if a match had been struck and dropped down her pants, she turned and ran screaming for all she was worth.

"It's just praying!" I shouted as I ran after her, but it still didn't matter.

It didn't seem to matter to Sally's Mom either, when she called later that evening. I don't know all the curse words in the world but I recognized most of them jumping out of the phone at Mom and her damned witchcraft. Mom hung up the phone shaken and puzzled at why her daily routine of praying would be considered so evil.

Sally went so far as to tell everyone in Sunday school that Mom was a devil worshiper. My chance of making a new friend was crushed, and now she was doing everything in her power to make sure ANY chance of making new friends was equally crushed.

Then, out of this single evil act on Sally's part, came some good. Earlier in our lives, church women invited us to attend, which we began to do faithfully. Sunday school was an escape for us from Dad and apparently the life that scared Sally so. Until this moment in time, the church wasn't much more than a passing curiosity for Mom.

But now hearing of this "devil worshiper," some of the good women from this Indiana Baptist Church came to our house the next week seriously intent on converting someone, anyone. They were aware of Dad's drinking, Brock's hospitalization, and Martin's death, but apparently it took Sally's rumors of fabricated Satan worship to move them to action.

One of the ladies was Kathy's nameless Sunday school teacher. I suspect that she came to check on Kathy who was, it seemed to me, acting more strange with each passing day. She was accompanied by another woman I only knew as Ms. Nevill.

"Hello Ms. Wesson! May we come in?" Ms. Nevill said as she stood smiling at the door. Mom looked like a frightened rabbit waiting to be pounced on but opened the door in response to Ms. Nevill's silent warmth and compassion. I tried to do my part by sitting prim and proper on the couch, strategically covering the large hole with my tiny bum.

"Amy-cochan, get cookies," Mom commanded as she brushed off the sheet covering the couch and motioned for the ladies to sit. I hoped that their bums missed the hole in the couch I had just vacated. But if not, oh, well... From the looks of Miss Nameless, she would cover the hole and never even feel it.

I ran to the kitchen just happy to have company. I also wanted Mom to make a good impression. There were three sugar cookies left. I decided to give one to each lady and Mommy, resisting the urge to stick one in my pocket for later. I smelled the milk from the fridge. Not spoiled, but on the verge. Pouring two glasses I loaded them with ice hoping the chill would take the edge off the taste.

As I reentered the living room Ms. Nevill was handing Mom a red book. She called it a "B-I-B-L-E," saying it really slow for Mom. As I put the cookies and milk down on the coffee table, I heard Ms. Nevill say, "It's the secret to love, the secret of life on earth, and the secret of everlasting life."

Mom did not want to be impolite so she took the Bible. Her Japanese culture had taught her that any gift giving should be accepted with all humility. I could tell she did not understand it all, but she did understand the universal word of "love."

After the cookies and milk, of which they only sipped so maybe it was spoiled after all, Mom thanked the ladies for the Bible. They departed as gracefully as they came.

After they left, I could tell something was different with Mom. She had been down for some time, not taking care of herself anymore and taking way too many pills. She said they helped her sleep. Then they helped her pain. Then they helped her depression over Martin's loss and Brock's illness. I also knew they helped her deal with Dad, but she never said that. At any rate, without ever having opened it, Mom clung to her new Bible as if she had found a long lost friend. In Japanese culture, being given the honor of a present called for a special reverence. She placed the bright red Bible on the coffee table as if it was the most precious possession she had, and a symbol of friends she never knew she had. Christian friends.

Sunday came in snap, and we soon found ourselves off to church. We could tell for some reason it was a special day for Mom. She had dressed Kathy and me in colorful kimonos. This was when I truly enjoyed being different from other boys and girls, even though Kathy and I looked alike today. Our hair was cut in the pageboy motif that seemed to set off the brilliant colors of our kimonos. I was proud of my heritage, even if I was ignorant to it.

"Why, hello Ms. Wesson," Ms. Nevill greeted us when we approached the church door. "You and you children look wonderful on this bright, balmy day!" She genuinely acted like she was so glad to see us; making us seem more special after her visit than other Sundays. I guess neither she nor her friends saw the hole in the couch after all, or at least she was kind enough not to say anything if they had. After Ms. Nevill came an endless line of church members, each greeting us with a loving embrace. I sensed in their hugging that they had talked amongst themselves about our family, but for some reason I didn't seem to mind - the way the grown-ups were treating us that is...

The kids on the other hand, seemed to find our Japanese outfits a little too comical to suit me. More than once a pointed finger and a laugh was returned by me sticking my tongue out. I'm old enough to know better, but still too young to stop it.

Church service passed enthusiastically even if it was uneventful. Mom was straining extra hard to understand the English words that are so foreign to her. It was a message of a "loving God," two words that were both missing and important in Mom's life.

When she returned home she was drawn like a magnet to the red Bible, still sitting on the coffee table untouched. It was big and thick with fancy rice paper for pages, and it seemed to be talking to Mom without saying a word. I watched Mom nervously reach over and stroke the Bible ever so gently as if testing it. It didn't bite back. It just lay there waiting to be opened. Finally, as if she could stand it no longer, she nestled in the couch with her legs tucked under and reverently picked up the Bible. As she opened the first page, her eyes grew in amazement. The Bible was in Japanese! She would be able to understand this story of love and life after all!

My heart leapt silently as I saw the thrill in Mom at finding the Bible in Japanese. She had never really found peace in Buddhism, I could tell. Something was missing in her, like a piece to a puzzle.

"Mom, what's for lunch?" I asked quietly after changing out of my red and blue kimono. Mom didn't move beyond the turning of another page.

"Mom?"

Another page turned.

I made my way into the kitchen. "Kathy," I hollered, "we have to make lunch. Mom's busy with her new Bible." I smiled to myself deciding that this new Mom was going to be a good thing to have around.

Well, that lasted about ten seconds.

"What the hell do you think you're doing, woman?!" Dad shouted at the top of his lungs as he staggered in the living room. He was still in his underwear from staying in bed all morning. Sometimes I actually wished he would stay drunk more often because at times like this, stone sober - he could be even meaner. "Keiko, don't you remember the old mythical teachings about how those who turn away from Buddha disappear! That's its power…the Buddha Gods will be angry and turn against us!"

'What garbage,' I thought as I peered around the corner of the kitchen, just to make sure that Daddy didn't get violent. The only thing ever angry around here was Dad. Mom continued to read the Bible without so much as acknowledging Dad's presence. She knew that anything that gave her strength was a threat to him. I had watched him fume when he first learned of the church visitors a couple of days ago, considering them interfering nosey busy-bodies. He was pretty much indifferent when we went to church but ever since they had invaded the sanctuary of his home, he was upset. Still he had been pretty confident that the fear of Buddha would keep Mom no more interested in Christianity than in doing laundry – until now.

For a brief instant, I flashed back to the old haughty bedtime stories that Buddha teachings must be obeyed in fear.

"For centuries, the myth has been so. In the middle of the night, Buddha would creep in and steal the bodies and souls of non-believers. Your Mother believed that the Imperial rulers would order the imprisonment or kill those against them and the Buddha God," he would say. In America there may be room for many religions, but I guess in Japan faith in Buddha rules alone. At least that's what Dad would have me believe.

Now I could see that its fear of other teachings such as Christianity, or threat to steal non-believers was a fear that may or may not have been history, but it was certainly a fear my Dad lived and ruled under. In any case, Buddhism and the fear of it suited Dad's beliefs a lot more than "love thy neighbor" or "do unto others what you would have them do unto you." Dad would never want to be treated the way he treats us, and you can forget the neighbors – most were only happy when we moved away.

I held my breath as Mom looked up from her Bible. I could see in her eyes the instantaneous reevaluation of her motives before she spoke... and her assessment of Dad's reaction. 'Yes,' the nod of her head seemed to say, 'I am a Buddhist teacher. But that doesn't mean I can't learn about other religions too.'

"Lichard," she began deliberately, "this church help. This church give us food in past. This church teach children love. This no bad religion."

"Bullshit. They are trying to turn you against the greatest God of all. That's evil. They are trying to turn you against Japanese, against your family, against me for god's sake – and after all that I have done for you!"

I looked around the dilapidated house and humble furnishings and almost laughed. My own heart began to wonder how much more we could have if we weren't under Dad's stifling thumb.

"After all you done! Ha! Church help with Social Services. Get money for bills. After all you done, ha! Get money when you can't!" Then Mom looked down and dove anew into the reading of her Japanese Bible.

I sucked air! Now you've done it, Mom. You've challenged Dad's manhood and he's going to explode. I involuntarily closed my eyes as I turned my back on the kitchen doorway. But my back was just met with silence, and then the sound of the television.

I peeked around the corner again, and this time I saw Dad sitting in his sleeveless undershirt and boxers in his recliner. It was as if Mom had actually given him pause to think. He could not deny that we lived more off of Social Services and food pantries than we did from what he provided.

Mom continued to read all afternoon and into the evening. Dad watched television between an occasional beer, and Brock, Kathy and I stayed away, fixing our own meals and playing outside. We knew an explosive moment was coming, we just didn't know when.

That moment came the next weekend.

Mom had awaked with new energy. She showered and dressed up on Saturday as if it was Sunday. Her personal hygiene had been a wreck for the longest time since the pill popping had started anew months ago, so she shocked us when she came into the kitchen in the morning with her freshly set hair and more than generous makeup. She looked at us and then looked at the kitchen sink full of dirty dishes. In the last week she had been so engrossed in the Bible that Kathy and I let our chores slip, and it was a cinch that Dad wasn't about to help. He would sooner eat with the pigs than clean a dirty plate.

But instead of a chastising, Mom sighed, and then without a word tackled the mountain of cruddy dishes. When she had finished, she fed us scrambled eggs and slightly burnt toast, then quickly swooshed us off to the bedroom to get dressed. If we hurried, she promised a big surprise.

We scurried to dress and make our bed. We knew the surprise couldn't be presents since there was no money for such foolishness; however, the bursting sunshine on a Saturday made Kathy and I buzz about the possibilities of a picnic. But as we rushed into the living room ready for our surprise, we were greeted by the not so surprising stone cold face of Dad staring down at Mom.

"Where are you going with that, Keiko?" he asked impatiently waiting for her response. She was cradling her Buddha Temple that sat passively in her arms.

"I go to burn the Temple!" she yelled in response with a set jaw and stiff upper lip. We had never seen her so determined, or so bold.

"Like hell you are," Dad said shocked. "You can't do that, Got' damnit. Stop this nonsense now, or you'll be sorry! We'll all be sorry if you do this! *Do you want the curse to come upon us?!*"

I couldn't tell if Dad was playing mind games with Mom or if he was genuinely gripped in fear of Buddha. I suspected a little of both with trying to scare us kids kicked in for good measure.

"You listen Lichard. This Temple evil to me now. I take from house," and without giving Dad a chance at rebuttal, Mom quickly sidestepped Dad and crashed through the side door. Once outside, she made her way swaggering down the hill in her tight dress and pump shoes to the end of the yard, with us kids in hot pursuit. Slowly recovering from his shock, Dad staggered woefully behind.

Under our lone apple tree, Mom quickly propped up twigs she had obviously placed there the night before. Gathering some old leaves, she stuffed them in between the stick chimney. I was impressed with such a well-thought-out plan and watched in awe as Mom brushed her wind-blown hair from her face and then striking a match, lit the brambly brush fire. She then lifted her Temple high above her head and with outstretched arms began to curse at the Buddhist god.

"I burn you, Buddha God! You lie to me! You no true God to me anymore! I take you from my life forever! In the name of true God, I send you away!" Mom was shouting at the top of her lungs all the while crying hysterically. You could tell her faith was truly from God. She was shaking violently, so much so I became worried for a second that she would burn herself as she lowered Buddha into the roaring flames. What courage she was showing to destroy such an important part of her life on faith and faith alone!

Dad was visibly shaken from the jog down the back yard slope. His cigarette charred lungs had him in a death grip for air, and he mumbled between gasps, "We'll all be sorry! You wait and see! We'll all be cursed forever!" he threatened as he backed away. "God, I don't even want to think about what will happen to us!"

How ironic that Dad cursed the very God Mom was now praising. He was transfixed on the blaze that now surrounded the burning idol, his eyes dancing with the speed of the licking flames. You could smell his fear in the air. He was trying desperately to scare us, but I suspect his fear was more of losing his death-grip control over Mom, much more so than any fear of this pot of clay melting before our very eyes.

I began walking back to the house in silence with Kathy and Brock. Hmmph! Some Saturday picnic surprise! And Mom... she wasted all those years praying to something that melts for gosh sakes!

I paused at the gate and looked down on Mom, her hands clasp to her chest as she chanted to her new God. Deep down I sensed this was life altering for Mom. I hoped that the church and Mom's new Bible would hurry up and teach her that physical, mental and verbal abuse sucked. I wondered how much more room for love Mom would have in her heart by emptying the part of it that lived in fear of Buddha... and of Dad.

Yep, it would only be a matter of time until everything would be all right. I couldn't be wrong.

...or could I?

Chapter 7

"never" finally comes

Everyone went to work the next day and I suddenly found myself alone for the first time. It occurred to me that I was STILL in a foreign country with little money and no car for transportation. I decided early that I wasn't going anywhere.

However, instead of panic I actually welcomed the solitude. The first three days had been jammed-packed full of action and memories. It was almost more than I could absorb. It was like I was a jigsaw puzzle spread out on the table and gradually being put together, but not without fitting some painful "past" pieces together first. I could feel myself becoming whole, but would I like the total picture when it was done?

The tiny apartment suited my needs right now. It afforded me peace and solitude without having to venture out. I had plenty of tea available and plenty of time to think about what I had experienced and record it in my journal.

I had gotten out of bed but didn't bother to dress when everyone else got ready for work and school. In contrast to my baggy housecoat garb, the kids looked neat, clean and colorful in their school uniforms. I could tell that they were being obedient to their parents in going to school, but their hearts were tugging at them to stay with Cousin Amy. I was truly touched. I could even tell that Miyuki wanted to stay with me rather than go to the car dealership where she and Maki both worked. Hidetoshi on the other hand appeared at breakfast in his work uniform, the consummate image of the Japanese businessman workaholic. He was stoic as the patriarch of the family, setting an example that work and school come first. I felt a twinge of sadness that I had not won his heart to the point of him wanting to stay the day with me as well.

Still, I was only a little disappointed.

I looked forward to relaxing in my Japanese slippers, listening until boredom to my Japanese language CDs and to weaning myself of my habitual overdoses of cohee by sampling primarily, the green tea. Concerned by going to work that they were making me stay alone too long, Miyuki had invited her family to eat out with us tonight at a local restaurant. So before the big party, I was determined to make it a very relaxing day to the end.

The day flew, literally...

I never knew relaxing could be so much fun. Lord knows I needed it, when rudely I found myself jolted out of my therapeutic state of euphoria with the ringing of the doorbell in mid-afternoon. It was Ai, home from school.

Then shortly after; IT hit.

The apartment began to rumble, slowly at first and then in the wink of an eye it began to shake up and down and sway back and forth at the same time. It was an earthquake aftershock! With each pulse the top of the building swung out like a carnival ride extending beyond its' base, and us helpless to stop the freefall to our death should the cables and concrete holding the ride together snap.

I grabbed Ai as my eyes darted around the room watching for pictures and ornaments to begin raining down from the walls. I contemplated leaving the building but the only exit I knew was the elevator, obviously not a very safe option. The shaking was so hard I could feel my hair swaying around my neck, sending bristles of fear throughout my body. My head shot to the left as I caught sight of the dish cabinet doors swinging open. Then my head spun to the right as I heard plates and cups and saucers rattling on the kitchen counter. The rumbling was deafening, like the freight train sound of a tornado back home. I slowly moved Ai to the couch where we sat down purposely tucking our legs up under us as if afraid touching the floor with our feet would intensify the tremors.

And then suddenly it was done.

No gradual subsiding, no winding down, just instant silence – as deafening as the quake itself. I stood up slowly as if sticking a toe in the ocean water to test the temperature and tempt the sharks. Nothing. I made my way in three short steps to the dining room table (a misnomer since it was in the same room as the living room couch), and immediately parked my quaking body.

'Okay, Lord. Am I supposed to be here? Was yesterday a warning and today a threat? Am I doing the right thing disturbing the status quo, delving into the past and desperately trying to buy into a heritage you're telling me I can't own? Give me a sign. Give me a sign I'm supposed to be here.' I thought to myself. Well, that's actually not true. Actually I spoke the words out loud just so I had the comfort of hearing a voice, any voice speaking English! Even my own…

Suddenly the doorbell rang, bringing my nerves to full alert! But it was only Ai's friend Mao. Both ran off to the bedroom babbling about the aftershock as I looked around for something to help calm my nerves. I finally decided upon making myself a cup of green tea. Rummaging through the cabinet proved to be frustrating, and I began to wonder if finding a simple bag of tea would be possible; after all, every container had the typical chicken scratches on the labels causing a rise of anger at my mother for not teaching me more of the Japanese language.

Then I spotted a small ceramic container on the cabinet in the kitchenette area. From a distance, there appeared to be bags of something peeking out. Maybe more tea or perhaps it could be sugar I hoped as I glided across the room. Upon retrieving the container, I pulled out one of the packets expecting to find more foreign writing, but to my surprise, I found another undeniable confirmation of my belonging in Japan.

My mind went numb, my hands still trembling as I zoomed in for a closer look. Gasping I covered my mouth in amazement at what I saw. On the face of the packets were bold black capital letters and in plain English was my name, AMY spelled out clearly on each bag of sugar.

I felt a moment of shame immediately understanding that God most definitely was losing patience with my lack of faith. I felt a jolt of adrenalin, actually flinging the bag to the floor almost as if I had been zapped with electricity. Staring me in the face was this simple packet of sugar. Only this was no ordinary sugar. In all of Japan, in all of the hieroglyphics of Japanese script, in a totally estranged atmosphere and falling only a few feet from my picture they had hanging on the wall, the name of the sugar was AMY. What were the odds? Just as I needed a sign, just when I begged for a sign!

"Okay, Lord. I get it. I'm supposed to be here," I said out loud. This time it wasn't a doubting question, but a stern confirmation. I no longer felt alone. Instantly I felt as welcome here as I had ever felt welcomed anywhere in my life.

As Ai, Mao and I straightened up the apartment, my excitement drifted to thoughts of what lay ahead to tonight and the party we were going to have with Miyuki's family. I felt a special bond with Miyuki. But due to the communication gap, I had some doubt as to how she felt toward me. However, tonight should go a long way toward answering that question. Tonight was dedicated to her family instead of Hidetoshi's, and I was really looking forward to it. Besides, the earthquake had taken away some of the appeal of being alone, and now I longed to be out of the apartment and surrounded by family. Bunches of family!

The restaurant they chose was on top of one of the tallest buildings downtown. After the earthquake and aftershocks I wasn't real sure about dining in a restaurant on top of a TALL building... I've read that Japanese buildings are built to withstand most quakes. Right...and the Titanic was unsinkable too. But as I wove my way through the building shops toward our nighttime meal, I began to discover that a lot of buildings were structured the same. Shops appeared to all be on the lower levels with several restaurants always on the top floor. To the point; there wasn't much I could do to avoid earthquakes and tall buildings – I was in Japan for gosh sakes!

Lingering at the end of the "family train" meandering past shops, up stairs and through more shops, I was soaking in all the colorful displays when Hidetoshi unexpectedly ran to the back of the line, put his arm around me, and ushered me to the front. Stopping, my eyes followed the invisible path of his pointing finger. Only then did I notice an elderly couple rushing out of one of the restaurant's entranceways to greet us. Without saying a word Hidetoshi pointed to the couple and then turning around, pointed to Miyuki indicating that this was her parents. I'm not sure if she was smiling at her parents or me, but by my acknowledgement of understanding, I was greeted by what was to become her trademark genuine smile. Close family was what I had been *missing and was the original purpose for my visit. You could tell she was proud of her parents, Quoko and Tehluheko as they were introduced, and that made me feel all the more welcome.*

Inside I was just as quickly introduced to Miyuki's brother Masakazu and his wife Chikako (pronounced Chicago – not lost on Rob who is a diehard Cub fan; or me for that matter since Oprah is broadcast from there). As we settled into our seats, I was ceremoniously presented with a four foot banner in Japanese Kanji symbols that translates to mean "bless this house of happy boys." They must have understood the advance trip emails explaining my family of Rob and three children – all boys, of course. The banner brought warmness to my heart for the thoughtful gift, and the missing of my children half a world away. Oh how I wished I could share my overflowing happiness with them. For a brief moment, I was overcome with pangs of worry about how I was ever going to make them understand the intense emotion and holistic healing I was experiencing.

The evening continued in grand style. The fare was buffet, and I didn't recognize one thing on it. Oh, I knew the food groups… well most of them, but none of the dishes looked like anything I had ever seen in America. I wasn't too surprised that the foods were foreign to me eating at Hidetoshi's home, or even other restaurants where meals were ordered for me. But here, at a buffet with dozens of choices of exotic and delicious looking foods, I couldn't get over the fact that I didn't recognize <u>anything</u>. I was finally beginning to understand that we were more sheltered in America than I had ever realized. As the greatest nation and only superpower on earth, sometimes a slice of humble pie on the buffet is still needed to help us remember we should honor and respect other cultures of the world.

I looked around the table as I sat to begin my meal, pausing to reflect at my good fortune. My "nevers" as in I will never find my family and I will <u>never</u> travel to Japan, has finally come. It came like a whirlwind, and now I found myself stuck right in the middle of it.

At that very moment I only had one thought on my mind. I had met so many wonderful people, family and now Hidetoshi's in-laws…but I regretted I could not meet his dad, my Uncle Ilotta. Ever since childhood I had dreamed of meeting my mother's only brother. He was dark and mysterious and handsome and debonair, or so I imagined.

Unfortunately, I found out that he had died at the age of 56 of cancer, just into his prime. I also wished my Mom could have seen me now. She died before she should have too. She was a victim of breast cancer and later, lupus.

Like brother, like sister...

I cannot get those horrible images out of my head as I lay in bed, the weight of the world crushing down on my petite heart. Just as it did with Kimmy.

I remember she looked as if she were a doll, all dressed in delicate pink and white, her frail body just sleeping in her bed – draped in her favorite blanket. Only this was a casket.

Kimmy was my best friend; *was* my best friend. I recall gazing at her silky blonde hair for the longest time, remembering her beautiful blue eyes now absent of their light. After years of search I had finally found someone like Kimmy who was willing to learn anything about Japan. We would talk for hours, and her interest seemed endless. She did not make sport of me or my family. Her sincerity to be my friend; *my* friend, was so genuine and so kind. She was my life, in many ways filling voids family could not.

Most days we flipped through Mom's Japanese catalog and let our imagination race with the turning of each page. I spent time teaching her Japanese songs that my Mom had taught me. She would watch with me in awe as Mom would craft beautiful Japanese dolls to sell for food money, marveling at the colorful silk costumes and wondering out loud about the first time Kimmy would visit Japan with me.

Her friendship allowed me to be somewhat socially accepted since Kimmy was the unopposed queen of the school. Because the kids liked her, they began to somewhat tolerate my foreign ways, and lower economic standing.

Kimmy...was everything to me.

And then one day Kimmy wasn't sitting at her desk in school. It was one of the longest days of my life. Teachers were whispering in hallways about her sickness, and we were all told to pray for Kimmy. So I went home and I prayed like I never prayed before. I tried to go to her house to see her, but she was in the hospital – no children visitors allowed. No children! If no children visited, who would? I imagined Kimmy lying in bed all day with no one to play with. It reminded me so much of Brock that the thought of it broke my heart.

It didn't take long.

In a couple weeks the announcement I didn't even give the time of day to consider came over the school intercom – a moment of silence for Kimmy who had died in her sleep the night before.

I was shocked and devastated and angry. Her soul remained innocent though her small body had lost the battle with a deadly mixture of polio compounded by rheumatic fever. I had heard mumps within the girl's restroom chatter too, but it didn't really matter. Whatever attacked her ganged up on her all at once, and even Kimmy, my perfect Kimmy, couldn't overcome their ruthless advances.

My parents had to drag me away from her casket at visitation, screaming at God and his unjust world. In Sunday School, they teach infinite patience and understanding so in my mind, if I watched the casket long enough, Kimmy was going to wake up. But it did no good, just like the prayers before she died.

Now it seems like Mom is always sick, just like Kimmy was. The horrible images of Kimmy's death keep me awake at night wondering if that might happen to Mom.

Mom's illnesses are too many to count, even for a smarter than average third grader. Ulcers, high blood pressure, all kinds of infections – I often thought if it hadn't been discovered yet, it was because it was hiding in Mom's body. She is living now off of prescription pills and rides a roller coaster of emotions. But I will give her credit. Ever since her conversion to Christianity she seemed less stressed, more at peace, and less tolerant of Dad's shenanigans. Me, I tried to understand God, I really did, but I was still angry over Kimmy.

Then after today I had the revelation that I had better not anger him against Mom, so I restarted the nightly prayers I had abandoned after Kimmy died. I restarted my prayers because after today, my Mom will never be the same again. How could she be? She wasn't even a woman anymore, was she?

It was breast cancer.

I lay there in horror thinking about what I had just seen. The darkness of night is always scary enough without images of such carnage branded in my head to go with it.

I guessed I had been in denial about any risk to Mom, until tonight when I saw what a terrible job the surgeons had done. At least it looked that way to me. Tonight was my first chance to see what no child should ever see. I could finger paint scars smoother than hers.

I thought nothing could compete with the red spots on her breast when she first discovered them. Both of them – breasts that is, not spots. She has more than two spots. She has a chest full of them. Over the period of a couple of days her breasts went from "sore to touch" to "sore to look at."

I pulled the blanket up tight under my nose and shuddered flashing back to the smell of rotting flesh when I got close to her a couple of months ago. The sores were rashy and seeping. Even the over the counter antibiotic cream seemed worthless and didn't help.

But the tomorrows came and went without Mom going to the doctor. Just more antibiotic cream and more pain killers. And then the REAL tomorrow finally arrived. The church calls it "a day of reckoning." Mom was out of painkillers with no more refills. The sores on her chest won. The pain was too much to bear, and Mom had to go to the doctor for an examination.

Mom told me later that the doctor was fidgety, like a boy who wanted to ask a girl to the junior high prom and couldn't find the courage. She knew then the news was bad.

"Ms. Wesson," the doctor had told Mom, "The holes in your chest are not going to clear up with any conventional treatment. No pill and no ointment will heal your condition now. You see, the silicone from your breast augmentation is causing the sores. But it's become so much more than sores now."

I paused in my thoughts cursing Mom for the stupidity of having silicone pumped into her body in Japan; long before she met Dad, or any of us kids were even a picture in her mind. It must have been vanity was all I could conclude.

I turned on my side wondering what Mom must have felt when the doctor said, "Ms. Wesson, you need a double mastectomy. The silicone is seeping out of your body on the surface, but what you don't see is that it also is seeping into your chest cavity."

Now I felt inadequate as a kid in a dangerous grown-up world. What kind of comfort was I going to be able to give? I put my anger for her self-inflicted pain aside for the millionth time and tried to concentrate on what the heck I could do to make it all better. Mom's been home for a couple of weeks now and even though her chest no longer was pronounced in the shape of womanhood, I solemnly made up my mind that I didn't care. Up until then my thoughts had been selfish. But I still had a Mom and that's all that matters. In the beginning how was I to know that her pain must have been horrible and her future uncertain?

She had been in the bathroom taking a sponge bath tonight when she came out and immediately went to bed. I guess my curiosity had finally been piqued. Barefoot and in my pajamas, I had pattered in behind her and had asked to see her scar.

I thought it would be a cut. I've seen lots of cuts. I've been raised on farms and have been around a lot of animals and suffering. This couldn't be much different. Mom was like a sick animal that just needed lots of love and time to heal, and lots more love.

"Can I see?" was all I had to say. Mom understood as if she knew I would ask someday, so without hesitation, she opened her blousy bedtime top and lifted the bandages.

The images of what I saw burned through my eyes and into my brain. Now I can't get the images out of my head. They're tearing at me and creating new scars in my mind. In fact, I was sure I could actually feel some of Mom's pain as I stared at the ungodly site.

Crisscrossed slashes ran across her entire chest where her once rounded breasts had been. In some spots, her ribs were barely covered with skin and others had an uneven terrain of flesh as evidence of the carnage. The colors ranged from hot white, to purple haze, to yellow pus, to red raw. From her collarbone to her belly, there was what looked like bullet wounds where the silicone seep holes must have been. She had several inches of long raised welts that looked like night crawlers. It was like someone was coring an apple or trying to dig the seeds out of a watermelon, and then tried to put it all back together.

I found myself lying in bed, thinking of Mom not as a woman anymore. The sight of her tortured chest involuntarily left me thinking she was something less. I was ashamed of myself as I ran from her bedroom, and I am ashamed of myself now as I lay here wondering in fear...

'What's going to happen to Mom, and could that happen to me? Was it more than just the silicone? Don't things like cancer run in your family?' I wished I knew Mom's family and whether any of them had cancer.

I finally dropped off to sleeping thinking, 'I'll never know...I'll never know...'

Chapter 8

japanese ants, florida roaches ... and blood

Hidetoshi arrived home late on Tuesday night. His job, like Rob's, on occasion calls for travel. I was thankful that he had driven himself to the airport when he left for Osaka. That way we didn't have to go get him. I had my fill of airports just getting here, and I still had the return trip home alone fishing around in the back of my mind already. In part it was my fear of having to travel halfway around the world without Rob, who was going on from Tokyo to South Korea while he put me on a plane to the States, but a bigger part of it was the people. Or better fitting, my insignificance in such a vast sea of humanity.

Not because OF the people, but because there were SO many of them. I was raised in rural farm communities and today still lived in a small ranch house out in the country. I hate driving in larger cities and I'm sure they would hate for me to anyway. But in Japan, even small cities seem large to me. The countryside in Japan is sparse compared to the Blue Ridge Mountains of North Carolina. And the people...all those PEOPLE. Like ants. Sometimes it's hard to see the concrete of the sidewalks or floors in the airport or shopping malls because you have a sea of "black ants" everywhere!

That is, a sea of Japanese businessmen in their black suits going about their jobs. Criss-crossing in every direction and moving at a pace of urgency. It makes the Japanese sometimes appears to be in orchestration, as if every person had a job to complement each other for the greater good; silent and ever efficient motion, like a wind-up toy that never winds down.

When Hidetoshi arrived home from his travels there were just myself, Miyuki and the children. For the first evening since my arrival we didn't have visitors or places to go. Aunt Iseko had been visiting earlier in the evening, but Miyuki had taken her home hours ago. We had a late supper with the usual gaiety, in fact, probably more so than usual. After the last couple of days, Miyuki and I had progressed to more than strangers; even more than family. We had progressed to girlfriends in Hidetoshi's absence. We were more than happy and close, we were comfortable around each other.

After supper Miyuki and I retired to my bedroom facing the daunting task of packing all the gifts I had received. I had discussed with Rob by phone and he had said it would be all right to give some of my clothes to Miyuki as gifts in return for all I had been given. Miyuki was my size so we both thought this would be the perfect gesture. We had also found out that with the tight import laws in Japan, American-made products where highly regarded.

However, when I motioned for her to pick something from my suitcase she lowered her head resolutely and shook it 'no.' I protested that I needed to make room for my Japanese gifts and pulled out a chiffon nightgown and accompanying housecoat. There was no way she could resist a second time. She could not contain herself as she jumped with glee saying, "Hidetoshi like!"

I then pulled out a line cut paisley dress with a crisscross bust line. It had a flattering hemline with a ruffle, making it very feminine. It actually could be used for a very sexy dress or worn with a pair of jeans as a long top. Miyuki slipped it on over her jeans and I told her it was sexy.

She acted embarrassed and said, "Me no sexy." I stood her in front of the mirror and raised my brow saying she was wrong and that Hidetoshi most certainly would think it was sexy. Miyuki turned and hugged me as a child would, squeezing me in thanks for her new clothes. I humbly thanked her instead and returned the hug. It was then I noticed Hidetoshi standing in the bedroom door. He seemed puzzled over our show of affection. It was obvious in sharing my life over the last couple of days, Miyuki and I had become very close.

Breaking our embrace, I asked Hidetoshi what was wrong. Straining for *the words but unable to comply, he went to the computer and with a sigh, typed his response. The language translator spit out the answer in bold blue letters on the monitor, "I feeling reservation right now because Miyuki has founding friendship with you."*

Leave it to a man. He was jealous.

I felt awful that our happiness made him sad. Suddenly, I was ashamed for not noticing that we were hurting his feelings. In a way it was the ultimate compliment. I had actually moved my cousin to feelings of "my belonging" in the family, and to the insecurity that he did not. Flattered, I immediately wanted to make him feel better.

I took my right hand and extending it straight out, I pointed to my wrist with my left. Looking him square in the eye, I made a cutting motion over my wrist and pointed between the fictitious cut and Hidetoshi. I said, "we cousins, we same blood."

Pointing to Miyuki, I tried to reinforce the thought. "Girlfriends. But you and I same Suzaki blood." To add the final emphasis, I took his wrist and rubbed it against mine. It worked like magic. The light went on in his face. I was special to him again. We had a blood bond shared by no other and the thought that I had traveled the globe to see him struck home. His smile was unmistakable and as he smiled, I smiled inside.

The rest of the night became magic. We ALL talked and giggled and swapped stories of our lives, our families, our countries and our cultures. In the wink of an eye, the night became a lifetime memory. It seemed as if instantly 2 AM was upon us; leaving my jaws tired but content.

Hidetoshi must have picked up on my more frequent yawns and bobbing head. Glancing at his watch, he pointed to the ever moving hands, and said, "Ahhmmy, you bath and bed. Even ants must sleep." I wasn't sure if he was moved solely for my concern or by his own exhaustion from work, travel, and now a night of partying with two crazy women. But I was touched that he was concerned.

I nodded my head and rose to do what he suggested, giving him a big hug goodnight. He gave a surprisingly gentle hug in return, and I meandered through the living and kitchen area to the small bath area. I call it bath area because it oddly contained a dwarf sized washing machine but no toilet. The toilet as noted earlier was in a closet square unto itself, also oddly at the opposite end of the apartment.

As I was drawing the water and undressing, I flashed back to Hidetoshi's comment that "even ants must sleep." What a quaint and sincere way to make the point, and a perfect ending to a perfect evening.

As I soaked in the tub, the ants made me flash back, this time to a less desirable chapter in my life –

Sometimes Dad's a real idiot. Forgive me, Lord. In fact, Lord, forgive me twice because you know what? Dad's a real idiot!

He'd made up his mind to find another job, even if it killed us! The last in a series of evictions had been humiliating for the entire family, but pulling up stakes and moving to Florida seemed more like running than grappling with the real problem. But since we had few possessions to transport, Dad made the move seem more appealing in his presentation to Mom, and after some badgering, she agreed to go. I think she was tired of the endless shame of moving locally in Indiana, and silently hoped new surroundings would make Dad a new person. I also don't think she really had a clue just how far Florida is from Indiana.

Sometimes I wonder why she continues to be with him. If I was her, I wouldn't. The only conclusion that comes to mind is that she still harbors some fear. Maybe not the *daily* old fear of Dad before the burning of her Buddha Temple, but a more subtle fear; the fear of being alone in a foreign country with three children. And perhaps the lingering fear of what Dad was still capable of in one of his now more infrequent, but still at times violent state of mind. Secretly I sometimes wished he would just kill us and get it over.

When we finally got to the Sunshine State, Dad immediately began looking for rentals. The good Lord knows we can't afford to buy a home with nothing more than the shirts on our backs and what little pride we possessed. We knew we needed the shirts to keep us clothed, but the pride was in short supply and we knew it would only last as long as the date of Dad's next drunk or violent out burst.

We pulled into the first junkyard we saw, complete with a "junkyard dog". Behind the piles of smashed and "would-be" smashed cars stood a row of bungalows in what I could only assume may be our next living quarters. Dad disappeared into the mechanic's garage and emerged a few moments later with a gleam in his eye and a smile on his face. He was so excited he could barely contain himself. Mom asked him questions but he told her to be quiet, she would see soon enough. He told her to trust him, and Mom openly laughed. She's heard that line before! And that look of his – it always preceded something that Dad thought was so great and inevitably turned out to be a bust.

Not far down the road we pulled into a majestic ranch style house. It stood at the end of a lane peppered with gorgeous flowers and ornamental palm trees blowing in the wind. The front yard had a statue of a small Negro boy holding one of those green mirror balls that looked so silly to me. The front door was laced with intricate carvings in the wood. Everything looked so shiny and neat. It reminded me of Dad's Army crew cut. I wondered to myself if it had the same hidden horrors underneath the surface as well.

Dad left us in the car and banged on the front door. In a moment he was met by a rather large middle age woman who let him in after some minutes of questioning. Dad returned a half hour later to his family he had abandoned in the car, all of us now sweating profusely. Mom yelled at him when he returned for being so inconsiderate as to sit in an air-conditioned home leaving his family to bake like dogs in a hot oven like the car. Dad just started the ignition and took off down the road, grumbling to himself for any hint of raining on his parade of what he apparently thought was going to be a revelation of good news. We rode in fuming silence as we made our way around the corner and began bouncing back and forth along a rough driveway adjacent to the ranch house.

At the far, far, far end appeared to be a small neighborhood which was indeed on the backside of the junkyard. The half-dozen houses lined up across from each other all the way to the dead end of the road. Each bungalow was identically shaped and faintly painted in a variety of pastel colors. As we got closer, we could see the paint peeling off of most of the houses. I noticed the rain gutter of one house hanging off kilter and another whose flower garden consisted of a singular weed begging to be pulled. Most of the houses looked barren and unattended. I tried to imagine how quaint the neighborhood would look if the houses were fixed up. Of course the owner's junkyard would still remain an eyesore. After all, who wants to live next to a junkyard? Then it hit me that apparently "we do."

Pulling up to the last house and practically dragging Mom out of the car, Dad explained that he had shrewdly bartered with the landlord to fix the bungalows for rent. He then proudly pulled out a set of keys and let us into his new castle. As I walked in I had to admit, it was better than what we had in Indiana. But better than nothing isn't much of an endorsement.

Mom walked completely around the house and then bluntly said, "when you start looking for a real job?"

"This is my real job. This is what I will do until something else comes up."

"Fixing dump no buy food," she retorted.

Dad, amid one of his arrogant and usually not well thought out plans, chose to ignore Mom.

In disrespect, Mom snickered at his silence and said, "I thought so."

Dad then turned to each of us kids and delegated the assignment of unloading the car while he looked at the other houses. We were tired and hungry and left to do all the work, but we were so thrilled to just have a roof over our heads that we obeyed in classic military style.

Already weak from travel fatigue, the unloading made us totally exhausted. I wondered what kind of a picture that must have made as the three children unpacked a beat up old station wagon in front of a beat up old house, in the middle of nowhere.

The houses were partially furnished so we had a bed to sleep in. It was the only thing about this trip that Dad did right, and he did it by accident. The sun barely setting, we went right to bed out of sheer exhaustion. We were too tired to eat, not that it made any difference; we had experienced going to bed hungry before. With very little money, there was no rush to spend it. The shopping would have to wait until tomorrow and with Dad having a job that paid no money, we would have to make that last a very long time.

No sooner had my head hit the pillow and I was asleep, and no sooner was I asleep than I was back awake again. I heard scratching followed by silence, and then more scratching. I was the lightest sleeper in the house so I always heard house-creepy noises before anyone else. But this was unlike anything I heard before. I felt my stomach muscles tighten as I strained to identify the sound. We had no lamps to turn on and I wasn't about to get out of bed to see what was afoot in a house I had never slept in.

"Kathy, wake up. What's that noise?" I queried as I gently nudged her. No response. This was no time for the delicate. I smacked her as my voice strained, "Kathy! What is that? Come on, wake up, darn it!"

"What noise?" she replied, half asleep and half curious. The noise had momentarily stopped at the sound of my voice. She lost her "half curious" in about a half a second and responded, "I don't hear anything."

"It sounds like someone scratching at our bedroom door, or at the walls, or at the floor. I don't know; it just creeps me out."

"I still don't hear anything," she replied back now in full disdain for me waking her. "Why don't you just go back to sleep?"

"I'm not going to sleep and you aren't either. I think it stopped when we started talking. You stay awake and I'll be quiet, then you'll hear for yourself." I was petrified because now it must surely be intelligent to respond to the sound of our voices. I also didn't want to be alone in the dark in case it started again.

Kathy immediately went back to sleep anyway.

'Thanks a lot!' I thought. Then my breathing virtually stopped as the annoying sound returned and even louder than before! Kathy's heavy breathing was overshadowed by the awful sound, but she didn't budge from her beauty sleep. I shook her again, but it was wasted effort. She was oblivious to everything but her dreams. Even though I was completely worn out from the travel and unpacking, I didn't sleep a wink all night.

The chirping voices of the early morning birds were never as pleasant as they were the next day. As the morning wore on through breakfast and a bath, I began to feel a little better. Maybe I had imagined the whole thing. 'Perhaps it's just my rebellious attitude and hyper nature playing tricks on me,' I reasoned.

After my bath I got dressed and sauntered tiredly into the kitchen to help Mom with the restocking of the house with what little staples and possessions we had brought. I thought I would help by unpacking the dishes first. But when I opened the cupboard I was greeted by a scampering critter that looked like an oversized ant, or beetle, or even alien creature about to invade! Startled, I dropped the dishes as my hands automatically flew to my cheeks to cup a curtailed yell! I had never seen such a thing, but before I could show it to Mom, poof; it was gone. It disappeared better than Houdini. I never even saw where it escaped to but I know one thing for sure, it was HUGE! Mom of course didn't believe me, and I resigned myself to cleaning up the pile of broken plates, sulking even more than ever about moving here in the first place.

In a few minutes it happened a second time, only this time it happened to Mom who dropped a frying pan and let fly her best Japanese bonzai scream! I felt redeemed at last! I was almost glad the critter reappeared; almost…

Dad came running from the bathroom with a face full of foamy shaving cream to see what was the matter. Mom explained it was a giant ant. Dad said she was off her rocker; there was no such thing. To prove his point he opened another cupboard and was greeted with the same type of ant we were. They stood eyeball to eyeball its antenna twisting in mid-air for a split second, and then it made that scratching noise I heard the night before and scampered away.

"It's only a cockroach, for pete sakes," Dad exclaimed in futile disgust. "They are always a handful in these climates. People just learn to live with them," he said in his best condescending *you're stupid and I'm smart* voice.

Mom was not amused. Dad had begun to tell Mom what for, when he had second thoughts. Probably because this time I suspect, he knew Mom was right. Living with a house full of bugs that don't pay toward the rent was too much to ask.

After a few short and heated words, Dad was off to see the landlord about spraying the roaches dead. I tagged along rather than stay there and continue to unbox things and run the risk of being greeted by a whole family of roaches.

The landlord laughed. "Why do you think the houses are empty? I was hoping with you fixing them up and a fresh coat of paint, I could get some people to move in, even if it's just for a little while. And don't you think I haven't tried to kill them cuz I have. I've sprayed until it began to cost more than the houses are worth, so I stopped. I guess they have built immunity to the insecticide. Most probably impossible to kill now," he stated matter of factly, sending Dad and me packing unceremoniously with an abrupt door in our faces.

I walked home with Dad not being overly satisfied with his "it will be all right Amy" assurances. I knew I wasn't. I managed through the day by helping make the beds and clean the floors thinking an overdose of Spic and Span might kill them; anything to stay out of the cupboards.

Come evening, I had settled down…at least as much as was capable considering my *energizer spirit*. After supper of flour gravy spread on toast, Mom made a pan of popcorn. It was cheap and filling and had become a Wesson staple. It must have been the next best thing to rice for Mom. Dad had worked getting the television antenna up that day so we settled onto the couch with our popcorn to watch a movie on the one and only TV channel we could get to come in. The reception was snowy, but the break from bugs and unpacking was welcome.

Halfway though the movie I was actually enjoying myself watching the small tube's bright light projection and the shadows it made stretch and dance off the walls every time one of us moved. It was a passing pleasure that we were actually snug on the couch eating salty popcorn and feeling content for the first time since leaving Indiana.

But contentment was short lived as suddenly a large roach shot across the television screen! I was startled by its boldness since I had drawn the conclusions this morning that 1/ it likes dark places and 2/ noise might keep it way. I hadn't planned to worry about the cockroaches until bedtime. And then I planned on sleeping closer to Kathy and her snoring (that she insisted was only "loud breathing") to help scare them away.

I was startled, but Mom was ticked off. She was going to get that bug and put an end to this. I could see the determination in the set of her jaw as she turned on the light to duel Mr. Roach to the death.

Her plan was short-lived. When the light flashed on, my heart stopped. To everyone's horror (even Dad's), we did not have "a" roach problem. We were the proud owners of what seemed to be the entire roach nation. The floor was painted in a sea black. It reminded me of an ant hill at the park – all marching out to attack any picnic basket that came into view. Only this time the basket was our living room, and the food might just be us! There were not just a few as we had surmised earlier this morning. There were millions, billions, jillions! We not only couldn't see the color of the floor because of the ocean of black, we couldn't see the floor! It gave you the impression that if you stepped onto what you *thought* was the floor; you would sink like quicksand into a vat of roaches.

Before I had time to scream, the light seemed to part the sea of black like Moses had parted the Red Sea. The roaches scampered to disperse in a circular pattern. It seemed as if we were in the sky watching the eye of a hurricane. The opening on the floor began in the middle of the room and got larger and larger.

In less than a minute, the black void had all but disappeared leaving us all in shock. One because it happened, but mostly because even though we witnessed the whole exodus, we still weren't sure WHERE they all went. With the floor cleared, I suddenly jumped up as the thought occurred to me that some could have decided to hide in the couch. Turning to survey my bottom, I quickly assessed that there were no roaches on me. Then with all the courage I could muster, I leaned over and peaked under the couch. Gratefully I saw nothing. It was as if half-dollar-sized bugs had vanished before our very eyes!

I went to bed afraid to go to sleep; *really afraid, scared to death, petrified afraid to go to sleep.*

Days turned into weeks, and my fear never subsided. I suffered allergies and was sure it had something to do with the roaches. Dad said it was some pollen outside and he wanted me to stay indoors more, but not me. Not with the roaches! Anyway, I noticed that I felt better outside more than in our roach infested death trap of a house so deciding I was a better doctor than him, I played outside every chance I got.

Mom escaped from the roaches by getting involved in a small church down the road. For all of her efforts, she could not get Dad to turn from Buddha so she spent her time learning more about her Bible and the stories in it. Her dream was to transform Dad into a person who loved God as much as she did. Over time her plans for his conversion slipped into tolerance, as long as the children were safe.

Job-wise, her patience was anything but Christian. She was tired of having to "make do" with Dad's job that didn't pay anything. Actually Dad also became disillusioned with his job, somewhat surprisingly because he was not one to openly admit he had made a mistake in coming to Florida. More often than not, he comes home all greasy and grimy and smelly, and fills the air for an hour with cuss words from arguments with the landlord and complaints of how little work got done. The only thing that kept Dad "employed" was that a couple of the houses got rented out. The landlord could have cared less about the plight of *our* family. All he knew was that *he* was better off than before we came, just so long as he continued to collect rent money from new would be victims of the assassin roaches.

And then suddenly as fast as the roaches appeared, we disappeared.

Dad finally decided he had had enough of Florida, so we packed up in the middle of the night and moved back to Indiana, I'm sure to the shock and dismay of our lazy landlord. I couldn't have been happier...

Or so I thought.

Chapter 9

my *god* and dad's *god*...

You can never be sure of what women talk about when the men are away.

In this case it was Miyuki, Maki her best friend, and me. Hidetoshi had just left for an overnight business trip. After all the events packed into such a short period in time, as if almost frozen in an on-going moment of euphoria, suddenly three women found themselves alone, staring eyeball to eyeball without men to lean on, look to or be inspired by, but I'm getting ahead of myself...

Shortly after Hidetoshi had left, Miyuki and I had that sudden and instant communication that women often have without saying a word. Eyes met, and our lips curled up in unison knowing each other's thoughts...and I could just tell she was thinking what I was thinking. 'Who needs men?!'

We giggled at this thought with our good morning greeting, at breakfast and one more time for good measure as Miyuki departed for work. In broken communication as she went out the door, I understood that she was making plans for her and Maki to pick me up for lunch. Just the three of us; after all, who needs men?

Without Rob, Hidetoshi and the kids (who were in school), Miyuki and I set upon a mission of some serious girl talk. Maki would be a great asset with both her understanding of English and her experience in the American culture from her studies. What she didn't have experience with was flood control as the gates of communication and affection were about to burst open.

The morning flow by and at midday I found myself sitting across from those two beautiful Japanese women ready to let my pent up words and feelings flow off of Maki's tongue. I say two Japanese women because though of Japanese descent, I still think of myself as American. I also say that because it's true in deed and action. Miyuki looks and acts the part of a doting Japanese wife. She is always smiling, either in politeness or perhaps in happiness during any task she is performing, but to me it appears she is most often smiling for someone else other than to herself. Her perfect white teeth complement her lean oriental features, and her crowning smile always puts me at ease. Kindness fills her eyes and her delicate face is kept in a perfect frame of lightened dark hair.

Maki on the other hand is a Japanese flower. She decorates every room with her presence and grace, and she is the most beautiful Japanese woman I have ever met. With perfect features, her smile betrays her with its openness of affection, and she gives me the feeling that she would be a companion for life. She would betray no secret of yours, but hold none back of hers. Her skin is porcelain without blemish and her delicate frame stunningly attractive. She is also single which immediately begs the question, 'What's the matter with Japanese men?!'

I was right about the floodgates of conversation.

Though slow waiting on translation, the communication was at light speed compared to Internet translators or pointing in dictionaries, and it was free flowing. We poked fun at husbands and their sometimes condescending ways; their egos and the endless list of things wives the world over do for their husbands – without thanks more often than not. It also might be that we were maybe a little full of ourselves as we privately crowed over who were really the brains of our families.

Maki also jumped in the conversation, explaining in part why she was still single. She explained that she was waiting for an American husband. She will always be Japanese, but after her exposure to Los Angeles, she will not settle for a Japanese husband now. It is nothing personal to the 75 million males in Japan. But studying abroad broadened her scope of the world and awakened new preferences she never knew existed before in her heart. I cautioned her that she was not living in a very ideal location for hunting an American husband

and for all the kidding we just had about Rob's shortcomings, he was taken. We all had a good laugh.

When the food came, the conversation didn't stop. Maki's voice filled the air as she remained busy explaining the variety of exotic dishes. Miyuki seemed to instinctively know what Maki was doing and wisely let her dominate the meal conversation as I learned about steamed noodles served on an arced flatbed crock and the spicy broth soup that we soaked the noodles in. The main dish was a type of beef (a pleasant relief from fish) over a hibachi burner. I learned that most food is imported. Beef I can understand, but I was surprised to find out that Japan imports a lot of their vegetables, fruits and rice too.

After the meal, we relaxed over a hot kettle of green tea, of which I was becoming an avid fan. As I cupped the tea with both hands, I leaned over and deeply inhaled its fragrant aroma. Sensing a good time to break the ice, I explained that when my Mom returned to Japan for the first and last time after 32 years in the United States, she met with ill favor from her two surviving sisters. Hidetoshi's Dad however, Uncle Ilotta, was much more understanding.

I explained that Mom returned after learning my grandma was deathly ill. But instead of open arms, she was met with open hostility by her sisters Chiaco and Minoko. The cause of the falling out was because she had turned Christian or more importantly, away from Buddha. I'm sure it also had to do with the fact that she had left Japan for America, had mixed race children and probably a host of other sibling criticisms that Mom shielded me from.

Still, I knew that Christianity was a sensitive subject. When Soshi had contacted my family in an attempt to help me find my roots, she had learned that my lack of success in finding them over my lifetime was not that they hadn't received my letters, but that "we were heathen Christians."

I was concerned about offending Maki with the subject of my religion, especially after her personal and intimate instruction to me at the Buddhist Temple. Sensing no ill will, I continued to proceed with caution. I did not want to lose the progress made with my family, regardless of religious differences – not on my very first visit. Yet God is important enough in my life that I could not ignore the subject completely.

With some trepidation, I continued to explain about Mom visiting Japan in 1989 after being away over half her life. She had returned to see her ailing *mother who died shortly after her visit, and I remember Mom talking about what an emotional trip it was. She, like me now, was happy to see Japan and her family after those many years. She had traveled to Kitakyūshū City to visit with her brother Ilotta and then on to Nagasaki where her mother and two surviving sisters were.*

The visit to her brother was as fabulous as the visit to her sisters was disastrous.

It was almost like a clash of the cultures I explained. Uncle Ilotta was open, receptive and understanding of Mom and her choice of life in America. He was genuinely happy to see her, confirming my life long belief that of all my Japanese relatives, he would be the one I would most want to meet. Rob calls it the "cool uncle" syndrome – everybody has one. But in my case, he turned out sadly to be the one I would never meet.

Aunt Chiaco on the other hand was condescending and judgmental. Aunt Minako was less so, spending much more time with Mom. I did my best to communicate how Mom felt ostracized when her sisters told her she was damned for betraying Buddha, especially since she used to be a Buddhist teacher. They told her she was the only one they had ever known who turned away from the Buddhist teachings and they were ashamed. I recall hauntingly how Mom recited the story of her visit – the scathing treatment of family who no longer thought of her as such, and how the daily Buddhist chants in her sisters' homes pounded in her head every evening. It was as if she was being punished for her years of denying her former God.

Ultimately, it was Aunt Chiaco that drove Mom out with her crazed rantings; out of the house, out of the country and out of their lives forever. She was supposed to stay in Japan for a month but called Rob for assistance in getting her home to the United States two weeks early. She could not take the persecution any longer. At the airport, her sister's parting shot was that "Buddha was going to strike her plane down on her flight home as payback for her refusal to see the error of her ways."

Maki and Miyuki were stunned. They denied that Buddha was vengeful. That was the old way. Immediately they were a bundle of emotions in response to my mother's sad story – sympathetic, remorseful, understanding, comforting, reassuring, regretful and apologetic.

And then somewhere in between the hugs and pats on the back and soothing voices, I heard something my Mom had not.

I heard voices of love.

The next day Miyuki asked if I wanted to have another girls' luncheon. With Hidetoshi still in Osaka and Rob in Tokyo, what else were we to do? It took me two seconds to agree. After all, it was as if after everyone had scattered their separate directions for school and work leaving me all alone; a feeling I welcomed a couple of days ago, but was fertilizing a restlessness upon my soul now.

And then the rains came, adding more anxiety to my being left alone during the day. Mother Earth decided to shake me up some more but unlike the earthquake, from above the ground instead of below. Rain came like there was no tomorrow. When I looked outside the balcony's sliding glass door, a sheet of water prevented me from being able to see the neighborhood tucked in the gentle hillside across the way. It also didn't help that Hidetoshi's apartment was on the top floor making the roof sound like I was trapped on rinse cycle of a washing machine.

'Surely the girls wouldn't want to go out in this weather,' I thought pessimistically, waiting for the phone to ring and call off our luncheon. But instead, as if not wanting to be cheated of time with me, I was pleasantly surprised when at noon I was greeted at the door - not to be picked up for lunch, but to assist with the sacks of "carry in" being held in Miyuki's soaking hands.

In the middle of rain and loneliness, they were my sunshine. We repeated yesterday's dinner routine as we quickly spread out the contents of the piping hot sacks, with Maki describing each delicious food and Miyuki again listening silently. After our stomachs were full and happy, we settled in the living room to visit.

Surprisingly, the conversation immediately turned to Christianity. Apparently yesterday's conversation had left them both interested, but Maki much more so. Her exposure to America had made her curious. She commented that there seemed to be something missing in her life. She was coy and respectful by not talking about Buddha's shortcomings, but instead asking about my Christian beliefs.

I explained that Christians believe in universal love and infinite forgiveness. The spirit of God lives in our souls and should be expressed in our actions. That others come before self and that we try to treat others better than we would have them treat us. In this way the rewards were endless. Not in monetary value or collection of assets, but in joy and all the intangible feelings that warm the heart and defy description.

They said they felt that way when something good happens at work or in Miyuki's case, when she shares an experience with the kids. They were not sure how Christian love differs from everyday love.

I found myself at a crossroad.

How can I make them understand and not offend? Then, moved by remembering one of the driving forces of my visit, I silently went to my bedroom and returned with a small package in my hand. I had planned ahead by wrapping the package before I ever left North Carolina, yet I had no idea if the opportunity would present itself – I had only hoped. But the voice in my head said "this was it." Hope went out the window, replaced by conviction.

I came back into the tiny living room and trembling, handed Miyuki the package. It was easy to read the puzzled look on her face. Through Maki I explained, "This is my Mom's Japanese Bible. I had given it to her many years ago to replace her original Bible when it became worn and tattered... and it is in Japanese." The Bible had special meaning to me over the years as it was a precious gift from me to Mom. To me it represented the culmination of every struggle and then victory for Mom over the years.

Held precious by me since Mom's death, I now felt moved to part with it. I had a sudden feeling that this moment was why I had kept Mom's last Bible all these years. I explained that my hand was shaking as I presented the package because of the fear I could lose my family in its presenting, and in that regard it was harder to share with my found family than it would have been with total strangers. Still, I am more compelled in my belief in Jesus and my willingness to share his teachings than to succumb to fear. Deep down I felt that warmth in my heart all Christians feel when presented an opportunity, and I was humbled by the grace of God in this singular, solemn act.

Maki translated my carefully chosen words of Christian love and cultural fear as I reverently presented my Mom's Bible as a gift. Miyuki accepted with a bowed head and a tearful eye. The tears made me realize that she understood, not the Bible's meaning yet, but its meaning to me. I also stressed that even though it belonged in the Suzaki family, I also wanted it shared with Maki and others that express interest.

Then turning to Maki, I asked if she believed in angels. She said, "Yes, the

Japanese know angels." I told her that I believed my God uses angels through people and that in my heart I know that God had brought Maki like an angel to me. She began to tear up and said she was honored and thankful that I thought of her in this way.

It is cliché to say "group hug." But I don't know of how else to describe three grown woman with their arms around each other smack dab in the middle of the living room floor. The driving rain knocking on the windows reminded me it was God's rain that had led us inside – and to this very moment.

My fear of offense and rejection about my Christian beliefs had turned out to be unfounded. I thought of it as Mom still reaching out, even after being absent from this earth for fifteen years. She had touched my life by her Christian faith, calming many of my fears in my lifetime. It was now my turn to help her touch others when she no longer could.

The tears flowed like the rain, and as God would say, "It was good."

Unfortunately it was not always so…

———————

I suppose I will always hate the night. It has never been good to me. More specifically, I hate the dark. Everything bad seems to happen in the dark. Why should tonight be any different?

Dad has started dabbling in the occult. Why does that not surprise me? He loves to always find a way out of work, churn up get-rich-quick schemes and aimlessly go through life because grass is supposedly greener on the other side of the hill…There is no finer idea than the last one he just had and now it seemed, his last idea was black magic.

The wind was nowhere to be found tonight, so Dad left the window to the front room down and locked. Closed windows made the house hotter but it either didn't occur to him or he didn't seem to care. Then after one too many complaints of suffocation or drowning in my own sweat, he instructed Brock and Kathy and I to pull up a chair in front of the window, and to be perfectly quiet.

Knowing Dad was up to something stupid, I stared blankly outside. In the horizon, the moon shone like a giant lollipop. In the foreground,

I could see the bush at the edge of the porch move every time our cat pounced at something. The cat was having more fun than me, that's for sure. In the back of my mind, I heard Dad's words of wisdom and insight on how he was going to show us wondrous things. Focusing on the dust and lint of the windowsill the word "wondrous" got my attention. Wiggling my scrawny behind in an attempt to sit up straighter in the chair, I tried to focus on Dad for a change.

"There are many powers in the world," he continued in a tone of voice that commanded my full attention now. "Excuse me, let me correct that. There are many powers in *all* the worlds. You see, I believe there is this world and many, many others. For example, there is a spirit world; and we can travel to the spirit world in our minds. It's called 'mind over matter.'"

I looked at Kathy and Brock. Brock was as riveted as Wile E. Coyote on the Road Runner, but Kathy just looked plain uncomfortable.

"Watch," Dad announced, sensing our skepticism. "I'll show you."

With that edict, he started to move his hand in a circular motion in front of the window. Slowly at first, clockwise with the back of his palm facing us. All the while he was making circles, he was chanting with his eyes closed. I could see the beads of perspiration forming on his forehead. It began after some moments to seem as if time had slowed. I don't know what he was saying, but the hair on the back of my neck was silently screaming as it stood at attention.

Faster and faster he was waving in the round motion. The faster he moved, the slower time seemed. Then as if by magic, on the next pass his hand had been turned completely around! Without breaking stride on his circular waving, the palm of his hand was where the back of his hand had been – facing us and still in constant motion in front of the window without skipping a beat!

My heart stopped. Kathy jumped back in her chair and Brock started to cry. Our semi-circle broke quickly as Mom entered the room to see what was the matter. I scattered first, not sure of what I had seen, followed quickly by Kathy. We went straight to bed, leaving Mom standing there to argue with Dad.

Neither of us wanted to talk about what we had just seen. Years of training had taught us it was best not to question Dad. Maybe he *was* a genius, maybe he *could* cross worlds…or maybe he was playing with something that ought not to be played with.

And maybe I could get the covers to my bed tucked tighter over my head…but I doubt it.

• • • •

"Lichard, you go to church. You have bad headaches even your magic no help. Church help. I already talk to them to make your headaches go away," Mom said, standing over a slumping Dad in the kitchen. His head was down in the crooks of his arms as if he got in trouble at school and had to put his head on his desk for punishment. Mom was in her Sunday best but I could tell she was frazzled and slightly anxious. It had been a couple of months since Dad's first trick with the hand over the window. Since then he has become more blatant in his "dabbling," over Mom's ardent objections.

I found myself in shock when Dad didn't say a word. He just got up from the breakfast table in his undershirt and boxer shorts and headed for the bedroom to get dressed. His headaches must really be bad for Dad to go to church for help.

The service dragged on. The pastor was a lady, but she was more preacher in the truest sense of the word than pastor. She preached and preached and preached. Mom was standing half the service with her hand raised to heaven. Just the opposite, Dad sat at the end of the pew reeling his head in a circle from his headache.

This was a new church. No surprise since we changed churches as much as we changed addresses. Well, let me clarify the word "new." Though the church was new to us, it was only in fair condition. It was solid in foundation, but outside it wasn't exactly what you would call spiffy white clean. Some of the paint was blistering from too much sun and neglect and the roof was in sore need of repair, but at least the bell worked. Inside, the pews were a woodened hue and only semi-full with the "flock." It seemed to me that the church was struggling as much as our family.

But I guess all prayers are answered because finally, the end arrived in all its glory! Hallelujah! Amen! Well, almost. The sermon was over but laying on of hands still remained. Mom approached the pastor lady in tiny Japanese steps and whispered in her ear for the longest time as the crowd restlessly looked on. Every few seconds the pastor would nod as if in agreement.

When done, the pastor lady stood erect, and turning to the congregation with Mom by her side, said forcefully, "Richard Wesson. Your wife informs me you have headaches." She paused for effect and then boomed, "Come forward and be cured!"

Dad didn't move. Not one to give up, Mom bustled down the aisle, grabbed Dad and tugged him out of the pew. He didn't look like he was objecting too much, but it was hard to tell. The grimace on his face could have been from the headache, or just from the fact he was in church.

There was a collective "whoosh" as half the congregation got up to join them in front of the altar. I sat on the edge of the pew to see what all the commotion was about. Kathy on my right was leaning forward onto the back of the pew in front of us. Brock was standing on my left, straining on tippy-toes to see what might happen next.

The congregation formed a semi-circle around the backside of Dad between him and the pulpit so he could face what was left of the congregation and his curiously gawking offspring. The pastor stepped down and stood majestically in front of the semi-circle of helpers.

"Lord, Jesus! We pray for your divine intervention for Richard Wesson. Please cure him of these terrible headaches. Please Lord, do, as we lay hands on him."

Stopping, she turned and forcibly pushed Dad by the shoulders down into a kneeling position. "And please dear Lord, Jesus...cast out the demons that are the cause of his headaches. The demons of evil Lord, the demons of the occult!" She bellowed in defiance. And in unison as if poking a cow for slaughter with a cattle prods, the entire semi-circle of people reached out and thrust their hands on Dad.

"Ahhh!" Dad screamed. His body convulsed as if electrically shocked. "Ahhh, ahhh, ahhhh!"

Mom must have whispered Dad's evil secrets of black magic to the pastor and used his headaches as a trick to get the laying of hands on and cast the demons out!

Brock, not knowing what was going on, started bawling. He was frightened they were hurting Dad, and he did his best to match Dad's every anguish. He was trying to get out to the aisle to run to his aid, but I held him firm. I found myself whimpering too. It was too awful not to. My eyes were riveted as Dad continued to scream and convulse. His voice went from the high shrill, to a low groan, to a frightening scream and back again. It was as if he were in constant pain, and still the hands continued to stay on him.

"Burn in hell, Satan, and take your evildoers with you. Free this man and his family from your clutches!"

The pastor was now shouting to be heard over Dad's wails.

Suddenly the violence intensified. His body went from limp to rigid to limp instantly and repeatedly. His arms were flinging at nothing in mid-air and made him look like a bird trying to take flight. Drool started to run out of his mouth and his pupils could no longer be seen, buried behind the yellowish whites of his eyes.

I stopped holding Brock, and I ran.

I ran out of the church for all it was worth. I ran away ashamed of my family, and I ran away from God. I was afraid I would be rejected by God if I stayed. I was afraid I didn't have enough faith. I was afraid the evil spirits would know that too and would leave Dad to attack me –

I ran all the way home, and I hid. I hid because my God and Dad's God were different, and I was afraid that one day they might become the same one….

> *Personal growth started when I stepped out*
> *of the sandbox. Personal growth continues*
> *every time I resist stepping back in.*

Chapter 10

how "it" all began

I love to shop. What girl doesn't? But I'm not the kind that shops till they drop or spends money frivolously. I work too hard for my money to spend it with reckless abandon.

Tonight was no different. Hidetoshi, now home again, wanted to take me shopping. Having been at work or on business travel the entire week he wanted to set aside time just for me now. He and Miyuki were adamant about me taking home more Japanese gifts to go with the heirlooms I had already received. He also wanted me to take home some of Japan for Kathy and for my children and grandchildren. He was working hard to instill Japanese pride in me and was doing a good job.

We went to multiple department stores and discount stores looking for gifts for my family in the late afternoon and early evening, hitting the last mall just as the sun was going down. Confidentially, I think between the restaurants and stores, everyone in Japan must go to the mall after work.

I had decided after much effort to communicate that I still wanted to shop for some authentic Japanese music to take home even though my feet were barking and my stomach growling. My youngest son loves music and is quite talented in writing his own songs. Even though he is of Japanese descent, he is not as enamored with discovering his heritage as I am. Sharing my world and blending it with his music seemed a logical connection to pique and perhaps nurture his desire to keep the family connection long after I am gone.

We settled on a combination music and book store. Not a bad choice since Rob loves books - he reads five at a time. I picked up a magazine and started to nonchalantly flip through it since reading in Japanese was slightly beyond human comprehension for me…and most of the world. I was deeply engrossed in the pictures of some Japanese stars of music and television when in the back of my mind I heard a distinct click of a camera followed by a muffled girlish laugh. I looked up and found Miyuki bowed at the waist with her left hand over her mouth stifling a giggle while her right hand hung limply holding her digital camera.

Looking up she read the puzzled expression on my face, and openly laughing, she pointed at Hidetoshi next to me. Hidetoshi for all his business grandeur had picked up the same magazine and was reading it as well, but as is the rule of the Japanese language, was flipping pages from the back to the front. Actually he was correct, but in my ignorance I had been guilty of the western custom of reading from the front and left to right…in essence what I was really looking at was the back of the magazine first. We must have made quite an impression on any passersby as we stood next to each other deeply engrossed in turning pages exactly opposite of the other.

I could not settle on anything to defend my ignorance, so, giggling, I returned to the business of shopping. The music part of the store was great to sample even though I understood none of it as it blared in the background. My American examples of Japanese music were easy listening flutes, the soothing sounds of oceans crashing and birds chirping in poetic rhythm. But contemporary music in Japan was something no American could possibly grasp on such a short visit – I simply had no idea what was popular in the clubs nor even who the local and national idols were. I ended up purchasing a couple of CDs with young-looking artists on them, not sure how many hours or seconds my son may tolerate them.

For Rob, I was looking for a pocket size "English to Japanese" translator for his travels but with less luck than my music shopping. Apparently understanding English was not a hotbed of activity on the western coast of Japan. In fact, the only thing I was able to pick up was the beginnings of a screaming headache. I was sure it was due to all the stress, lack of sleep, change in diet, and perhaps something else.

Ever since I started shopping earlier, I was missing Kathy. She and her daughter Abby are the ultimate-shopper shoppers. I wasn't sure if it was their prowess with the dollar or the fact that living with four men had dulled my shopping senses. But Kathy however can kill hours, buy nothing and actually enjoy it! I almost felt guilty that I was here and she was not. I may have been made in Japan but born in America, while Kathy was born in Japan and actually lived here the first two years of her life. It was her native home even more so than mine.

On top of her natural heritage, she had afforded me protection at home and school and filled the motherly gaps my foreign mother could not during most of my childhood. For that I will always heap intense obligation and loyalty to my infinite love for her. I only hoped and prayed that I could do an effective job of communicating all that I was seeing and doing so she can share the experience with me and perhaps someday, see fit to return to Japan with me.

We left the music and book store and headed for supper before going home. It was my hope that eating would make my headache go away. But no, that would have been too simple. Instead, after eating I felt worse. By now I had picked up a touch of nausea and the bouncing in the back seat as we made our way home made sure I had one more thing to do before bedtime. Every bump in the road confirmed that my stomach had a date with Hidetoshi's commode.

I lay back in my seat trying to forget what had now become a full blown migraine and a tsunami of a stomach ache. I tried to suffer silently so as not to concern Miyuki and Hidetoshi. I also didn't want to worry Ai and Uuto who had fallen asleep in the middle row of seats in the bouncing van.

I was trying desperately to do likewise; sleep, not bounce – but the queasiness reminded me of past feelings buried deep within me. It was the same queasiness I felt 35 years before. It reminded me that shadows of the past never remain shadows forever. Like a bad omen they will appear and reappear to remind me of "the dark side" of my life and of my family's. This particular time reminded me of how bad I felt the very first time I found out why my sister had protected *me during my childhood. It's a secret that has remained in my heart for all these years and makes me feel nauseous every time I think about it.*

Kathy was manipulated…and she was only a child…

———————————

Mom has been sick, again.

Not with the breast cancer, or in her head, or in the heart, but another life threatening experience nonetheless; one that resulted in a hysterectomy. Plenty of rest, plenty of rest and more rest is the doctor's main order of the day. No lifting, no work of any kind, and of course, no intimate relations.

That didn't seem to bother Mom any or me for that matter. Ever since we moved back to Indiana from Florida, Mom and Dad seemed even less affectionate than before. Dad was virtually non-existent by Mom's side since her mastectomy. Not that I would know anything about it, but there was no holding hands (not that there was ever much), no sitting with each other on the couch (Dad always heads for the easy chair now), and no noises coming from the bedroom at night. But then again, it could be my imagination. As any person knows, imagining your parents having intimate relations is pretty disgusting.

Kathy, on the other hand, acted worried or at least defensive of Dad. "He has to have his manly needs satisfied," Kathy commented the other night before we went to sleep. "If he doesn't, he could get sick. Once you become capable of sex, even women have to have it, but it's even more important for men. Dad told me so."

"How so?" I had asked only half interested. Our parents' sex life was not high on my priority list of casual conversation.

"If a man's satisfaction is delayed when he, you know, has an erection, then the man's body will react negatively. It's related to numerous illnesses and is one of the causes of prostate cancer. And Dad says when he has an erection that means *treatment* can't be withheld."

I propped my head up in bed with the cradle of my hand to get a better look at Kathy, skeptical of what I was hearing.

"Yup," she replied, picking up on my skepticism.

"Kathy, do you remember when we were little how he used to come into the bedroom to tuck us in with his thing sticking out."

"So," she answered with a sudden twinge of nervousness. She turned her back on me as she rolled over to face the wall.

"I remember him making you touch it to prove it was natural," I pressed on.

"So?" she repeated defensively with a crack in her voice this time.

"What did it feel like?"

"It's not like any other part of skin. It's much softer, but hard underneath. That's all. See, perfectly natural like Dad says."

"You suppose he went to bed then and he and Mom, you know... did it?"

"Probably. I think he would get awfully sick if he didn't."

"Seems kinda weird to me that if they both do it together, Mom gets sick and Dad doesn't."

"Well, the doctor told Dad that he has to release his, well you know... to keep his prostate cleaned out. I don't think a woman has one of those so I don't know how it affects a woman."

"Maybe we should ask Mom. She would know."

"No," Kathy said firmly. "Don't mention it to Mom."

"Why not? She's a woman, isn't she?" I retorted.

"Well for one, she's sick. No point in making her feel worse than she does. And Dad knows what he's talking about. He fixed up that bandy chicken with the broken wing in Florida, didn't he? He may not have a college degree, but Dad's smart about a lot of things."

"Fine. I just don't want to get what Mom's got someday. That's all." I let it rest. There were no more answers to be had from Kathy, and I'd honor her wishes not to ask Mom, but I sure as hell wasn't going to ask Dad.

The next day I meandered alone down the lane to our house from school pre-occupied with wonder as to why Kathy had to come home early. I had been notified by my teacher that she had gone home ill but they didn't tell me how ill or what illness she had suddenly come down with.

When I got inside the house I immediately threw my books on the couch. It had been a long hot, humid day, the kind where the dust sticks to your sweat when you kick it up walking down the lane, and I was exhausted. I had tons of homework to do but wanted to check on Kathy first.

"Anybody home?" I tried not to raise my voice too much in case she was sleeping. I noticed all the blinds in the house had been drawn. As if in a cave, I gradually maneuvered down the hallway half blind, half feeling my way against the wall.

I could hear Mom's heavy breathing as I passed her bedroom. She was taking a lot of medication again, and slept all hours of the day. Pausing, I hoped she was feeling better. She spends way too much time in bed and needs fresh air. At least that's what she always tells me when I'm in bed sick. Chicken soup and fresh air is God's universal cure all.

Continuing on I turned the corner of the hallway and gently opened the door to our bedroom not wanting to disturb Kathy if she was asleep too, but what I saw froze me dead in my tracks.

"Oh my God, what are you guys doing?" I gasped in total shock. There before me was my father squatting on the floor next to the bed touching his privates while looking at my sister's naked body. She was just lying there, stiff and uncomfortable.

My head was spinning, my mind shorting out, everything momentarily going black. I thought I was going to faint. I wanted to run but my feet were invisibly nailed to the floor. Instead, I found myself straining to ask, "Why didn't you lock the door!"

"Get the hell out!" Dad said in a hushed scream as he groped the floor for his pants. I started to apologize like a deer in the headlights for accidentally crossing their path, but I couldn't find the words.

When I heard Kathy begin to sob, I was startled back to reality and bolted out the door. I ran to the couch and buried my head in a pillow, my stomach tied in knots. My entire body was racked with sickening waves of nausea. Why was this happening? Why did I have to find IT? WHY didn't they lock the door? Mom was sick asleep in her bedroom for gosh sakes! My mind raced with a thousand questions and no answers.

In a few minutes, I gathered myself as I heard voices. The door still gaped open to our bedroom, and I could hear Dad talking to Kathy.

"Kathy. You have got to make Amy understand. She must not tell! If your Mother finds out, you kids will be put in a foster home; maybe separately. You have to make her understand the family must stay together."

'Damage control. That's what it is,' I thought. Make it *my* fault if the family splits up. And the sad thing is, it *will* be, unless I stay quiet. I thought of Mom and Brock and how I couldn't live without them. The innocent will be punished. How sick is that?

The bedroom door creaked open, and a knot began to swell from the bowels of my stomach, rising to my throat with each approaching step. I was relieved to see it was Kathy. The drag of her feet told me how much she dreaded each step toward me, but the military training from Dad was working on her now. Obey at all cost.

I couldn't look at her. My head was still half buried in the pillow when I blurted out, "Why didn't you lock the door? Why?!" I began to cry into the already damp pillow again.

"Amy, we did lock the door. I don't know what happened." She paused weighing her words. "It doesn't matter anyway. Dad didn't touch me," she stated with as much resolve as she could muster.

I raised my head from hiding and looked at her in shock. "What do you mean it doesn't matter? You were both naked. What does touching have to do with it?"

"Amy, you'll be reaching womanhood soon, but you're still too young to understand. I'm two years older, and Dad has already explained it to me."

"Explained what?" I asked confused.

"You and I talked about this just the other night. If a man doesn't get a sexual release from his body, he could go into shock. Mom's too sick to help him stay healthy. You don't want both our parents sick, do you? What would become of us?"

Was it true? Or was Dad just manipulating us? I don't know. What I do know is that I was more confused than ever. Since Kathy had already talked about this to me, it slowly occurred to me that this must not have been the first time! I thought again of losing Mom and Brock. I stared at Kathy through my tear-matted hair. In all her sincerity, I could see she thought what she was doing was the right thing to do; at least in her *presentation* to me. She was trying to keep the family together. She was doing her part, and now she was asking me to do mine.

Kathy moved closer and sat at the edge of the couch in her rumpled dress; silent, her eyes cast down at the floor. At fourteen, she had indeed matured for her age. I flashed back to when she was in elementary school wearing thick glasses and shabby clothes, the brunt of cruel ethnic jokes. Everyone thought she was Chinese with those thick glasses, like in the comics.

"Ahhhsooo! Bow to me, China Doll!" they would say.

I remember telling her to fight back, to be funny, and to do any-thing that would not let them see her feelings were hurt. But instead of fighting back, she withdrew to be the loner on the playground. Secretly, I was even ashamed to go over and play with her. Now I was ashamed of myself for not giving her more attention.

It was beginning to dawn on me that this had been building for years. The touching when Dad was tucking her in bed. It all led to the fateful event of finding them disgustingly naked with each other this afternoon. I'm sure it has been an emotional roller coaster for my sister, resisting her own subconscious beliefs in favor of what Dad was teaching. Dad could be convincing. For all his faults and my calling him stupid, he was pretty smart – just no common sense. Through his cruelty, his anger, his drunkenness and all his botched jobs and endless parade of homes, we never really doubted his intelligence. After all, he *was* my Dad.

I snapped out of my brief daydream when I faintly heard Kathy say, "Amy, are you listening to me? If you tell, we'll surely be split up. You know what they say about foster homes. We will probably be sepa-rated and then ALL of us will get abused, including Brock – and he's too sickly and frail for that to happen. Do you want that to happen? We may never see each other again! And besides, Dad didn't touch me! It'll be all right! I'll be all right! I have to keep us together. WE have to keep us together!" she pleaded.

Still, I wanted to scream. I felt betrayed. I had come home all full up with worry about Kathy for having to leave school sick and instead I got   this.

"Kathy, are you crazy?!" Like a volcano bubbling over, my emotions erupted. "Do you think this is how a Dad's supposed to act?!"

"But he says it's not his fault. Mom's been sick. Most Dads have wives who can take care of them. We just need to know that you won't tell. We can't be separated. Even Mom has said 'never let the kids be separated' when she thought she was going to die with breast cancer. You know that was her dying wish. Do you want to go against Mom now that she's fighting for her life again? She just had another major operation, for gosh sakes. You know," Kathy gravely stated almost against her will, "it will be your fault if that happens."

If it was the last ditch intention to scare me with her resolute words, it was beginning to work. She had been either brainwashed or threatened into the belief that what she was telling me was true, and now she was even convincing me against *my* will.

With resignation, I succumbed to her arguments. "I won't tell. But I want you to know that I'm doing it for the family. ALL the family, EXCEPT for Dad. And you can tell him that for me," I said with as much rebellion as I could muster.

In the days that followed, the weight of hidden embarrassment began eating at me daily; to the point I can't focus on anything.

Today in school I was trying to concentrate on a math problem when I flashed back to "the scene." I didn't want to but something invisible made me. In disgust I was ashamed that I couldn't get the scene out of my head. Yet a small part of me was curious. Like watching farm animals mate where you really could care less but yet you can't stop looking. Maybe that's what Kathy meant about me coming into womanhood soon. Maybe I was just starved for affection that has never been given to me. Kathy had her delicate emotions and her budding age working for her to get affection but at times it seems I never receive any; least of all from my father.

I hardly see how I could be budding into womanhood anytime soon.

I'm smallish without one womanly physical trait. Then again, maybe Kathy meant on the inside. My insides were a mess, all churning, all mixed up and now thanks to Dad, all turned upside down. If this is what becoming a woman means, I'm in no hurry.

And all of this makes home life suck. I have no way of knowing if Dad is ever telling the truth or just manipulating. What I do know is that I have a hard time looking at him. I want to disown him for what he was making me be a part of, almost as much as for what he was doing to Kathy.

In the absence of love, I began to hate; with passion and without discrimination.

Most people go through life not understanding that
you're supposed to go through life not understanding.

Chapter 11

to "protect and serve"

I couldn't believe it when I awoke the next day to find that Hidetoshi was going to take the day off work. My visit was winding down, and we had several things that he still wanted to cover with me before I left Saturday. On today's agenda was to visit a real Japanese teahouse and participate in an official Japanese tea ceremony. You know, like the one in <u>Karate Kid</u> Part II, or was it Part III?

At any rate, I had requested visiting an authentic Japanese Teahouse earlier in the week. My mind had just been locked into this "gotta learn my heritage all in one trip" mode. I have since realized that was impossible, but I still wanted to learn all I could. Who knew when I'd get to return?

We took the whole family and Maki, so she could translate the intricacies of the ceremony to me without me asking too many questions. Apparently my continued queries had already taught my Japanese family that a translation dictionary can only do so much to keep up with me! Maki, as I have said many times before, was a Godsend.

The Pagoda Teahouse was located about an hour's drive from where Hidetoshi lived. It was tucked into a small rise of a hill, in a city which I have long since forgotten the name.

But what I will always remember is the beauty of the Teahouse and its delicate and ornate setting in the hill, like a jewel hidden in nature's painting. I was awestruck with the dainty structure and sculptured garden as we approached up the walk. It was a little early for spring bloom but the spiraled trees and year-round green foliage was still breath-taking. If I stood back and looked long and hard enough, I decided it truly was a painted image of nature. Nothing else would explain its symmetrical beauty.

Peppered between the trees and shrubs danced snow white pebble stone. Not a shred of paper or litter of any kind could be found on the ground. I wasn't sure if that was due to the fact that litter was absolutely forbidden, or if someone cleaned it up in a daily manicure of the gardens. In either case, it saddened my heart to think of some of the beautiful countryside back home, ruined by unwanted trash and disrespect.

I pointed and asked a question or two about how the Teahouse came to be as I wandered the grounds. When satisfied with enough polite conversation, I stepped up on a three foot wooden deck or walkway that encircled the Teahouse to soak in my foreign yet nostalgic surroundings, and to take a few pictures. Instantly, I was greeted with gasps. Ai rushed over compassionately, tugging my arm with her small hand.

"No, no Ahmyco-chan," and she proceeded to pull me down off the deck. Maki who had been distracted by the caretaker discussing the tea ceremony for me once inside, turned around and came scurrying in patented Japanese baby steps.

"You cannot walk on the side step of the house with shoes on. To walk with unclean feet is to offend." She was visibly distraught for not explaining that beforehand, which would have saved me the embarrassment and my family the shame.

I could think of nothing else to say but to reach into Rob's patented universal language and offer, "Stupido Americano" while slapping my forehead. I'm not sure if it was the "stupid" remark or the slapping of my head but the proprietor broke into a wide grin of acknowledgement. I was just relieved I wasn't offered a Samurai sword and expected to disembowel myself!

After replacing our shoes for slippers at the entranceway, we proceeded inside. We walked down a narrow hallway between glass on the right displaying the beautiful pagoda garden and a rice paper wall on the left, hiding many rooms or chambers of some sort. The smell was fresh and clean, with the slightest hint of wood that framed the sliding rice paper doors to the various rooms. It seemed as if I were cast in Shogun Relived *as I passed solemnly down the hall*

We entered the last chamber on the left and were instructed to sit in a circle on the floor in Japanese style, with our legs tucked under our buttocks. Cut in the floor at the center of our circle was a covered opening. The remainder of the room was sparse, with no furniture and little decoration. The proprietor or "ceremony master" was ordained in a black business suit and white shirt, complete with a black thin necktie. Men in Black-Revisited *came to mind but I stifled a comment on my Hollywood analogies.*

Solemnly, he explained the process as Maki translated. Removing the cover from the floor revealed a teapot in a hot oven just below the surface. Hot coals in the oven chamber warmed the water until the tea was ready for serving.

The tea service was hand-decorated bowls that added dignity to the solemn service. The "ceremony master" immediately poured enough bowls for everyone three quarters full with the bubbling hot water. I was given a brush (similar to what a barber uses to lather shaving cream) and commanded to stir it briskly in a separate cup of tea leaves. As I admired the detail of the brush it was explained that the bristles were actually hair-split bamboo. I was instructed to slowly pulverize the leaves, which I did until I thought them acceptable. I then handed my leaves to the host who carefully sprinkled the remains into the bowl of simmering water. When satisfied that the blend of water and tea had reached its full body, the host took the tea bowl and ceremoniously rotated it halfway around in the cup of his hands. With a bow of his head, I was presented the tea for drinking.

The tea was thick green, like pea soup. I bowed my head in return and accepted the offering without hesitation. I hoped my eyes would not betray my shock at the viscosity of the tea as I tilted my head back and sipped cautiously.

It was delicious! I took a second sip that turned more into a gulp. Mmmm! Without fear I reached down and picked up the rice dough ball served on a saucer with the tea and took a big bite.

Uggghhh! It was anything but delightful!

Its aromatic aroma overfilled my nostrils, but its bittersweet taste made my mouth water with a pre-vomit sensation. It was like a fine wine that you must develop a taste for; not bad for the daily consumer but odd in taste, smell and texture for a first-timer. Fortunately I saw Hidetoshi to my left wolfing down his rice dough ball in sheer delight. I could tell he was still hungry so after my obligatory bite, I discreetly offered him mine out of politeness. No one seemed to notice as he nonchalantly picked up the remains of my rice ball and dropped the thing down in one gulp, followed by a "cat that ate the canary" toothy smile. I began to breathe as I marveled at his intestinal fortitude at being able to handle the pungent sugar aftertaste.

Polite conversation followed about the pagoda, the ceremony, and what kinds of Japanese food I liked (maybe I was noticed passing the dough ball to Hidetoshi after all). As we exited, I stopped to take a couple of parting pictures and suddenly found myself crying.

I was as surprised as anybody. Hidetoshi asked, "Ahmyco-chan, you all right?"

Maki followed with a quick "What's the matter?" as she gently touched my elbow and leaned over to gaze into my spring-dew eyes.

"I wish Kathy were here. She should be here," I responded with tears flowing openly. "She gave so much for me in my childhood. She was my protector. She deserves to be here instead of me."

I am fortunate to have Rob today, but in my childhood, it was Kathy. I was overwhelmed with a feeling of unworthiness as I stood on sacred Japanese soil, and the true meaning of "sacrifice" came crashing down on me.

At the epicenter of that sacrifice, Kathy was brave, she was brainwashed; most dangerous of all, she was seduced...and physically she was no longer a child...

I have watched silently (in preference to a backhand) as Kathy was treated differently than me. She has been "preferred" over the last few years. But now I find myself wondering if it's not so much a matter of preference, as a matter of being trained for something much more sinister.

I have suspected ever since my discovery of the two of them together that fateful day after school that Dad has also taught Kathy masturbation and introduced her to oral sex but I wasn't positive. How could I be? I had not witnessed the acts, but things have changed. Kathy has changed. Years of conditioning were showing visibly, as were her womanly attributes. Curves showed on her body that mine could not. More and more frequently I woke at night when Dad would come into the bedroom and get Kathy. I simply chose not to notice her suspicious absence from bed, wishing for the best and silently wondering why Mom had to take so many pills for her illnesses. I hoped and prayed she would wake up if Dad tried anything with Kathy.

My fears are fed lately by the display of their affection for each other that had migrated to a public boldness. Lately Dad was treating Kathy like a queen – well, in my eyes. Actually I had to remind myself we were dirt poor, so any small attentions showered on Kathy like a new dress particularly grates me. He was giving her some of the motherly responsibilities since Mom had taken sick for the hundredth time. Kathy assumed most of the cooking and their affections were more open; a touch here, a hand held there – She was even sitting in the front seat of the car when Mom wasn't around. All this appeared to please Dad immensely.

I told Kathy yesterday that it just didn't look right, her sitting up there with Dad (almost like a girlfriend I thought) when she told me with soulful eyes, "You don't understand, Amy; you can't."

It's as if Kathy unwillingly or unknowingly had been turned into a trophy for Dad. Or she was doing what she thought was right to protect me or maybe, just maybe, a little of both...

Either way, today it was brought to a head.

I will never forget today as long as I live. I had just walked in the house after a particularly playful day in the field across the road with a particularly playful butterfly, when my ears filled with Dad's shouting curse words.

"Son of a bitch, woman! Are you trying to kill me?" I heard Dad shout full throttle from the bathroom as I entered the house.

"Lichard, I no understand," Mom said puzzled as she stood in the bathroom doorway. Kathy stood silently off to the side of Mom. Dad was nude but partially hidden from my view by Mom and Kathy. I immediately knew what happened. I had cleaned the bathroom, but Dad thought Mom had. It was my way of trying to elevate myself in family esteem. After all, Kathy didn't have to get all the praise around the house! Stepping in without being asked, I had tackled the bathroom scum. But it had been disgustingly filthier than I thought, and I soon discovered that normal cleaner simply wouldn't do. It was a natural progression to think of what worked on the worst thing that needed cleaning and migrate that into action on everything. So I elevated Sani-Flush toilet cleaner to outside the bowl. It was the only logical thing to do if I was to stay on task of stealing some praise and still have time to play.

Amazing stuff, Sani-Flush. As long as you keep it off your hands it will kill, cure and remove most any germ known to mankind. It apparently worked wonders on the bathtub.

As the argument elevated, I took a step back in the hallway hoping no one would see me suppressing a giggle. I had rinsed the tub thoroughly but I must have missed a few traces.

"The skin is coming off my ass now, thanks to you!" He screamed. Mom confused, ignored his ravings and instead immediately turned to Kathy to vent her frustration.

"Kathy. What matter with you? He your Dad. You no love him like a woman!"

My giggle stuck in my throat as I felt all my suspicions come crashing down.

"He takes care of me and I take care of him. Isn't that what family is all about? We have to stick together and protect each other and take care of each other's needs," Kathy pleaded.

Seduction.

Mom stood there stunned. She was at a loss for words. Instead she pointed at Kathy's wedding finger and at the small diamond ring adorning it. Her mouth moved but no words came out.

"Families do what we are doing. Everybody does it. Maybe they don't talk about it but it happens. We are no different behind closed doors than the neighbors. You'll see. I'll be proven right," Dad interjected as he rubbed his backside with a wet towel. I couldn't believe what I was hearing, thinking maybe it was just the burn from the toilet bowl cleaner talking.

"That's right Mom. As long as you're always sick, I'll have to take care of him," Kathy repeated. "I have to…we're family."

Brainwashing.

My jaw dropped watching this incredible scene. The years of mental brainwashing, of military obedience and of physical abuse now culminated in this torn and twisted perspective of family life. Being sheltered all of our lives from outside influence; I found myself wondering, 'Is he right? Are we just a normal family?' The thought of it made me chill. What a sad world it must be if that's true…

Swiftly and with the purpose of making Kathy think about what she was saying, Mom delivered a crushing slap across her face! Kathy, in a reflex reaction mustered all her strength and delivered a return blow to Mom's face.

"Kathy! No!" I screamed as I saw the arm retract. It was more than just seeing or hearing the indignant slap. It was as if I felt it too.

Everyone froze.

Then Mom looked down for the longest time…as if defeated. Her hair was frazzled. No makeup adorned her face. Her housecoat had become slightly open in the exchange of blows exposing the jagged landscape of a missing breast. She looked sick and weak and lost. Gradually she looked up and stared at Dad for the longest time as he stood naked in the bathroom doorway. Her look started out with sadness and disappointment and finished in angry defeat. He had done this. He had sent her oldest daughter into betrayal. Relieved, I sensed that Mom knew it wasn't Kathy's fault.

Then as if a slug slowly moving against the beating sun, she made her way into the bedroom and closed the door. On the other hand, Dad broke out in a smile and stepping through the doorway he gave Kathy a pat on the derriere; as if rewarding her for standing her ground.

Kathy pushed his hand away and ran into our bedroom crying.

I turned and ran out the front door, leaving Dad standing naked to the world. I ran to the field and went in search of my butterfly. But soon the physical chase and the weight of blocked emotions drove me to take a rest; just a little one, a wink or two or ten…

I had fallen asleep in the grass hoping to wake up and find this was all a dream. Suddenly I sat upright in a jolt - in the distance were sirens! And dogs barking! And more sirens! 'What was going on?' I wondered as I scrambled to my feet and broke out in a dead run.

I rushed toward my house following the sound of strained and incoherent voices and fearing the worst. Had Mom, Dad, Kathy, or everyone but me done something crazy? As I got closer I could hear and see Mom shouting at two uniformed policeman, spewing unintelligible words through the screened front porch door. Dad was on the porch with Kathy as I approached from behind the officers. Dad was looking extremely uneasy.

"What's going on?" I asked out of breath. "Is anyone hurt?"

Mom continued with her spewing of half English and half Japanese words from behind the door, most that didn't even make sense to me. Dad began shuffling his weight from one foot to the next, acting embarrassed by the whole ordeal. Kathy continued to stand perfectly still beside Dad, her amber brown eyes cast down at the floor.

The look on the policemen's faces told me part of the story. They were puzzled and concerned about Mom's incoherent behavior. When Mom paused for a breath, Dad leaned over to whisper something to one of the officers. I couldn't hear what he was saying, but I know my Dad. He was manipulating the police.

In some kind of male code recognition the policemen nodded in unison as if to say, 'yea, we understand now' and immediately turned to Mom to calm her down, as if she was a rabid dog.

"It'll be all right. It'll be fine, lady. Just calm down," Officer #1 offered none too convincingly. He opened the screen door part way and made a feeble attempt to pat Mom's hand.

"Yeah. Settle down, lady," Officer #2 brutally said, none too patient with the whole ordeal.

"He crazy man. He trying to have sexy with daughter. Take him out house now! Jail! No... jail too good for him! Do something, anything," Mom was finally able to plead in choppy English. Her eyes were flashing back and forth and her nostrils were flaring. Dad shook his head in fake disbelief at the site of Mom, and Kathy recoiled away from Dad in apparent horror at Mom's blatant outburst, as if she didn't want to be identified as the other "culprit" in Mom's ranting. I was still standing behind the police watching the whole matinee unfold before me. 'They got him now,' I thought.

But I thought wrong.

Instead of probing Mom for details, Officer #1 turned to Dad and apologized profusely for bothering him.

Curtly Dad responded with an air of authority, "Thanks. Don't worry officers. I can handle it from here. I've been handling her for years."

I was shocked. With her unruly and unkempt hair and her rumpled housecoat, at a glance she sure fit the profile of a crazed woman but she wasn't! My mind was pleading and my hands were wringing, but my mouth failed to move as the intimidating uniforms turned and faced me. I was even more shocked at my actions as I found myself casting my eyes down and looking away as the officers passed, gripped by shame.

The bathroom scene a few hours ago was like a movie in rerun again. Mom stormed off to her bedroom, Kathy vanished into the house sobbing, and Dad was just standing there smiling.

I also found I was not as strong as I thought I was, and I was ashamed of myself. I hadn't said anything, 'and Kathy knows that,' I thought. Her job was now that of a police officer of sorts...a police officer to *our family*. To *protect* the family.... and *serve* Dad.

Left standing on the porch with only Dad and his evil grin, I turned and ran to the field for the third time today...

> *It is true that the rain falls on the just and unjust*
> *alike. It's just the amount that is the question.*

you can't stop the rain...
or puberty...or dad

That evening Aunt Yoko decided to pay a visit and assist me with the "how to" of dressing in the kimono; a <u>simple</u> 45 minute ordeal! I'm sure it took me a little longer than the average Japanese woman since I have to fight the "Stupido Americano" factor, that expression that had already once gotten me out of an embarrassing situation. In reality I had stolen it from Rob; it's his tongue-in-cheek reference to the ignorance of Americans to other cultures around the world. In other words, no matter how starved I am to learn my heritage, my actual knowledge is pretty limited. Hence the 45 minutes of dressing in a kimono – half of which is actual work and half of which is continually repeating instruction to me, again, and again, and sometimes (and I know this is hard to believe) again.

The final product of my dressing was acceptable to everyone but me. Aunt Yoko thought I was beautiful when fully and finally clad in the complete ensemble. I thought I could look better. I think what was lacking was the addition of the facial makeup, key to the presentation of the traditional Japanese costume, which turns the Japanese female from woman to a piece of art.

Aunt Yoko is a piece of art herself. She is a collage of many personalities and activities that have shaped her life. She is a professional photographer, and as I've said, in my house today hang two beautiful photographs of breath-taking Japanese foliage; one amber hued fall landscape and one spring picture of mint fresh white cherry trees. She also is a lounge singer. She has a club circuit that she regularly headlines; her voice is like a bird that complements her landscape photos. She is bubbly, supportive and surprisingly youthful for a grandmother.

The rice paper partition that can separate the living room into two rooms was pulled closed part way to afford us some privacy as Aunt Yoko put the final touches on my unveiling. A pull back of the partition revealed me, the geisha wannabe to Miyuki, Ai and Ai's friend, Mao.

I was greeted by "oohs" and "ahhs" and a couple of schoolgirl giggles to make sure my ego stayed in the right proportion.

In response to my reception, I took center stage and pirouetted, hamming it up for effect. Then on the third or fourth twirl, I noticed out of the corner of my eye, rain starting to fall on the balcony glass door. I immediately stopped, and reaching over to the dining table, grabbed the paper umbrella Aunt Yoko had brought to finish accenting my kimono. I surprised myself by breaking out into a song in rhythm with the gentle patter of heaven's teardrops against the window panes. The song in turn, stopped Aunt Yoko dead in her tracks. Then surprisingly, as if beyond her control, she joined in.

The song was a child's Japanese "rain song," and one my mother used to sing with Kathy, Brock and me in our youth. Aunt Yoko and I clutched each other's hands and bounced around in a circle as we joyfully sang our hearts out:

Ame ame fudi fudi kaasonna
Chianomene omekaldi udeh shidina
Pichi pichi choppa choppa lun, lun, lun…

The song ended in a climax of hugs and clapping. I was excited to share something halfway around the world that related to my past, and Aunt Yoko was just as happy to learn that my mother had extended "Ami Uta" (the rain song) as part of the Japanese culture to her children.

We were joined in the middle of a second singing by Ai and Mao, both of whom are at the wonderful age of not yet leaving childhood, but on a freight train at "full steam ahead" toward puberty. Mao goes to the same school as Ai, and is two years older. She is tall and slender with that patented Japanese shoulder length blazon black hair. She not only is two years older, but acts much older than Ai in maturity. She formed an immediate bond with me, and I'm not sure why. I suspect it developed more from the womanly plane. However on this day, maturity went right out the window as both sang and clapped with total abandon, at least until Mao and Ai both replaced what I called dancing with uncontrolled bouncing up and down after their contemporary idols of music.

In retrospect, the rain, playing "dress up" in costume, and the children on the verge of puberty played on my memory strings one more time.

I was thirteen and behind my peers in physical maturity...

I could not help it from getting wet.

Tom and I had just run from the field as the cloud burst happened.

We are both thirteen but totally unalike. Tom has shoulder length long brown hair, constantly having to push it out of his eyes. His skin is soft looking and tanned. He has a confident swagger and tough mini-biker edge to him. Tom was a neat freak who wore Tide-clean T-shirts and crisp new blue jeans.

Me – I'm a smallish thirteen year old without much confidence thanks to either my Japanese genes or my lousy life at home. I have ash dark hair that is also long. I use it to mask all my glaring body's faults; acne, crooked teeth, slanted eyes and underdeveloped but straining to get out breasts. I am shy and quiet at school, contrary to my argumentative attitude at home. But Tom makes me feel different. Skippy heartbeats, lack of sleep and the need to wear low-riding Coca-Cola bellbottoms every time I am around him would have never happened a year ago.

We had been meeting at a secret location periodically all summer as we had gotten to know each other. He had given my first blissful kiss last month on my porch after saying good night to popcorn and a movie with my family one evening. I was in heaven with the gentle touch of his lips to mine while our bodies pressed slightly harder together than they should have before breaking apart for the night.

Today we had decided to go exploring a pasture near our secret hiding place. It was Tom's idea. The pasture stood next to the road that split our two homes, and it was void of anything save some tall grass, a wooded area peppered with trees and brushy area toward its very back. We made our way to the wooded area, wanting to reduce the chance of us being seen. Disappearing into the camouflage of brush and shade, Tom immediately noticed something as he hunched over at the knees, out of breath from our scamper to hurry up and reach the woods before being spied by his father, or mine. Pointing, he took me by the hand and led me on a safari over to one of the most distant bushes. There lying face-down in the bush were some magazines. But these were no ordinary magazines. As Tom picked up the first one and flipped through rapidly, I picked up the second one out of curiosity. There to greet me on the first page was an unabashed photo of a naked man and woman lying together. Tom quickly flipped through his pages as I stared at mine in disbelief. 'Do people actually do those things?' I wondered. The pictures stunned my senses.

They had also stimulated Tom's. We both sat with our knees folded Indian style resting the magazines on our legs as we flipped quickly through the pages. Tossing his copy aside, Tom immediately wanted to "make out" after he finished looking at the last picture. I was hesitant as I cast my magazine away, looking him squarely in the eyes.

"You like looking at this, don't you?" I asked picking my copy back up and flipping to a particularly graphic scene to hold in clear view of Tom. It was apparent it was a pretty dumb question because obviously he did.

"Of course I do. How could you even ask such a thing? Any red-blooded man would want to look at beautiful naked women," Tom answered in a somewhat disappointing attitude that I'm sure was directed at my telling immaturity.

Chemistry had brought Tom and me together and having fathers neither of us could satisfy brought us even closer. In a silent 'I'm sorry' gesture, I leaned over and cocked my head to one side, offering Tom a consolatory kiss. Quickly, the kissing began spinning into heavy petting. But unlike before, the heavy petting began to take on a new life in itself. I sensed in Tom's trembling touch that he wanted something more and I became a little edgy. I found myself thinking in the middle of an intimate embrace that I had instantly been thrust at a crossroad of my life. Tom was now heated in his advances, and I wasn't quite sure I could stop them.

The summer drive toward fall had already been building a fire inside of me to be known as "Tom's girl" when school resumed. Today Tom seemed to feel that this was his moment. He moved in closer placing a firm arm around my waist, all the while probing the buttons of my blouse with his free hand while locked in a crushing kiss.

I hesitated, breaking the kiss and turning my cheek. I rubbed my sore lips from the pressure of his advance. I was confused with the turmoil boiling inside.

"Jeese, Amy! Don't tell me you don't like it. I know you do. That feeling of a rush, all dizzy inside. Think how great it would feel to go all the way. You can't tell me you don't feel it too."

I pushed Tom back in the chest to create some distance. "It's not that I don't feel something for you, and it's not that I won't go all the way someday. I'm just not ready today." Buried in the back of my mind were insecurities about sex I could not tell Tom, and that I needed time to sort them out.

"Look, I can't wait forever. We've been getting closer all summer. I don't understand you. Why don't you just go with the flow?" Tom's plea was edged with frustration.

In my own frustration, I began to think, 'I may lose him and not even know what I'm missing. I may be making the wrong decision. I may even regret saying 'no.' I may'.....and then the rain abruptly interrupted my maybe, maybe nots. Suddenly I realized I didn't have to answer Tom's eager anticipation of sex. The rain gave me a reprieve and began cooling Tom down somewhat, at least for the time being.

Glancing at the sky and then without having to say another word, we simultaneously jumped up and ran hand in hand for home.

It was early evening, and I stood there soaking wet watching Tom fade into the sheet of rain and cover of darkness. He had left me standing there frozen on the front porch without as much as a peck on the cheek good-bye. For the briefest of moments, I found myself wondering if he had planted the magazines for me to find. Even though I didn't let their stimulation show to Tom, I had to admit some of the pictures had an affect on me. I just didn't know if it was a good or bad feeling.

'If the rain hadn't come, I'm not sure what I would have done – what I would have decided,' I thought as I fought back the beginning sniffles of a good cry. I was so unsure of myself and what love really is. As I wiped my eyes and turned to walk into the hot humid house, I wondered if I would ever know...

For some time I had been doing what all teenagers must be doing as nature struggled to work a young girl into womanhood; sorting out feelings toward sex and my relationship with Tom, and I suppose with men in general. I was hampered with what I had seen with Dad and Kathy, clouding my image of what was right and wrong.

Still wet from the rain, I guess I realized full well what I would have done if it hadn't come to my virginity's rescue. I guess I might have said no one more time, but then again...

Stopping in the kitchen I drew a full glass of water to help me catch my breath and cool my feelings. As I finished my second glass of water and I turned around from the sink, I was greeted with a set of eyes piercing on me. They were Dad's. He could see I was emotionally shaken. My eyes were moist and stinging from the mental and physical drain Tom's advances had generated. Trying my best to avoid Dad, I reached up under the kitchen cabinet and ripped off a paper towel, intently blowing my nose.

"What's the matter with you?" he asked as he walked over and took his usual place in a kitchen chair; or more correctly, in *his* chair, at the head of *his* table. The only one appropriate for *him* to sit at. He had a shot of vodka in one hand and a cigarette in the other. Black and white ashes dotted the yellow table where he had carelessly missed the ashtray several times, in part due to the spillage of excess butts overflowing its brown tobacco-stained rim, and in part due to the unmistakable shake of an alcoholic's hand.

My mind raced with conditioned guilt. I wonder if he had seen Tom and I go into the pasture? Am I in trouble? What am I going to say we went there for and whatever I made up, would he believe me?

But the explosion never came.

Instead he downed his drink in one gulp, stood up and looked out the window to my back, toward the clouds from the rain that made nightfall even darker. Then facing me, he took me by surprise by picking me up under the armpits and placing me on top of the freezer next to the kitchen sink. He took three steps backward, looking at me for the longest time and admiring his handiwork of placing me at eye level to him. It was the first time I think I had ever really been able to look at him at equal height. Until this very day, every one of Dad's one-sided conversations had been conducted from an intimidating and dominant posture, with me on the short side of the receiving end.

He took one step closer.

"You're becoming a beautiful young woman, and you don't even know it. Now, tell me what's the matter?" he said with all the concern he could muster.

Maybe it's been the age thing all along that's kept us distant. Maybe he's just been waiting for me to catch up with him in stature to be included in more adult conversation. I found myself wishing he would do the fatherly thing and give me a hug and tell me everything was going to be all right as I confided in him my honest emotions and adolescent struggles.

Taking a chance with nowhere else to turn, I told him I had a fight with Tom. "It seems like all he wants is sex," I blurted out.

"There is nothing wrong with sex, Amy. What are you afraid of?" he asked me cautiously as he moved another step closer.

I shockingly found I couldn't restrain myself. "We found pornography in the field today, and Tom was so turned on it scared me."

"Amy, that is the natural way for men to act. They can't help it. There isn't anything wrong with sex. You can do anything you want as long as you don't copulate. Do you know what that means?"

"No," I responded blankly. I was so naïve. I didn't know anything about sex. Only how Tom makes me feel all dizzy inside and out.

"It means that you run the risk of pregnancy if you allowed the man to complete the sex act inside of you. You can't do that. It would ruin your life."

Another step closer.

I tried not to cry, but I couldn't help it. I actually wanted to hear him say I was too young for intimate physical contact, but instead he was giving me permission. I was really confused now. Maybe I was ready and I didn't know it.

"How did the pictures make you feel?" he probed, his eyes more intense than I had ever seen.

I said nothing as I gazed at the ceiling in silence; struggling to have an adult conversation and fighting the storm of emotion inside me.

"On the other hand," he continued without my reply, "I've had a vasectomy. That means I can't father any more children." As if us children were an unwanted curse, he finished by saying, "after so many unexpected pregnancies around here, I took care of that ever happening to this family again."

I didn't ask what his pro-creation abilities have to do with anything. But his comment startled me to attention. The free offering of this unwanted information made me feel uncomfortable and even more confused.

He took one final step closer.

Then without warning he ran his hand up my skirt! I pushed him away at the shoulders, but not fast enough. His hand struck dead aim between my legs allowing him to discover how warm Tom and the magazines had made me.

"Dad, don't do that!" I said shocked as I held his hand at bay by the wrist. I wanted him to treat me as a grown up, but not in that way. After all these years of dysfunction, I knew that I desperately sought his love as a father, but more than anything I wanted his respect.

Rebuffed, he said in a low stern voice, "Fine then. Let's go to the garage." His eyes had switched from somewhat caring to his usual disinterest in me. "There is something I need to show you...now."

Military training told me to obey as I hopped down and followed him in silence.

I heard neighborhood dogs bark as they sensed us slipping into the unattached building, my bare feet tingling along the way in the rain damped turf. The door squeaked as Dad opened it, and I saw him wince. I entered, and he immediately closed the door behind me throwing us both into total darkness.

I could smell the grease permeate my nostrils as Dad said, "I want you to sit on the floor."

"What for?" I asked puzzled, being my normal confrontational self.

"Just do it," he commanded, his voice distant. In the pitch black night something hollow in its tone frightened me into reluctant obedience.

"The floor's messy. I'm going to ruin my clothes," I weakly protested as I eased myself downward. I had no idea what he could possibly be up to, or what he could show me in the pitch black darkness. Somewhere in the back of my mind I heard what sounded like the opening of a zipper tearing at my subconscious. Knowing that was not possible my mind was pre-occupied with trying to figure what else that sound must have been when out of the darkness of night I felt his full weight thrust upon me, barreling me backwards. Without warning one hand raised my skirt in unison with the other hand that was shredding my underwear to expose my innocence.

"Dad don't!" I screamed but the skirt-hand quickly found my mouth, muffling any future pleas.

"Whot aree yo dooin?" I mumbled as my mouth stretched to form words.

"Amy, be quiet!" he hissed like a viper. "If someone hears you, I'll just hurt you worse," he threatened. "Now lay still..!"

My mind paused for a moment to gather and try to process all the physical and verbal information that was crashing down on my brain. The whole of life – catching Dad abusing Kathy, Tom and his more intense advances, the graphic pictures, coming in and stupidly asking Dad for understanding, naively expecting comfort in the kitchen, and now this, hidden under the cover of darkness in this foul stable of a garage. The millisecond of flashback seemed to replay in slow motion.

'What was happening? What was going on?' my mind queried as I snapped to reality, realizing I couldn't move. Dad was a good foot taller and at least 100 lbs. heavier than me, with his full weight now bearing down full throttle. He continued to force himself upon me as he crushed my face with the one hand over my mouth. I couldn't see or feel the other hand, and I couldn't breathe!

A sting, followed by a burning sensation, and then finally a rip sent a nauseating shockwave through my body …and my life's worst nightmare commenced. My Dad was raping me!

I shaped my limp hands into fists and started pounding weakly on his shoulder blades. I continued pounding but grew weaker with each cascading blow. My outcries were still being muffled. I tried to bite but was too weak from his giant hand partially covering my nose. I was suddenly dangerously aware that I was having an even harder time breathing, suffocating under his enormous frame.

I wanted up! I wanted out of that stinky grease pit! I wanted to take it all back, but it seemed as if I were caught in the eye of a hurricane with everything else whirling around me. All those adolescent mixed up emotions with Tom, my screwed up family, speeding faster and faster in a circle around me – suspended in the air as if I was having an out of body experience; wishing for this moment to end.

And then I got what I wished.

Dad suddenly felt heavy as if he had fainted, his breathing fast and irregular. His breath filled the air with alcohol and tobacco making me want to throw up. He rolled off of me, and then standing up, he commanded, "Straighten your clothes and get yourself to bed. And for God sakes, pick up all the shreds of your underwear before you leave. We can't have that laying around for anyone to find."

His voice was cold and disconnected as if he were talking to a dog and expecting full obedience. I heard his zipper again, clear and distinct this time closing somewhere in the air above me as I tried to cover my half naked body.

And then he was gone.

I lay there alone feeling as dirty as the grease on the floor. Dad had managed a new low. I had been scared before, but always on the outside. Now I was robbed of my virginity and scarred forever on the inside; both wounds irreversible.

I cried in short sobs as I groped in the dark, gathering the tatters of my underwear, somehow realizing that all my dreams were as shattered as my panties...

• • • •

The alarm clock slowly shook me out of my slumber. A single ray of sunshine shot over my head as I reached up and pulled the shade aside. For an instant I thought it was just another normal school day until my mind processed the fear and humiliation I had experienced yesterday.

As I swept the morning cobwebs from my mind, I was slammed with a panic attack. What the hell happened last night?! Did IT really happen? I looked around in instantaneous fear. I wanted to talk it over with Kathy, but somehow couldn't. I wanted to tell Mom, but I didn't want to compound her medical worries with emotional ones. Brock was a boy and too young to understand.

'Somebody help me, please!' I thought as I sat up and dangled my sore legs over the edge of the bed. I need to make sure that the topic of my incestuous father never comes up in school, but I hated bearing this all alone. But who would listen and not tell? I couldn't risk breaking up the family and way deep down subconsciously, I knew I couldn't take the beatings that would surely come with such action – even if I lied to myself and bravely tried. Nope, I'm left all alone with my thoughts, which was a dangerous place to be right now.

Rubbing my eyes, I got out of bed hoping to be the first to get to the bathroom. The door to my parents' bedroom was directly across the hall, and it swung open just as I walked into the hallway.

I froze in my tracks as I unwantingly locked eyes with Dad. I felt my stomach turn in the impenetrable silence. His eyes burned through my shame in what I *knew* was a warning. After an eternity of silent threats he slithered back into his bedroom, closing the door quietly behind him.

I ran into the bathroom, and falling hard to my knees, I threw my head in the toilet and was immediately overcome with convulsions. IT had really happened! The nightmare was here to stay …and I had nowhere to turn.

Withdrawing my head from the toilet, I leaned back onto my rear haunches, my arms reaching far behind, touching the floor to prop me up. I tilted my head back letting my long hair dangle within inches of the bathroom floor and inhaled as much oxygen as my tiny lungs would hold.

And then it hit me.

My mouth stiffened from last night's oppression as I hissed under my breath. The magazines in the field, letting Tom confuse me with his advances, and then Dad waiting patiently alone in the kitchen for me to return…

Could Dad have planned this all along?

Chapter 13

there is no "school" like an old "school"

Every day, the school bus would pull up to take Uuto to preschool. It was a pink and white mini-van with the cutest little blue and white bunnies on the side. Just to look at it made me feel fuzzy warm. The first couple of days, "Mommy" would take him down to the bus each morning, but as the week progressed, the job migrated to me. I felt privileged. It meant acceptance into the Japanese society, trust in me from the Suzaki family but most importantly, love from the children. As I said before, Uuto felt a bond with Rob, but he had to "warm up" to me. I think it's a universal "guy thing."

On this particular day, it was raining (imagine that), so I had gathered an umbrella and a cup of hot cohee for the trek with Uuto down the eight stories to the curb where the "bunny bus" waited. Or sometimes, we waited on it. So much for Japanese promptness. School schedules may be rigid, but children's preparations in getting ready for school is universally disorganized...kind of like the universal "guy thing."

I swear someone has written a code of conduct somewhere that says kids must not find homework, must misplace book bags, must oversleep and eat half a breakfast and must always whine about not wanting to go to school, or about how Mom's demand for proper clothing is going to make them miss the bus. The only difference in Japanese preschool that I can see is those darn little Japanese bunnies. They just make me feel fuzzy, fuzzy, and fuzzy all over!

What was different about today is that I was going to accompany Miyuki to pick up Uuto from pre-school. As I deposited Uuto on the bunnymobile, I glanced at the weather thinking, 'I'm going to need the umbrella and a second cup of cohee when we go to pick him up.' I also thought I was beginning to see a Japanese trait in spring weather. It looked anything but hospitable.

And I was right.

It was pouring rain when we hit Uuto's pre-school in the early afternoon. I am sure I looked extremely silly making a mad dash to the school, only to find out I had rushed to an EXIT ONLY door. Except of course it was spelled in Japanese Kanji that looked like hen scratchings in the dirt after looking for worms. I practically pulled my arm off when I yanked at the door to escape another daily pounding of H_2O. How was I to know?

Once inside (the right way), Miyuki gave me the grand tour. For all the disorganization of getting kids to school, the school itself was run like the military. A place for everything and everything in its place. I was impressed.

You didn't hear a sound in the hallways, nor when we walked into the classroom. Once in Uuto's classroom, I was astounded by what I saw. These little four year olds must have had a degree in Organizational Management. Every color under the rainbow was represented in the shelves, books, puzzles, desks, chairs and walls. It was the primary color wheel on steroids! But what was amazing beyond the need for sunglasses to be able to look at all the bright colors was the symmetry. Each little cupboard for each child had exactly the same thing, organized in the same order right down to the slippers below and on the left; blue for boys and pink for girls. And the floor – you could eat off the floor or use it for a mirror. They must have hundreds of janitors whose sole purpose in life is to make visitors gasp at the floor's sheen.

The next stop was the restroom. You heard me right; the <u>restroom</u>. Not plural as in girls' and boys' "restrooms" - this was a co-ed <u>restroom</u>. I didn't know that neatness counted in school restrooms; back where I came from, if there was no graffiti on the wall it was considered a clean restroom. My first thought was White House Dining. Why? Because the white urinals were as spotless as the classroom floor and rivaled the shine of the best white china at a State Dinner. It looked like you could eat off of either if you were so inclined…To *put the restroom over the top there were pink little bunnies on some toilet stall doors and little blue bunnies on the others – the connotation was obvious. Pink bunny stalls for the girls and blue bunny stalls for the boys. Lined up in front of each stall were slippers. From what I could tell between home and school, Japanese kids have more slippers than Oprah has shoes!*

With the hustle and bustle of school children, I was taken back to my not so distant past with three boys of my own in school. Fond memories of each. My mind's stop in the 1990s was brief – for the most part school with our children was enjoyable; class plays, awards, scholastic and athletic participation. All except the last few years of school with our youngest son who gave us our own trials, tribulations and crossroads to meet. Crossroads Rob and I tried to meet with him as parents, as family and ultimately, as his friend – which we are now for life.

As if a tidal wave that cannot be stopped, my mind continued on, marching back into the early 1970s and settled on Mrs. Fillmore's algebra class...

"Amy, I'm talking to you. Answer the question!" Mrs. Fillmore's masculine voice boomed.

'Question, what question?' my mind raced, snapping back to reality.

"Obviously some of us don't put a whole lot of effort in studying, do they, AMY?" her deep monotone voice seemed to rattle the window I was staring out of into nothingness.

'Question, what question?' my mind racing now in circles. My mind was so glazed over from last night I couldn't think straight. 'Was I in Algebra class?'

Like a stalking bear, Mrs. Fillmore moved down the aisle until her looming shadow engulfed me. Looking up I saw the whole class looking at me, some of them with genuine concern on their faces.

"Ringggg! Ringggg! Ringggg!" went the bell signaling class was over. Thank goodness I didn't have to make the decision between crying and retaliating. With Dad on my mind, I'm sure I was about to make the wrong choice. Grabbing my books, I streaked out of the classroom practically breaking the sound barrier as I sped down the hall. The only sounds keeping up with me were the sound of Dad's zipper and the creaking of the school's old wooden floor as my frightened feet gave them a good pounding.

I paused at my locker, too dazed to remember my combination. Taking a deep breath to clear the fog from my head, I slammed my back against my locker. The physical force brought me back to reality, because I instantly was mortified with the sensation of wet panties. Mom had coached and equipped me for when my period would start. Dropping my books on the floor, I made my way to the nearest girls' bathroom just as the buzzer for the next class period sounded. Great! I was going to start the next class in trouble too!

Stumbling into the first empty stall, I checked my panties for blood, but there wasn't any. What I found was the remains of "evidence" from the night before; the final consummation of what I had really, really hoped was a nightmare. But I could no longer deny what my father had done to me. It was a grim, ugly-truthed nightmare. I became frightened and crazed at the same time. Frantically I ripped at the toilet paper and began rubbing myself raw trying to clean away my shame…again, and again, and again…

Relieved at the day's torturous end, I meandered home more out of habit than desire. But the hits just kept on coming. Once home, I found out that Mom had packed her bags and moved in with a neighbor down the road. Panic set in for the second time today. Mom was our lifeline to security. I had planned on using her as my island of safety. If I was never far outside of her presence, I thought I would be all right. Instead, I found myself drowning in fear as Kathy and I clutched each other on the couch while Dad explained Mom's actions. He delivered his speech on cue and in his controlled, domineering voice.

It was a double edged sword. We did not want Mom to leave but now that she had, both edges of the blade showed itself. First, Kathy and I secretly cringed at the thought of Mom telling everyone about our "house of madness" now that she has escaped. How were we going to face our classmates? The other edge of the sword being the fact that without Mom, I was going to have to use Kathy and Brock to protect me from any future advances from Dad. From my perspective, I now was glad that Mom was not aware of Dad raping me. Her moving out made me more resolved than ever to keep it silent now!

Dad also informed us matter-of-factly that the police report from the earlier visit to our house had registered Mom as "hysterical and out of control." There was no mention of sexual abuse. Then ruthlessly, he announced that as a "concerned" husband, it was his intention to have Mom admitted for psychiatric treatment.

Imagine that! After being deathly ill on numerous occasions, drugged for half her life, society ignoring all the signs of mental and physical abuse, Dad had manipulated authorities into believing that our family was normal and if there was anything to be concerned about, he was innocent; everything on record was Mom's fault.

In shock of his announcement and disgust of his arrogance, I broke away from the couch without saying a word, leaving him stunned as his mouth gaped open – hopefully drawing the flies to his mouthful of crap. Delirious with shock from the ill twisted state of events, I stumbled outside until I found myself standing at the foot of my favorite tree. Planting my feet firmly on its elderly trunk, I began climbing to its heaviest branch. It was an old friend; one that always makes me feel safe. Curling up in a ball, I concentrated on my ears, straining them to listen to the rustling of the leaves.

In time it worked! For the briefest moment I was invisible – from school, from my family and from the horrible future. I was invisible from everything and everybody, except my own pain and sorrow... and the gentle whispers of the fall leaves.

• • • •

Months of school passed, and I can honestly tell you that I don't remember a thing. Time was like liquid and could never be captured in one place long enough to solidify a memorable memory. I hated school with a hatred that bordered on passionate. I hated my cliquish classmates. My hate for *going to school* was only exceeded by my hatred to *come home* from school.

I also hated my personal life, if you could call it "personal." It seemed more like my life belonged to everybody, *but me*. My relationship with Tom had become close to zero – he stopped pressing for intimacy, not understanding that Dad's secret rape had traumatized my feelings about sex. Tom interpreted my resistance into thinking that I didn't care enough to take our relationship further. The thought of sex revolted me now, and our relationship had sunk to a new low. It seems like I don't know much about anything.

What I *do know* is that today I am sitting in court, having rushed to the courthouse with Kathy and Brock from school to anxiously wait for a judge's decision that would return us to our Mom. Unbelievably true to his word, Dad had succeeded in having Mom committed to a sanitarium. But Mom's psychiatric tests in the end had turned out clean, and she was returned to society a new woman, with a singular resolve – to regain custody of her children.

I always stopped by her new apartment when I didn't think Dad would catch me. She was working in a factory and had found the courage to file for divorce. I could see her developing into a stronger, more independent, Christian woman. Her time away from Dad had proven therapeutic, and her entire life was now consumed with getting her children away from their father. I could hardly wait.

I sat there confident that Dad's days of abuse were numbered. I looked forward to moving out and starting in a fresh school with Mom and her new life. Exhilarated with hope, I fidgeted in the public seating section and gazed around taking in the high cathedral ceilings and linseed oil smelling woodwork to help deaden my excitement. I had never been in a courtroom before, but I knew the courts were always on the side of justice; I learned that from television. Even though I'm a half-breed, I am a proud and loyal American. I was on a natural high as I waited the judge's decision to dole out the "justice" Dad so richly deserved.

The gavel fell like my heart; cold, fast and hard, pounding my bountiful faith in the system into oblivion. The judge gave us over to our Dad! I was stunned. I couldn't believe my ears. What system would allow such a thing? My natural "high" transformed me into a dead zombie – not able to move and unable to speak. I felt Dad grabbing at me to usher all of us out of the pew and through the courtroom doors.

130

Mom was sobbing violently to my left. I tried not to look but I couldn't help myself. She was so pretty in a new print dress. She didn't look like the shell of a woman she had been for the last several years. Now all I can see is her screaming for her children. She disappeared out of my sight as Dad dragged us through the courtroom door, not even allowing for a good-bye kiss.

I wasn't sure if she wanted to kill the judge, her lawyer or Dad the worst. What I did know is that it wasn't over... for any of us.

"Why didn't you scream that loud sooner, Mom? Why?"

> *The price of your soul is free. The*
> *cost of losing it is priceless.*

Chapter 14

possessed, possessions....
or both?

Hidetoshi was the reason I had the nerve to venture to Japan. Plain and simple.

He was the one who responded to my contact when finding my family, and he was the one who welcomed Rob and me into his home. It helped that he was somewhat similar in age and somewhat similar in circumstance, with his father deceased and being an only child. As I stated earlier, Hidetoshi was also as estranged from both his aunts in Nagasaki as I was from my paternal family in the United States. He, like me, was closer to his in-laws than his bloodline. Maybe I should say, our lives half a world apart were more than similar, they were "eerily similar." This made him as curious about me as I was about him...and as needful.

As time marched toward my very fast approaching departure date, Hidetoshi overcame the insecurities of my relationships with Miyuki and Maki. We became very comfortable with each other and ultimately, very close. He would always escort me by the elbow when we were out, pointing to different things in shops and stores, either telling what it was in Japanese, or on rare occasion showing off by pronouncing some object's name in broken English.

He was intimidating to look at with his six foot frame full of serious expres-

sions. But in Japan, he was my lifeline. He kept me safe in a strange land. Without him, I would have been as alone as on a deserted island. He also became quite funny as he got used to having me around, betraying his stoic face and worldly air about him.

One evening in getting ready to go out to eat, Hidetoshi asked me if I could get ready in 30 minutes or less. I said "yes." He looked at me and then looked at my hair and then wrinkled his brow in doubt. I got it, my hair was a mess.

"Shame on you! You only asked because I am woman. I will wear hat like Rob!" I retorted, and grabbing one of Ai's hats, I covered my flying hair and announced I was "ready to go." Hidetoshi broke out in a broad smile.

While at the Pagoda Teahouse, there was an extremely low crossbeam over the hallway entrance, a crossbeam that none but Hidetoshi had to navigate by ducking his head. I had turned to Maki to warn Hidetoshi to duck, adding that "although if he hit his head it may knock some sense into him." Maki began faithfully translating but as if understanding what I had said, Hidetoshi immediately flashed me a fake scowl and struck me a blow to my right shoulder knocking me two steps sideways. I almost fell through the crystal-clear paned glass catching my balance! What a sight that would have made!

Later that evening we had fallen into deep conversation – about Mom and my similarity to her. Hidetoshi had met Mom as a teenager in her one and only visit to Japan. Everyone commented on Mom and now what seemed to them my adventurous spirit. They admired the courage it took to make the trip to Japan, and to not allow the language barrier to come between families – as Mom had done struggling with English when coming to America. We were alike in so many ways, except according to Hidetoshi, his Aunt Keiko would never sit on the floor with her legs crossed like I was doing in my most comfortable blue jeans.

"After all, Japan woman legs fat," he surprisingly offered. It was such a contrasting comment to the seriousness of the conversation I almost fell over backwards laughing.

I told him that "men should not speak of such things! Sumimasen. Americanjean des! Sorry, but I am American!" I said in my best Japanese and then automatically translated in English. I was trying to convey that sitting like this was acceptable in America and in any case, my legs were not fat like

Japanese women. They laughed heartily either at the meaning, or my poor Japanese language skills.

On another evening Hidetoshi was in one of his feeling neglected moods; in other words, not being more the center of attention when surrounded by all females. Sensing how desperately he wanted to fit in with me in the short time we had together, I pondered for a moment how to make him feel better. Trying to separate our relationship from everyone else present, I took my right hand and made a karate chop in my left hand. Then I pointed to me and him trying to communicate that I was half Japanese; his half.

"We same," I had tried to explain. Hidetoshi seemed to pick up on what I was trying to say and acknowledged that I was correctly only "half Japanese" and then went on to say to my shock and amusement, "the half that is Japanese is the smart half." Immensely pleased with himself, he broke out into his wide toothy grin.

However, the most memorable witticism surrounded talk of my returning to Japan and the skepticism that Hidetoshi showed that I would ever come back. To set the stage you must understand that possessions are like an unwritten code of worthiness. From my understanding, Buddha teaches that possessions are not the true path to Nirvana, but it is undeniable in my observation that possessions afford a certain amount of pride and stature in the Japanese culture. That's why when explaining the finer aspects of his Toyota Estima and proclaiming "Toyota #1," Hidetoshi asked with guarded envy, "what you drive?" As this was earlier in our visit, it was Rob who responded "Jaguar." Not only did Hidetoshi's eyebrows raise, so did Miyuki's. No amount of explaining that it was an X-type, the cheapest brand Jaguar makes and a used model at that could take away the respect that was generated of us by owning a Jaguar. Silly, I know.

After what seemed like hours of being badgered now by Hidetoshi that I would probably never return – the travel, the time, the expense; I responded emphatically that "I will return. I will do whatever it takes, no matter what!" Hidetoshi seized the moment.

I still recall fondly how he leaned back in his chair, folded his arms and stroked his chin in his best Confucius imitation saying, "ahhh sooo… you sell Jag to return?"

I laughed until I cried. Outwardly I laughed at Hidetoshi's wit. I think *the crying started not from excessive laughter, but at the vision of Rob selling our car to send me back to Japan. Regardless of love for my car, inwardly, returning to Japan was a promise I intended to keep.*

It reminded me that people do unusual things to get what they want – and how ironic it is that worldly possessions are at the center of their actions…

I had just taken out a piece of paper to start my homework in study hall; study hall had become my haven after the divorce – my only escape, no class and no home – when the fire alarm went off.

Exiting with no particular urgency, practice fire drills were routine in every school I had attended and almost always ended in being herded into the narrow hallway, like too many cattle trying to get through the slaughterhouse door I began to notice that my steps were becoming smaller and smaller as I stared at the shoulders of classmates. My body curves had finally blossomed, but my height was either lagging behind or I was cursed to be short.

As we came to a standstill, I craned my neck in hopes of seeing the crowd progressing to an outside door and freedom to move about. Feeling claustrophobic, I didn't notice that all the shoulders I was staring at were of the male gender until someone's hand cupped by left breast. I tried to pull away but couldn't move! As if splashed with cold water in the face, I suddenly realized that I was encircled tightly by nothing but leering boys.

My mind began racing as someone behind me grabbed my buttocks. Then the sea of testosterone pushed in closer and I quickly had a dozen hands on me.

"Hey, feel here!" someone snickered. I jumped as my crotch was violated. I began screaming and kicking for all I was worth! If any teacher was in earshot the attack would stop, and if no teacher was around I was confident enough girls would hear to come to my rescue.

Wrong!

My punches were easily deflected and then returned with more violating gropes. In the back of my mind, I can hear my screams being returned by the nearby girls in the forms of snickers. I can feel the hot embers of my cheeks burn with the added humiliation that other girls were allowing such a thing!

'They probably were going along with this game because they are secretly happy it wasn't them!' I rationalized as I fought back. My arms and voice tiring, the bell rang again just as I was about to succumb to the opening of my trousers.

'It must be that I'm yet again, new in this school,' I reasoned as I straightened myself up and returned to class. Angered beyond compare, I still decided not to report the incident. I didn't want to become the target of retaliation. I barely saw faces and knew no names, and in high school I desperately wanted to fit in. Starting a new school required a quick acquisition of friends, and turning anyone into the office would be the fastest path to never gaining any. Besides, compared to home, being groped in school seemed easy enough to handle once. All I had to do was invoke my trained "shutdown" mode. Somehow it just seems to fit right into the disgusting pattern of my whole damn life.

Or so I rationalized…

• • • •

"We had to move," Dad tried to explain. "The apartment was being sold, and we were evicted. But don't worry; you're all going to love this place." How many times have we heard that line before? Oh, only ten or twelve times by now…

The new apartment is really a huge eighteen room house with another family of four (with two small children) living on one side; the other side to be ours. It's out in the country centered in the middle of a barren field, with a pointless shed and a rustic barn. The house looks 100 years old and is in dying need of attention. The barn is worse. I don't think it's dying for a paint job anymore; I think it's dead. But the house is roomy, and the more room between all of us the better.

The father of the other family next door traveled much of the time, but his wife Bess appeared more than friendly. Bess stood 5'4" and weighted 150 lbs., most which she carried in her double-D bra…when she wore one. Her shoulder length shoe polished black hair and matching personality sent a sultry message; one that I was sure wasn't lost on Dad.

We settled in quickly and quietly over the weekend, as I secretly hoped for the millionth time, for good. Dreams of a home instead of just a house still dance in my head like Christmas sugarplums. And the Christmas presents? They're always the same – a personality makeover for Dad, a healthy Brock, and a Mom who never wanted to leave again.

But Monday came and no Christmas with it. Just the same old grind of getting settled in what I'm sure will be another temporary situation.

Brock and I were home from school before Dad and Kathy got home, and we were immediately greeted with a knock at the door. It was Bess in a denim long sleeve shirt with enough buttons left undone to expose a large portion of cleavage. So much for what I had hoped would be transparent neighbors. She was molded in shiny jeans as if poured into them. When she smiled she had two halves of pearly whites, separated by a large space between the top front teeth. Her skin was olive brown like her rumored Cherokee ancestors. Save the teeth and twenty pounds, she was very attractive.

"Hello," I greeted Bess unsure of what she wanted.

"Hi hon. Got time to talk?" she queried indifferently as she made her way past me and into our side of the house without invitation.

"I suppose. Why?" I answered with an air of annoyance as I closed the door.

"Thought you might like some history of this place. It's an old Amish house you know. Or maybe you didn't. Doesn't matter. I'm going to tell you about it, just in case…" her voice trailed as she made her way to the couch in her best Marilyn Monroe strut. "All right to sit here?" She asked, and then without waiting for me to answer, sank forcibly into the couch.

"In case of what?" I asked, trailing a safe distance "in case" her walk might be contagious.

"Well, this house was built by the Amish with every intention of two families living here. In-breeding you know, or maybe you don't.

How old are you, hon? Oh well, from the looks of you you're old enough. Anyways, about the house..."

"Yes, about the house," I repeated, ignoring her personal prying as I sat on the edge of Dad's recliner opposite her opposing figure.

"As I said, the house was built for two families, split right down the middle, only connected by a door through a closet upstairs. It's the walk-in closet in the master bedroom."

"I've seen it," I announced. "It has a zillion locks on it. I have no clue as to why so many?" I said, thinking I was making polite conversation.

"It's because we are unable to keep it shut all the time, dearie," she said, my response playing right into her manicured hands. "We have that many locks on the other side too." It was a fact that she announced with a prideful grin.

I sat up on the edge of the recliner. "What do you mean you can't keep it shut?" This was sounding very interesting or very scary, I wasn't sure which.

"I mean no matter what, no matter how many locks we put on that door, there are some mornings it's gaping open," she said expressionless as she stared at an annoying hang nail on her left index finger.

"Are you saying this house is haunted? As in ghosts?" I asked shocked. No wonder Dad got such a good deal.

"Yes, that's exactly what I'm saying, dearie. Why do you think I came over? To tell you it's haunted. You do believe in spirits, don't you? They're everywhere, you know."

"Yes, I believe in the spiritual world. God is spiritual, and I believe in him."

"Do you believe in witches?" Bess abruptly tossed out. She sat silent waiting for my reply.

"Do you mean in real witches, or like Halloween witches?" I replied trying to keep my heart at an even pace. Where was she going with this?

"I mean good and bad witches. There are such things you know," she replied with an air of certainty.

"How do you know? I'll bet you've never even seen one have you?" I shot back.

"I am one, dearie!" Bess laughed heartily. It was as if this was the real reason Bess had come over. To see the shock on my face when she made her grandiose announcement. Well she got her wish! Reading more than shock on my face, she continued, "Don't worry, I'm not a bad witch. Bad witches do bad things to people."

I stood up and paced for a second trying to act nonchalant. Is she nuts? Should I kick her out, run, scream for help? And Dad had *MOM* committed! I decided to go along, just a little farther. "I've never heard of good witches, except for Glinda in the Wizard of Oz you know, the good witch of the North. Can you put a spell on anyone?" I challenged.

"Of course!" Bess snooted. "I've put lots of spells on people. Love spells to get couples together. That's a good thing, don't you think?" She shifted her weight causing her to tilt to the right as she leaned on the arm of the chair. Trying to get comfortable, she crossed her slightly chubby legs and then stared me down for a response as she curled her hair behind her left ear, exposing a half a dozen piercings.

"Isn't that like taking God into your own hands? I mean like controlling destiny or something that we don't have any business messing with?"

"Oh, we got business messing with it all right! We believe in, what was it you called 'God', Amy? We just believe that God's love needs a little coaxing. It's what makes the world 'go round' you know? Or don't you? Probably not. We have lots of love in our group, in fact we have orgies," Bess announced. She let her confession hang in the air shifting her crossed legs, and waiting on a reaction from me.

I had paced to the window and was concentrating on a blue jay on the sill, when I suddenly felt uncomfortable having my back to Bess. Shackled by her bold claim I turned and a shrill voice asked, "like in a bunch of naked people? That kind of orgy?" I was astounded at her blatant approach to the subject of sex.

"Yep."

"Bess, I think you better leave," I stuttered as I turned and walked toward the front door. I had a fearful idea where this was headed, and I had heard enough.

"Well, I never!" She exclaimed. Following my command, she stood and sashayed across the living room, pausing at the door to stick her finger under my chin as I held the door open. With a quick upward motion of her finger, she said, "Don't knock it until you've tried it, honey! What the hell, you're just jailbait anyway!" and then she tartly left.

I repeated the episode to Dad when he got home from work, stupidly thinking he would come to my defense. Instead he found it amusing. I suspect he found it exciting, both the orgy and potential new partners in the occult. A few days later he went on a buying spree, adding new books on the spirit world to his meager collection.

It was like the floodgates of hell had opened. Thankfully I haven't been bothered by Bess again, but now our living room is lined with twice as many books on cults, psychic phenomenon and witchcraft. I keep reminding Dad that the Bible says to stay away from the dark side, but it's like an evil demon has been unleashed in him. He is convinced he has psychic and magical powers. His latest kick is predicting that someone in the family is going to die. Last week a great aunt died, the third prediction of a death in a row. Dad claims victory, and that it's a gift. I think he or the demon inside of him is pure evil.

• • • •

'I can't believe I'm doing this again,' I find myself wondering out loud as I sit at the kitchen table with Dad and Brock and Kathy, all holding hands in the dark, except for the candle in the middle of the table. It's like an annual séance with him, and it creeps me out – evil, Evil, EVIL. I attend because of the threats of what will happen to me if I don't. The heat is suffocating tonight because of Dad's insistence that all windows be clad-iron shut (to keep the spirits in and the outsiders out), a cruelty unto itself.

Once the "master" felt the mood was just right, he broke our circle of three fearful kids and one pompous adult long enough to produce what looked like one of Dad's homemade contraptions. It had a sharp needle in the center of a wooden spool and a strange looking pendulum made of paper. It actually looked like the top of one of those miniature umbrellas in one of those exotic drinks you see on <u>Hawaii Five-O</u>. Carefully, as if any wrong movement would disturb the spirit world, he hung the umbrella on top of the needle only to have it fall off. I wiggled my butt in the chair and sighed a deep, loud sigh hoping that Dad would just give up this silliness. Besides, I didn't want to see anymore. He had made his hand change sides before, but this is the first time he has tried to use something other than his stupid chanting.

Just as I was hopeful Dad's patience would wear out, he finally got the delicately balanced object to teeter, waiver and then hang on, as if it was anxiously awaiting Dad's next command. He explained that with his powers joining the spirit world through the pendulum, he would be able to communicate with the "haunts of the house." He was going to ask questions to the spirits, and the umbrella was going be the translator between the two worlds; rotating clockwise for yes, and counter-clockwise for no. It was imperative that we remain silent, as if we have a choice.

I was skeptical, but after looking left and right at our shadows darting all over the walls, I began to feel a tad uncomfortable. Dad commanded we join hands. As I took Brock and Kathy's hands, I could tell they were both nervous from the sweat in their palms. Brock gave my hand a slight reassuring squeeze that he wouldn't let anything happen to me, which I found comforting. I squeezed back to indicate I would take care of him too. Kathy's hand was as limp as a noodle, and I wondered if that was a good sign or bad.

Rejoining Brock and Kathy's hands, Dad took a deep breath and said, "Spirits of the house, we come to you for answers."

No answer.

"Uhhhmm, are you in the room? Do you honor us with your presence?" Dad beseeched the unknown spirits clearing his throat. Any unknown spirit. We all sat stiff, waiting on a response.

No answer.

Ignoring the spirit's rebuff, Dad continued on as if he was speaking to long lost friends, "Spirits, does this house have evil in it?"

Then as if awoke from the dead, the pendulum moved slowly to the right. It was only a jiggle, but it definitely moved. We all stared in disbelief. I felt Kathy's limp hand go rigid in fear, while Brock's reassuring grip was like wax. It wasn't the dumb umbrella we were scared of, it was whatever moved it that we couldn't see! I glanced at Dad whose eyes gleamed with delight.

"Spirit, I feel your evil!" Typical of Dad's turbulent life, he plowed ahead into the unknown. "Does this house have a history that involves an accident?" Dad seemed almost hopeful in anticipation of the response. The pendulum wiggled at first and then as if someone was blowing on it, picked up speed. It spun to the right and began moving so fast I thought it was going to fly off the needle.

"Dad! Stop!" I begged, unable to keep his commandment of silence.

"Quiet! You'll anger the spirits!" he threatened. "I know what I'm doing. I've studied. Why do you think we have all these books? It will be all right. We *have* to help them communicate. Trust me. And whatever you do, DO NOT BREAK THE CIRCLE! Any of you!"

I looked around at the frightened stares of everyone else. I couldn't tell if they were more afraid of spirits or Dad, but no one was moving, so I stayed put. Besides, I knew who that "any of you" comment was directed at.

Again, clearing his throat for effect, Dad continued solemnly, "Did anything happen in the main part of the house?" This time without hesitation the device spun to the left. NO.

I leaned left and right, straining to see in the dark if Dad had some fan or something to make it move, but I couldn't see anything. In my look around I was sure that as things got more intense, it got darker in the room somehow. That's when I noticed that the complete calm outside the house had begun to bluster up into a sure fire "brewing storm." I was suddenly startled by the cat on the porch jumping up on the outside windowsill, trying desperately to avoid the storm. I jumped back in my seat, almost breaking the circle!

"I feel something wrong in the basement. Is that the place of the accident?" Dad said pressing on into the unknown. The device violently began spinning to the right, faster and faster until it flew completely off the needle!

With my heart in my mouth, no amount of threatening could keep me nailed to my chair any longer. I jumped up and ran out of the house, away from my evil father, and whatever spirits he had conjured up! I found myself several blocks away before I stopped and thought about what I just witnessed. As I looked back into the past, it seemed more like mind games and parlor tricks. But now....I couldn't tell what was more important to Dad. Was it worldly possessions and the sexual gratification he coveted, or did he relish being a possession of the evil spirit world?

What I did know is that I was standing under a dimly lit light post in the middle of the night, violently shaking with fear at the possibility of the joining of the two....

Chapter 15

and the "hits" just keep on coming

Time was winding down and I couldn't believe it. Or maybe, I didn't want to believe it. All my fears of ever finding my family; the travel, the language, and their hopeful acceptance…every fear had melted away like sugar in a tall glass of water. And the most surprising of all – I was fitting in! My comfort level increased each day as I acclimated to the culture with no fear of interjecting mine. And then a new fear began to creep in.

The fear of leaving.

I didn't want to go, but the calendar loomed larger each passing day. With only a few days to go, time was of the essence, and I found myself motoring our way to the next item on my "wanna see" agenda - to my mother's house as a child.

I also still wanted to visit the family cemetery where my grandparents and Uncle Ilotta were buried. And of course I needed to say good-bye to everyone; a proper good-bye, leaving my thoughts, my feelings, my appreciation and my love.

Damn that calendar.

When we turned the corner to what I thought was my mother's house, I was puzzled by the anxiety in Hidetoshi's face. He looked reluctant to continue as he parked the van in an alleyway instead of in the front of the old house. We were in a residential area, a rare sight from what I could see since the only one I had been in was Aunt Yoko's. Most of my limited exposure to Japan gave me the impression that a majority of the general population lived in coastline city apartments. But this was more like rural America. Houses were smallish and one story and surprisingly, not very well kept. As we parked, I realized that dirt alleys in Japan were something my stereotyped opinion had not processed.

We got out of the van in silence. I somehow sensed that even though this was a solemn occasion to me, it was causing Hidetoshi much consternation. I turned to Maki, who had made a personal sacrifice to spend as much time as possible with us for the last half of my visit and asked, "What's wrong?"

A wrinkled brow on Maki's beautiful face told me she read my puzzlement and immediately interceded on my behalf. Approaching Hidetoshi, they digressed into rapid conversation. After what seemed like minutes, Maki turned to me to explain.

"This is home of your Grandmother. The home of your mother as a child was destroyed years ago. Your Grandfather lived a very short life and your Grandmother a very long one. Your grandmother live here 40 year alone. You understand?"

"Yes," I replied. I was disappointed not being able to see where my mother had lived, but since I had never met my maternal grandparents, this was still exciting to me. "So, why is Hidetoshi acting nervous?" I queried.

"Someone else live here and Hidetoshi think it impolite to be on another's property," Maki explained. "He no want to offend and considers it improper to go to home of someone when you are not invited."

My cultural indoctrination just took another setback. Back home we would waltz up to a house as politely as we could, introduce ourselves and announce that "we were in the company of some relative who use to live here, and we want to show so-and-so around the old homestead." Granted in some areas of the country you may get a shotgun in the face, but 99 times out of 100 you were warmly greeted and welcomed in, replete with offers of cookies or coffee or both.

However in Japan, politeness rules, and in retrospect I suppose that's not such a bad thing.

In the end, Hidetoshi's loyalty to me won the day. We did not "knock" on the door and introduce me as "so-and-so," but we did visit the house. Like thieves in the night, we snuck down the alley and found an opening at the backside of the home. With hopes of not being seen, the second rule of Japan overcame the first rule of politeness. That is the rule of "you must have picture taken at all cost." To that means, I was escorted to the back patio of my Grandma's house and placed in a stoic position for pictures. Many pictures. How strange we could not announce ourselves but found it perfectly all right to be stealthy as spies trespassing on another's property.

The house was clean, but run down. Ratty clumps of brown grass dotted the miniscule back yard which was boarded on two sides by a tall fence, and on one side by a row of concrete blocks that had hidden the house from the alley. The house itself had the texture of grayish smoke made of slate or concrete, and as dull and drab as the dark gray sky.

For my ceremonial pictures, Hidetoshi placed me in the middle of the three foot by three foot "patio" amongst the clutter of folding chairs and a canvas umbrella. I stood there rigidly while cameras flashed, feeling nostalgia for both my Grandmother and my past.

Gradually I lost count of the seemingly infinite camera clicks, drifting instead to another place in my memory. The musky smell of the canvas umbrella reminded me of the smell of alcohol on my Dad's breath, and of a fateful camping trip...

After the divorce, Dad isolated us from as much outside contact as possible. All school activities were discouraged or refused, and the séances increased in frequency.

I feel oppressed most of the time, and I could sense that Kathy is becoming more and more manipulated. Dad no longer has to sneak into the bedroom to pull Kathy out. She is now under orders to retire to bed with him.

I denied any sexual activity between them to Brock. If everyone thought I was too young to understand, then *I was sure he was.* Besides, I really didn't know what went on behind closed doors. Periodically I found myself popping off to Dad about how unnatural his actions were with Kathy, but only once in awhile. Each time I did, Dad shot me a fearsome and fateful look that sent shivers down my spine. I can't sleep after one of those looks, fearing for my life and replaying my own tragic indoctrination into Dad's imaginary world of "what a family should be." After one of those looks, I sense that an ideal family might just be one less daughter. After abating my mouth, survival instincts usually kick in, and I don't say anything more about it for several weeks.

Last night was one of those nights though…I just couldn't help myself. Most nights I sleep with my pillow on my head and block out the images of my Dad and what he might be doing to Kathy behind closed doors. But last night I couldn't take it any longer. I recalled the first time I had heard something and didn't know what it was a few years ago, when Mom was still home and drugged into a catatonic state. Back then Kathy had urged me away from the bedroom door with me not understanding fully what was going on.

This time though, as I lay in bed I couldn't take listening to Kathy's sullen cries and whimpers behind Dad's closed bedroom door any longer. In what must have been a temporary moment of insanity, I found myself in an "out of body experience." I can't believe I risked all the pain and anger Dad could turn on me; it was as if I watched myself leap up out of bed and run out into the hallway, pounding with both fists on Dad's bedroom door.

"Kathy! Are you all right, Kathy?!" I wailed uncontrollably.

"Shut up and go away!" Dad shouted at the top of his lungs. It was as if I could feel the spewing fire out of his mouth as his angry words burnt my ears.

"Is he hurting you, Kathy? Dad, you leave her alone!" my entire body cried as I continued to pound away, even though my arms were already tiring.

"Get the hell away from that door if you know what's good for you!" he threatened one last time. The tone of his voice sent *that shiver* down my spine. I stopped cold, and seemingly watched from above as my body slinked away from the deafening sobs of my sister.

The last thing I saw was me crying myself to sleep.

• • • •

In one aspect, Dad never fails to let us down. Every few weeks he would routinely purchase some kind of liquor. He sadistically joked to me one time that "Kathy was his one true love; after Smirnoff." I was confused both at the sickness of his possession of Kathy, and my feeling of being neglected from his callous attitude. I obviously wasn't ANY kind of love in his life.

It has become a game for the kids to come up with distractions to keep Dad from getting drunk. Kathy and I both knew that Dad drunk spelled 'S.O.B.' But I gotta hand it to my sister. This time she came up with an idea that will keep everyone busy, and hopefully, Dad sober.

We are going camping.

Our equipment is limited to two pup tents and a frying pan. The rest we are determined to make up as we go. Kathy threw some food in a sack, some water in old milk carton jugs and grabbed some old sheets and blankets to sleep on. I thought of the flashlight and toilet paper. Brock thought of marshmallows. There was a forecast for rain but Kathy was adamant that a sober evening in the rain was infinitely better than a drunk evening at home. I couldn't agree more.

We settled on a free government sponsored campground. It was isolated and out of the way, but it was just the right price. I have to admit with everyone pitching in and staying busy with the setup, cooking and cleanup, we were too busy to fight, and seemed to genuinely be having fun. Finishing off the last of the marshmallows I actually felt satisfied that we had experienced a good evening...for a change. I looked at the campfire and then tracked its flames in the form of darting shadows on the trees, the sun having sunk below the horizon hours before. Yes, this was a good idea, Kathy. There had been no rain and most of all, no booze.

Late, tired and our bellies full on this rare occasion, we doused the fire and began heading for our tents. I grabbed Kathy by one arm to come to my tent and immediately found myself in a tug of war with Dad, who had firmly grabbed Kathy by the other arm.

"Dad, you promised!" Kathy pleaded, standing between us. Her face was full of hope, but her eyes were full of fear. I gazed at them in the dark noticing how empty they were. Then I glanced at Dad, whose eyes seemed to glare red in anger at me. I dropped Kathy's arm without a word of protest. Gathering Brock in my arm instead, we retired silently to our tent.

Intent on eavesdropping, I strained to hear Kathy and Dad's whispers rising above the creaking branches and twigs – most likely snapping under the weight of a scavenger raccoon. My mind eased that nothing explosive seemed to be happening between Dad and Sis, so I turned my attention to nature's critters of the night.

Or should I say, to the prevention of animal cruelty; primarily to me!

I turned on my flashlight momentarily illuminating our tent, then peering out the crack of the tent opening I placed the flashlight at its base, pointing in the direction of the snapping twigs – just in case it was more than an old raccoon. Nothing was getting in our tent unless I knew about it!

Feeling relatively safe hidden behind my makeshift spotlight, I soon could feel myself nodding off to sleep. After what seemed like hours, my head bobbed to one side in my sleep, abruptly waking me with a jolt. The first thing I noticed was that the air had cooled considerably for a hot summer night. I reached over and tucked the sheet around Brock's side, who was slumbering like a hibernating bear. The wind whistled, and I whistled back. It answered me with surprising force. I looked up at the hole in the top of our pup tent and prayed it didn't rain, then rolling over, I tried to concentrate on going back to sleep.

I must have dozed off for the second time but not for long. When I awoke the wind was howling. As I glanced outside, I was rudely greeted with falling branches and tumbling debris scooting across the deserted campground. Faintly hidden in the whistle of the wind was Dad's voice hollering outside, "Run to the car!"

The rain began just as I opened the tent flap in the black of the night, searching desperately for the direction of the car. I grabbed Brock who was still half asleep and stumbled out of the tent with the rain pelting us with hail-like drops. We crawled in the back seat of the car aching from being pounded and watched with wide eyes as the rain bounced off the windows.

Almost instantly, the wind kicked into overdrive and the car began to rock like a boat being tossed on the water. The torrid rain on the roof of the car made me feel like I was the clapper inside a bell. It was deafening as I swung to and fro from the unbridled force of the wind and rain. The windows began to steam over from our rapid breathing, and the lack of fresh air made it hard to breath.

"I'm miserable! Let's go home!" I blurted out in frustration. My hair was soaking wet having matted itself to my round cheeks, not to mention that my pajamas clung to my shivering skin. "We've had our fun. Why do we have to ruin it by staying here couped up in the car?!"

Not heeding my whines, Dad chimed in with "I've got an idea!"

I held my breath with skepticism at one of Dad's ideas.

"The trunk is clean. I know because I just cleaned it out last weekend. Why don't you sleep in the trunk? I won't actually lock you in it. We'll pull the back seat open a little and let you crawl in. See?" he demonstrated without waiting for an answer as he tugged on the seat and popped it loose. "I'll give you a pillow and a blanket, okay?"

Except the "okay" was accented with the brashness in his voice I had come to fear.

"Okay, maybe it will be fun," I lied not wanting to appear frightened. Soon I found myself clambering through the opening in the backseat into the trunk of the car. What a childish idea I thought, and I know I can never trust anything Dad suggests as a "good idea." I fought back my natural panic of the dark when Dad replaced the back seat, only leaving a small crack of an opening exposed in the middle. I found as long as I lay perfectly still I was able to calm my fears and actually catch some sleep, at least in between Kathy and Dad's now incessant arguing. What a difference a couple of hours makes!

I didn't have to listen too hard to know what they were arguing about. I could smell it. Mr. Smirnoff. I forced myself to sleep on several occasions, just to block out the possibilities of what might happen next. The rain, with its rhythmic dance on the trunk of the car, drowned out the rise and fall of their voices somewhat helping me shut out their bickering; at least until I found myself stabbed awake with the next fit of rage.

"BAM!" I was startled by the slamming of the car door. I heard

Kathy bawling in the front seat so I knew it must have been Dad that stormed off.

"What's the matter, Kathy?" I asked gently through the crack between the back seat and the trunk.

"Ohhh, Dad's drunk, and he's out of his head again," she responded between sobs. "It will be all right. Once he's done stumbling all over the woods, he'll come back...if he doesn't hurt himself too bad. He always does, you know."

"Know what? Hurt himself, or come back?" I asked through my peephole. I wasn't sure if she was trying to comfort me or scare me.

"Both," she said slowly in a trance, as if searching her mind for another answer but having to give this one instead.

Sure enough, the prophet in her was right. Within the hour, the car rocked as Dad lumbered in. I couldn't see Kathy through my dungeon hole, but I could see the driver's side of the car. Dad's face was bright red with blood, most of which was running down his face mixing with streams of snot and flowing like a river toward his mouth. He smelled of dirt and grass and Russian white whiskey.

I couldn't stand to look at him. He must have stumbled on every log and his face must have found every mud puddle. The smell was equally revolting. He was blubbering incoherently, wiping his slimy face with his dirty shirt sleeve periodically. Sickened at his sight and exhausted from the earlier fighting, Kathy turned her back on him and appeared to doze off, or was doing a heck of a job faking it to avoid another confrontation with Dad.

As I lay in my trunk prison, I knew something was terribly wrong, with the both of them. I thought about perhaps him demanding sex from her as the reason for their argument. What Kathy said earlier, 'Dad, you promised' flashed in my head for a brief moment and hoped I was wrong. I didn't want to know. And besides, what could Dad possibly pull with Brock and I both in the same car?

With that final thought, I was motivated to offer an olive branch. A consolatory gesture to try and make things better – as a family. With all my will, I stuck my hand out of the trunk peephole in the one visible direction I could see; toward Dad. He saw me out of the corner of his eyes and as if having suddenly remembered I was there, reached back. As he extended his shaking mud caked hand to me I said, "It will be all right, Dad. Please, just stop crying." It was all my stomach could do to hold onto his hand and not throw up.

They were the last words spoken all night as I groggily drifted off to sleep.

I awoke the next day with my hand now mud crusted from his. As I pulled myself drearily out of my slumber, I thought for a flashing moment that things *could* get better! I thought that some understanding of a verbal message from Kathy, and some silent message from me was received last night, and that Dad realized what he was doing was destructive to our family...

...and then *he* woke up. Gruffly, he jerked his hand back out of mine, as if in remorse of ever showing me any emotion.

When he rather reluctantly released me from the trunk prison, I only had to look at him once in the bursting sunlight to see that the evil gleam was back in his eye... and so was the "shiver" down my spine.

• • • •

EDITOR'S NOTE: Kathy revealed to Amy later in life the reason she was upset that fateful night was not because their father was drunk, but because he had physically abused and raped her - in the back seat of the car and less than five feet away from her brother asleep in the front seat and Amy a prisoner in the trunk. Shame made her cover up the real reason at the time. If any good can come from such a thing, her Dad's arrogant attack signaled to Kathy that this must be the beginning of the end.

Hide your feelings and you will
always be seeking happiness.

Chapter 16

the truth wins out

If Hidetoshi is the reason I went to Japan, Miyuki is the reason I stayed. We became as sisters sharing a common bond with her family and children. Out of all the people I spent time with, I spent more time with Miyuki than anyone. She went everywhere we all went as a family: school, malls, the temple and the Teahouse. She was also there for the lunches and girl talks with Maki. But most importantly, she was there alone with me late at night when Hidetoshi was still not home from work or traveling.

We also had the common bond of motherhood. We talked, we drank tea and we shared more pictures of our families. She would also do her household chores after everyone else went to bed, leaving me to watch Japanese TV or translate on the computer or write in my journal. Helping her with housework would not be tolerated. It was almost as if she did not want others to see her doing laundry or cleaning the house but to do it in front of me was acceptable to her. Understanding the Japanese culture of "face," I considered that a big step for her and therefore, a comfort to me.

We have so much in common. We both work part-time but our families are the center of the universe. And Miyuki has such a supportive and loving family beyond Hidetoshi and Ai and Uuto. It reminded me of Rob's. Large and loving. I had met her parents, brother and sister in-law eating out when I first arrived. Though not directly related, they had treated me like royalty.

In fact on the next to last night of my stay, we were all going to her brother Masakazu and his wife Chikako's house for supper.

Masakazu loves to cook, so he was honored to have me into his home for a personally prepared, authentic Japanese meal. Masakazu and Chikako don't have any children so they shower Ai and Uuto with special attention and affection. When we arrived, Masakazu greeted us at the door with a larger than life smile and a bow of royal proportions. He was dressed in a sweat-shirt and blue jeans, both of which were mostly covered with a flowing Disney character apron. Adorning his crown was a Disney kerchief tied karate style around his head. The background color of the ensemble was a frightening bright mint green color. I was sure if the lights went out Masakazu could serve as a florescent lamp. And what made it even more special is that in his hand was an identical "junior" outfit for Uuto. They were so cute running around the tight apartment; one cooking and one pretending to cook.

As usual, I didn't know most of what I was eating, but I do know I still loved it. He prepared some type of little breaded meatballs that were cooked in a muffin style pan on an open fire, right on the dinner table. I ate so many he had to fix a second batch. And the salad, mmmm! There is a type of dressing in Japan I would kill for in America and was determined to find it when I got back home.

Miyuki was her usual quiet "behind the scenes" self. She herded the kids, helped with the serving of food and managed to film the meal on videotape. She had been trying to capture key events of my visit on tape for me and promised to send me a copy. I noticed that she filmed a lot more when we first met and didn't know each other. I take that as a strong sign of our growing affection. Plus the fact there usually wasn't anyone around to film her and me together when we spent most of our quality "girl time." It would have been boring cinema anyway. Who wants to see two grown women acting childish and hanging laundry while I miserably attempted to speak broken Japanese, second only to Miyuki's struggling English?

We wound the evening down at Masakazu's drinking tea and discussing my emptiness from lack of family nurturing. I wanted to convey to them my desperate need for this exact type of family time – time never afforded me in my childhood.

I felt so loved that night. I could easily imagine falling into this type of family routine and exotic Japanese culture. In fact, I imagined so hard I suddenly became ashamed of my desire to not go home so soon. But I was not nearly as ashamed of my selfish desire to stay as I was of my childhood, and how little love my life before Rob had contained. REAL love; not the kind that Dad showed - based on old lies and continually suffocating from the piling on of new lies.

I learned that night that truth and true love will always win out; if you have the courage to go look for it...

Finally! It only took until my middle teens but I have actually gained a curvy figure. Alas, nothing to brag about compared to Kathy who is the cocoon turned beautiful as the butterfly. In part, in dropping the thick eyeglasses for contacts her beauty has become an instant miracle. Trading in her ugly frames, she no longer is nerdy looking. Her fresh face brings out her cute waist-line, full flushed bust and her long dark hair which is darker than mine. Even with my puberty in full bloom, Kathy's carved figure and oriental features make her the woman *I wanted* to be.

To her credit, she has graduated high school and now has a job. But most importantly, she had taken two major steps to get there:

Step ONE: Shortly after the camping fiasco, she had demanded a separate bedroom from Dad... and not just moving back in with me. She demanded her own bedroom; a concept that until then had been unattainable. I think her resolve was strengthened in part by her now adult size. She simply was less intimidated by Dad. She also started to break away from Dad's iron fist control, in no small part because her impossible to hide beauty afforded her attention from other men. For the first time in her life, relationships outside the family seemed possible. Her room was a "hide-away haven" complete with a lock, and sent Dad the message she needed her space. I loved visiting in her bedroom, with its shaggy red carpet and soft lighting. It kind of reminded me of our Asian descent for some reason. I hoped it gave

Kathy in the short time she's had it, the calm it gave me when I was fortunate enough to enter.

~~Her own locked room! The world will never know how I coveted such~~ a luxury. What it didn't give Kathy was much peace. That "message" it was sending Dad, *was not* being well received. He continued to try and drive her back to him, only this time it backfired.

Instead, he drove her away…

Step TWO: As a continuation of Step ONE, it was only a matter of time and Kathy finally moved out. She later moved into a small utility apartment against his protests and advances once and for all! She knew as she unloaded the last box of her scant personal possessions that he would not give up his efforts easily, but to her credit, every time he showed up on her doorstep loudmouthed and drunk, she courageously turned him away. Kathy knew that the first time she let him in, he would cajole and manipulate and try to twist his way back into her life and if he couldn't, the physical abuse would follow. She simply knew that no good could possibly come from his further domination and so she held her ground. The one mistake Kathy made was thinking she had successfully held all of Dad's attention on her and away from me. When she moved, I truly believe she thought she had successfully broken him and after her life of bondage she was free!

The thought of any danger to me now never seemed to have occurred to her.

• • • •

The house was eerily quiet.

Stone deaf quiet. The kind of quiet that shouts at you. I was already uncomfortable with Kathy gone. Nowadays I always tried to make sure that Brock was around the house whenever I'm home, just to serve as Kathy's surrogate protector of me. My guard is never down, never…because I know what Kathy does not – that *she wasn't the only* victim.

But Brock was nowhere in sight today when Dad came into the house. He had been out in the barn working on something unimportant; unimportant to everyone but him.

While stepping up to the kitchen sink to wash his mangy hands, I was greeted with a cheery and benign, "Hey, guess what I found?" Then before I had time to put my guard up, "That bitch of a beagle had her pups. I found them in the barn. Come on, I'll show you."

"Puppies? Really? How many?" I asked excitedly as I followed him out. Animals are still a kindred spirit to me; especially newborns. They are so fuzzy and fresh with their whole life ahead of them. They're my envy of innocence, my comfort for love and they speak of hope in life; all qualities that are missing in mine.

Making our way into the barn corridor that separated empty wooden stalls, I saw something move against a bale of hay in the distance. I quickened my step past Dad and bound toward a larger loose pile of hay near the stack of bales.

"Oh, they're so cute and cuddly," I exclaimed as I bent over at the knees hovering a safe distance over three precious beagles. Making sure that mommy beagle was nowhere in sight, I reached out and stroked their little peach-fuzz heads. They were so cute! I simply had to make sure no harm came to them! I will help feed, and train, and bath, and protect...

Suddenly out of nowhere I felt a tug on my shoulder. Shrugging my shoulder away without turning around, I said, "I don't want to go yet. I want to spend some time with the puppies and make sure their mommy returns."

Without a word, the tug turned into an urgent yank. In half a breath I was twirled around and to my shock, was slung onto the hay. Falsely, I had assumed that as long as I kept my guard up and threatened to tell Kathy, I was safe from another attack. But the puppies had lowered my guard and now that Kathy was gone, Dad's demons ruled his loins. "Never again" had come calling....

I felt my backbone bruising as Dad immediately crushed his weight down on me. I was instantly forced to sink deep into the prickly hay. As we tussled, the hay dust flew and as it settled back down to earth, it began to suffocate me. I tried screaming and choked. In fear, I discovered that the more I fought, the more the dust was kicked up in a swirling tornado and the more I choked. I twisted my head left and right looking for any object I could get my hands on. I was frantic to find something, anything that I could wield in my hand that would strike a blow!

Through all of this Dad somehow managed to get his bibs down around his ankles. He was wearing no underwear, immediately telling me the whole puppy thing had been staged to lure me to the barn.

Then out of nowhere – mice!

Like evil friends of his, they came in a herd, as if called to surround my head and aid Dad in his despicable act. I couldn't see them, but I could hear them and feel them. They were squealing in my ear and pawing through my hair! Our fall in the hay must have crashed on their burrow. I choked a scream for Dad to get off before the mice bit me! A film of "panic sweat" beaded on my forehead matting the hay particles onto my face and neck as they flew in a swarm of dust.

"Please get off of me, Daddy! You're hurting me! Get off! I can't breathe!" I took my arms and gave one last push against his massive shoulders. "The mice are going to bite me! Please!" I felt one and then another burrowing with their tiny claws into my hair.

I was so panicked about the mice that the unveiling of my womanhood and penetration seemed secondary. And then as fast as the dust storm began it was over. Like before, I was distantly greeted by a threatening look as the thing over me gruffly panted, "Get dressed and get your ass back to the house."

Like a ghost he disappeared, leaving me crumpled and broken in the hay. I scrambled sorely to my feet and brushed my hair with both hands to make sure the mice were out.

Glancing around to ensure that Brock was nowhere near, I sat back down. Clutching my ripped shirt and crumpled pants, I cried with the puppies until supper. When I was all spent, I gathered my broken body and bruised spirit and slipped into the house to clean up.

Dad had ruled Kathy with twisted lies and now me with an iron fist. In the beginning, that iron fist was full of fears and threats and pain. But now, even though childhood beatings remained in the back of my head as I went through my early years, as I got older they began to fade. My courage was slowing developing from childhood defiance

158

to something new and bold, with only one ingredient missing. And I knew what that added ingredient was…confession. After the last rape, I was determined to tell Kathy and no fear of my childhood whippings was going to stop me.

Dad seemed to sense my every thought… and so the intimidation began. It was as if he knew that childhood beatings were not going to be good enough. To keep me in line and quiet about our dirty little secret, he coldly began beating me with fresh resolve. He would smack me across the face. Then he would grab and punch me, christening my arms with bruises and swear a stifled, "you better never tell or you'll be sorry."

In the meantime, as he knew his hold over me was slipping, he continued to try and woo Kathy back home with his showering of vain affection. When that didn't work, he sunk to a begging drunkard at her doorstep. And then, through all of this manipulation of me and failed wooing of Kathy, Dad had what he thought was a stroke of genius.

He invited Tom, whom I had broken up with without ever really being "his girl" out for a "family and old friend" weekend. He knew that it had been a long time since we had hung out with Tom. Regardless of how my personal relationship with Tom had ended, Dad knew both Kathy and I could not resist seeing him. He was the only outside friend of the family we had ever really gotten to know. And what girl doesn't always carry a torch for her first kiss?

Dad set the whole thing up and it was agreed we would meet Tom at the old abandoned excavation gravel pit we used to live next to, and Tom still does. It would be on Saturday night for a cookout. The week flew by as Kathy and I spent the time planning on what to cook, what to wear and what to say when we saw Tom again. Saturday arrived and so did Tom…at the gravel pit, and right on time.

When Dad broke out the Colt 45 malt liquor, everyone was shocked. All minors but him, Dad assured us that no one was around and it would be all right. We all took a can and sipped. The pungent taste bit my tongue and I really couldn't see what all the attraction to drinking was all about.

"Don't worry. You'll get used to the taste," Dad assured.

'Well you're certainly an expert,' I thought as I guzzled some more. By the time everyone was on their second beer, I was already feeling light

"Whoa kid, you better slow down on that stuff," Tom said with some concern. "You'll regret it later."

"I don't know what you're talking about. I can't stand the crappy taste, but I like the way it makes me feel; like I'm so carefree. I feel like, hmmm...for a change nothing can hurt me." I sat there and traded back and forth my staring out into the calm of the night for the licking flames of the campfire. The gravel pit looked like a home movie playing before me. It was a brief sanctuary in our vagabond life where we used to swim and fish and run to get away from Dad. I sighed, enjoying the cool night air and the warm memories and absently drinking my beer like water.

Somewhere after losing count of how many beers I had, I jumped up and began waltzing around the grounds. I held my arms out and pirouetted around in the gravel's dust. The wind kissed my cheeks warmly as I gently cocked my head back. I smiled as I caressed my empty beer can.

"Amy, you better cool it," Tom warned laughingly. "You're going to have the hangover of your life!"

I stopped my waltz and wondered out loud "what makes you such an expert?" It was then that I noticed all eyes on me and my flailing ballerina arms. I suddenly felt panic, as if silently I was the butt of their jokes and simply didn't notice until now. I backed away from the fire. The beer had made me free to embarrass myself, and they all looked at me like I was stupid. Without thinking, I found myself standing on the perimeter of the clearing ripping off my shoes. The tender skin between my toes was greeted with the warm feeling of oozy fresh tilled soil. I curled my toes squishing the dirt between them. Then with the tension of the moment, I felt the need to withdraw from my audience. In shame and embarrassment, I abruptly turned and bolted into the darkness through the brushy opening and into a nearby corn field.

Mildewed stalks lashed at my face as I stumbled forward into the abyss. My arms began itching from each lick of the stalks' dried leaves as I plowed onward. Behind me I heard voices calling. The voices made me charge even harder into the blackness. I'll teach them to snicker at me!

Tripping, I fell face first into the dirt. I lay there with my mind whispering that I really wasn't running from their ridicule of me, I was running from me. Instantly I was consumed with one thought, 'Truth. I must tell the truth.' My mind flashed back to Dad's cold uncaring eyes when he attacked me in the barn. The beer must have been working its black magic because I felt totally out of control. I began sobbing, my tears mixing the dirt on my face into a sea of black.

"Amy, where are you? Amy?" I heard Kathy's voice shout nearby. Jumping to my feet I ran, too embarrassed to let anyone see me so out of control drunk. My mind raced faster than my feet, and I stumbled again. I stayed face down for just an instant, but it was an instant too late.

Kathy pulled me up by my shoulders, and slung her arms around me. "Settle down, Amy. It'll be all right," she soothed as I went limp finding a safe haven in her tenderness.

In time, she was able to get me to my feet. Silently we stumbled back to the campsite together with the only conversation the whole way back being my crying like a river, and Kathy's quiet reassurances. At the pit, Kathy coaxed me to sit in the car for some privacy.

It was as if the dilapidated front seat afforded me just enough privacy for release. With Kathy still holding me, I let my emotions go. My crying turned uncontrollable again and Kathy took to rocking me like a baby. My hysteria was so much more than my embarrassment of drinking by now. It was my life; my damn sucky life – from the first physical beating to my last emotional rape. Now that it was just the two of us in the car, it was now or never. I had to make Kathy understand. I had to! Leaning over and placing my head in her lap, I looked up into her loving eyes and tried to get control.

"Oh Kathy, I love you. You're the only one that was always there no matter what. But I have something to tell you before you make another mistake and before I shut down on hopes of a normal life...

and accept a living hell. This whole evening was a setup by Dad. Don't you get it? Just to get close to you again. His plan was to get me drunk enough to put me out of commission for the night... I see that now. Or perhaps give me over to Tom to have his way, although I don't think Tom would do that. But Dad is conniving to get you! He wants to attack you again, and I can't let that happen!" My voice sounded hollow as if I was in one of my "out of body" experiences. "He hasn't given up on adding you back to his trophy shelf and you need to know...his sex drive hasn't stopped just because you left!"

My emotions were spilling so incoherently that Kathy looked at me skeptically, not sure what she had just heard.

"Kathy! Are you listening to me? You HAVE to listen to me!" I began crying all over again. I was having trouble forming my words due in part to my state of mind, and in part from the alcohol. My tongue seemed as huge as a wad of cotton and I struggled to gain control of my speech.

Kathy rubbed the dirt and tears from my face with the sleeve of her blouse as I continued to slobber. 'I must make her understand,' I thought. 'I must tell her the truth.'

Suddenly Tom stuck his head in the window, not understanding my behavior at all. Embarrassed for Tom to see me this way, I struggled to sit up and get out of the car while Kathy remained seated. Regaining some composure, I walked up to Tom and cupped his cheek. "You still care about us, don't you? That's so sweet."

Then turning my attention toward Dad, the composure I had gained turned concrete hard. "Kathy, I have something to tell you...but you must make 'him' go away first!" I pointed at Dad and then turned my back on him in a defiant revolt. Shocked by my boldness, Dad strangely complied by walking back a few steps. Tom followed Dad, and then together I could hear them whispering as they walked toward the pit, and away from the car. Dad was already trying to manipulate Tom. Damn him!

My shame hung thick in the air. I had hoped Dad was beginning to realize that he had finally lost us both but if he didn't, that's okay. He was about to find out. The moment of truth had finally come.

With one last deep sigh to regain my composure and a safe distance from Dad, I was overcome with a sudden calmness as I let it all out.

"Kathy, Dad raped me; more than once. He's never been the person he tried to make you think he was. He said I'd be sorry if I told you, but I can't keep his secret any longer. I'm sorry, Kathy, I'm so sorry!" Falling to my knees, I hid my face in her lap as she sat on the car seat with the door gaping open.

I knew she was stunned. I knew now that what I had sensed all along was true; that what she had been doing as her part in Dad's play was to protect me. The sum of our lives was nothing but cold calculated manipulation by our father. *Our father!* Without looking up, I could feel her anger begin to boil at Dad's betrayal to her, to me and to all of his family. And then as quickly as I could see it rise, it subsided. Instead of getting out of the car and confronting Dad, she turned her attention lovingly back to me.

"You have nothing to be ashamed of. You're a victim," and then almost reflectively, she said quietly, "just like me."

I gave her a bear hug around the waist; my face still guarded by her lap.

"Don't you worry," she continued. "No one is going to ever hurt you again."

The weight of the world seemed to rocket skyward and out of my life. I knew I had done the right thing in telling her. *Oh, why hadn't I told earlier?!* She not only was going to protect me, she had a suddenly new, revolutionary and clear direction on her life.

In an instant she lifted my head by the chin and said, "You're moving in with me, immediately."

Overhearing Kathy's edict, Dad turned on a dime and started moving in our direction shouting, "You can't do that. She's not of age yet." His finger pointed right at me as he continued his stalk in a feeble effort to regain control of the situation. It was as if when he couldn't have Kathy, he wouldn't be cheated out of making me his private whore – even if I wasn't his first choice, and even if it had to be forced.

My newfound calmness bolstered by Kathy's support turned

into courage. My soul complete with confession, my courage rose to respond. Jumping out of the car, I pointed a finger back at him and shouted, "You better back off! The only reason I didn't tell until now is because I was afraid – afraid you would beat me"…and then after a long pause, "and afraid that Kathy would hate me. Well guess what? Kathy doesn't hate me, and I don't fear you anymore! You make one false move toward either of us, and I'm going to the authorities!"

Dad stopped cold, involuntarily letting his half full beer slide out of his hand. It splattered all over the ground running away from him, beyond his control - just like his plans for us. Tom stood in the background, shocked by the soap opera motif the evening had taken.

My horrible hidden truth for the last four years had finally lost, and my courage had won.

I was seventeen.

Chapter 17

one photo equals
two memories...

*The final day in Kitakyūshū City was as full as the first one; after all it only
took 21 hours to get here! It began much as it had begun over a week ago – an
endlessly full day of renewed greeting and experiences lasting long into the night;
squeezing every encounter for every drop of love we could find.*

*That final morning was a bustle of activities in the small apartment. With
sharing of one toilet and one bath, I could tell I had become an added strain
to daily living, and deep down inside I wondered if my departure was not
only imminent, but somewhat welcome. The breaking of routine is sometimes a
refreshing change, but let's face it...I shattered the family routine the moment
I passed through the Suzaki front door.*

*The morning was left free to get their disorganized life back somewhat in
order; bathing, picking up the apartment and some quick marketing; as well
as that one last round of picture sharing.*

*Lunch was already planned. It was going to be a final get together with
only Hidetoshi's immediate family; his mother Aunt Iseko and of course my
adopted sister, Maki. Sadly, the afternoon was planned for a visit to the
cemetery to pay my respects to the family members I will never get to meet.
Then the evening will be left to a private and quiet supper and packing before*

getting up at 3 AM to catch my 6 AM flight to Tokyo, where I hoped Rob was waiting anxiously to greet me.

Once the table was cleared and the breakfast dishes done, Hidetoshi, Miyuki and I cozied up to the table and dumped out our final stash of pictures. I had brought tons of pictures, but had only shared a few loose ones at Aunt Yoko's earlier in the week and a couple with Miyuki. I wanted my visit to end with lasting memories of sharing our lives beyond this trip, and I still had sooo much to share. It seemed odd as I sat there and gazed at the mountainous pile of pictures; the mosaic of our lives. So much has happened in our lifetime of separation, and now it was all reduced to covering this one small tabletop.

Over the week I had gradually been weaning myself from cohee. Instead I had been adopting hot green tea and now poured myself another cup. I took a long satisfying sip and surveyed the pictorial terrain before me. Hidetoshi, Miyuki, Maki and I all paused to look up at each other. Then instantly as if sucked into the eye of a hurricane, the hand grabbing started and the pictures flew. At once everyone was grabbing one and studying photographs with the utmost intent, throwing it down and grabbing another, periodically stopping to point at someone in their "papered frame" and sign language a question or two. Like sponges, we absorbed each other's lives before the witching hour struck and this Cinderella had to go home.

I had brought pictures of my family, Rob's family, pets, houses I'd lived in, scenery of the United States and a wealth of Mom's pictures from her only visit to Japan just before she died. In the pile on the table sat all of my offerings, save Mom's pictures. I held them back on purpose; until the end of the "picture show shuffle" this morning. When it seemed like everyone had filled their curiosity, only then did I pull them out. I did this for two reasons – I had specific questions about some of them, and I wanted to show proper respect. Mom's pictures were a guarded heirloom to me. Although Mom had passed away, I wanted them to know that my Japanese family has always been important to me, as witnessed by my keeping Mom's pictures of Japan for these many years after her death.

Most were of Mom's sisters; my aunts in Nagasaki that Soshi had so prudently warned me not to make contact. She had stated that at least one was "crazy," and not to bother visiting. From what I could tell Nagasaki was beautiful and our not going there was a disappointment to Rob. Rob loves history and wanted to pay his respects to "Ground Zero" from that fateful day of August 9, 1945, where the second atomic bomb that ended World War II was dropped.

But the photos that intrigued me the most were of a traditional Japanese wedding which turned out to be Hirokazu's (Aunt Yoko's son and Hidetoshi's cousin). The pictures were beautiful as the bride and groom were dressed in traditional Japanese garb for the happy occasion. To add to the array of colors and patterns of the costumes were two distinct and separate costumes; one for the wedding and then a arduous change into a whole new costume for the reception. Twice the Technicolor, and twice the viewing pleasure.

Embedded in the stack of wedding pictures was one that had captured a cocky yet handsome male Japanese teenager. He was slim and had slicked back "Fonzie" hair. He was garbed in a black Miami-vice type outfit, right down to the Don Johnson tee-shirt underneath his smokin' black jacket. I pulled out the picture and admired it at arm's length.

"Who is this?" I asked innocently enough since I had often admired this picture for the last fifteen years. Then truthfully continuing, I mused, "He is very handsome."

Miyuki broke into an unrestrained giggle. She could tell I had absolutely no idea what I had just asked, or said. "That Hidetoshi," she responded with another slightly more reserved chuckle. I looked at Hidetoshi who smiled sheepishly. He wasn't saying a word. I couldn't tell who was more embarrassed, him or me.

His picture took me back in time to where I had broken away from Dad's clutches. I had established my freedom. And over time, I had made two choices for a beau. One was right and one was terribly wrong...

———————————————

Here I am – alone again.

I am lying on the couch and mindlessly watching the local news. The *news* for gosh sakes! I'm 22 years old, and I'm watching the news for entertainment!

That's what I get for praying for a husband.

You heard me. I prayed for a husband and I got, well...the news!

I've had my fill of the single life, the night life and now the lonely life, so I've decided to marry. Only one problem...you can't marry the news!

Actually my mind is not on the news, but on Rob. Rob is my new boss at work. I'm not sure if he's the one I prayed for, but the girls at work aren't laughing at me so much anymore; not like they did the day I announced I had prayed for a husband. I'm not sure "laughing" at me is the right word, but it's the kindest one I can print. No one believed me then, and only some now...yet; I'm not convinced it's Rob. Still, he DID show up after I prayed.

'What are you waiting for girl,' I chastised myself standing up from the couch. What was on my mind was not a relationship, but a Good Samaritan act of kindness. Rob was home sick, and he has two small children to care for...and well, he's home sick. He just moved to Indiana from another state and has no supporting family. Since he has no one, he's GOT to have help with those two little boys...I rationalized!

'Why couldn't that help be me? Why?' the optimistic voice in the back of my head suddenly spoke out loud. 'Because he's getting a divorce,' the pessimistic voice said in answer to the question.

I sat back down on the couch and toyed with my hair. I pondered back in time to when I met another man at work. I thought he was IT too. Then again, I've thought a lot of things since leaving home five years ago. But I had to be sure. This time I HAD to be sure...because I was sooo sure with John....

• • • •

My senior year. Dad demanded I quit school to support myself now that I was living with Kathy. He refused to give me any money for school or money for any means of support. He was repeating a theme I had witnessed many times before – he was going to be cruel to the last.

If I moved back however..."it would be a different story," he had ruefully said. Yea, right! Like hell I was moving back! Who needed him?! Kathy told me I was graduating no matter what and with her help (not Dad's) that dream is coming true.

Socially…that word sticks a little in my throat…. socially, I had no idea what I had been missing. My job helps that. Since my leaving home and Dad's absent generosity, I took a job in a local factory which was willing to give a second shift job to a seventeen year old. I now meet and interact with people outside the family for the first time in my life in a social setting. At least I called work a social setting since that's where I met John.

I can't adequately describe the feeling the first time John came to the factory in his full dress Marine uniform; all full of muscles and loaded with charm. He walked tall, straight and held his head high. I immediately fell in love with the uniform, just as Mom had mistakenly done with Dad so many years ago. That alone should have warned me, but his baby blue Paul Newman eyes spoke differently! They were piercing and as shiny as the brass buttons on his uniform. His hair was coal black, and he drove a tiny convertible MG; an imagined "perfect fit" for my 5'1" 95 lb. frame. I boldly asked around about him and to my surprise discovered that both his Mom and Dad worked at the same electronics factory as me.

He was just out of the military after serving his second tour in Vietnam. I shamelessly pumped his mother during work for details but all I could get from her was that he was often out late, and she didn't know anything about his social life. That should have signaled warning bell number two, but it didn't.

John landed a job at the same factory and weeks passed with no initiative on his part toward me. Then one day after hope was all but gone, John walked past my work table unexpectedly. In a *time stood still* moment our eyes caught, each staring slyly at the other. With a shy smile, I diverted my eyes downward at the sterile widgets before me. As he passed on by, I looked up to follow his walk only to be greeted by his full front facing me as he walked away backward! We both broke into a laugh, and the flirting at work began.

But then much to my dismay, nothing more…

I waited impatiently for John to make a move but he either lacked the courage, the confidence, or the good common sense to ask me out. Either way, I was determined to get around his problem…and made it my problem. The Sweetheart Dance where the girl asks the guy out was fast approaching at school. I had never been – thank you Dad, but I was not going to miss it my senior year. All I needed was a date.

I fretted over how to approach my quarry and then hook him. I replayed a meeting and then asking in every location, and at every time I could imagine. I wanted to be prepared in case the right moment approached unexpectedly. I was a nervous wreck waiting for the right moment. I had never asked anyone out before. Not even Tom.

Finally, when no right moment presented itself and the dance coming ever closer, I settled on the direct approach. I picked up the phone and called. It was simple enough, but it sure didn't seem so at the time. However, John was calm and casual and immediately put me at ease. He said he had friends going with some of the other girls in my class and that he would love to go. He was almost five years older and here he was…going to the Sweetheart Dance with me! I wondered why only briefly…and then I decided I didn't care.

That should have been warning number three.

I had no money for a dress so I swallowed my pride and borrowed one – red with black dots. The dots complimented my oriental hair and the red was only rivaled by my flushed tone of excitement. It was a perfect fit for the perfect occasion. John's "Wow!" was my confirmation when I climbed into the car.

My premiere entrance was like a princess at a ball. I was immediately elevated in social status in the eyes of my peers. Jealous girls whispered in huddled masses, and envious guys catcalled from darkened corners of the gymnasium. I smiled, imagining happily that 1/ the guys were sorry they didn't treat me with more respect at school, and 2/ the girls wished they could have someone "half as hunky" as my escort. John's friends mentioned earlier were there and not surprisingly, with the coolest girls in school! They were witty popular, not cheerleader-jock popular, instantly elevating my social standing further.

I was hanging out with the queen bees and I felt like the belle of the ball. Life had definitely been too serious until now. I danced my heart away until the last balloon dropped. I floated home imagining how John rescuing me was going to be an endless parade of excitement, changing my life forever.

Well, it definitely changed…

Having a boyfriend made me feel like a princess all right, but only for a little while. With John as a returning veteran, he walked in the stratosphere of hero status. We were invited to all the parties and social gatherings, or rather more to the point, he was invited. But he always took me, so I was never at a loss for attention – the one thing I was robbed of all my life. The parties, though, involved alcohol and very soon, the alcohol became the party. Since it was a favorite past time of John's, I overlooked it at first. After all he had served his country and he deserved to blow off a little steam. At least, that's what he told me. I saw how hard he worked so affording him the luxury of partying every weekend was okay, I reasoned.

Warning number four.

Weekend drinking became weekdays, and soon his reputation became notorious in our small little community. It seems the more he drank the more intense his behavior – and the more his war story flashbacks became a living reality. And the more the flashbacks the more the drinking – until they fed on each other.

I became secondary, and was no longer *always* invited to be by his side.

Alcohol had become more important in John's life than me or anything else. I couldn't make him see that it was a whirlpool of self-destruction. After I graduated, I began using work and college classes to my advantage keeping me busy to fill the void of John when he was "missing in action." Over time our relationship became strained. Rumors began to fly that John was having a relationship with Sherry, one of my classmates. I confronted him and got the *I'm consoling her because of a boyfriend problem* answer.

Warning number five.

John began disappearing evenings, and on weekends he was gone all night more often than not. I finally listened to my friend and co-worker Lane, who told me that John was having an affair on the side. Well, sort of… since we weren't actually married. In one regard, he could date whomever he wanted, technically…but a very, very small "technically" from my perspective. He had given me a promise ring so we had an understanding, and I felt like he was playing me for a fool.

The night of my eighteenth birthday party I decided I couldn't wait for proof of his affair. Halfway into the party, I dragged him outside and wailed into him verbally and physically, pounding into his rock chest as I confronted him about Sherry. But instead of the denial I was praying for, he confessed.

I immediately broke off our relationship, and John not so surprisingly was stunned. Convinced he was invincible, he refused to let me go denying the harm he had caused me. But I could not live with the humiliation of betrayal.

Yet like the phoenix, problems rose out of the ashes of parting. Avoiding him became a problem since we both worked at the same place. It didn't help that I continued to wear his promise ring. I don't know why – stupidity I guess, but I was reluctant to remove what I had fought so hard to gain. Unfortunately he picked up on my still wearing the ring as a sign to his self-feeding ego.

Translation – *I must still want him*. How arrogant and typically male. He would make a nuisance of himself by hanging by my car after work and telling me that "I knew I wanted him back." I decided that if he knew so much about what I wanted he should have been smart enough not to sleep with Sherry.

When he didn't get through to me or better said, I didn't break under his constant badgering, he decided to take more drastic measures. One night he showed up at my place – alone, drunk and high. I hadn't seen the signs early - the red eyes and bloody noses and erratic mood swings, but I saw them now that I was away from him.

It was a cold wintry night when he showed up at my doorstep holding a huge plain brown wrapped rectangular object banging loudly on the door. I had answered the door in my housecoat with the wind cutting to my bones. Concerned the other apartment tenants would call the cops for disturbing the peace, I bargained for him to lower his voice and I would let him in.

Once inside, he instantly tore off the brown wrappings of his oversized package revealing a peace offering of sorts. It was a painting of a boat being tossed at sea. Lacking in poetic skills, John attempted vainly to relate the tiny tossed ship to us. He wanted me to hang it over the couch as a symbol of our turbulent relationship.

As I gazed for a moment at the violent frothy waves and half tipped boat, I realized that it was not a peace offering. Contrary to his hopes, the painting was a symbol of just the opposite. It was not an apology or a symbol of undying love; instead it jumped off the canvas at me as an ominous warning that more storms lie ahead. I was amazed at his bearing of gifts in a blatant attempt to buy me, and at his very poor offering to correct all that was wrong with our relationship. In fact, there was no offering; verbally, or in the form of an apology or even a commitment to reform!

As I looked down at the promise ring still transfixed on my finger, I had to admit that some part of me still loved him. But I was determined not to cave to emotion and let my head rule my heart for a change. Instead of accepting his gift, I refused it. Then before I could change my mind, I followed up with a curt request for him to leave. I was amazed at the steely resolve in my voice.

I was not amazed at his strength.

Anger filled the air instantaneously as John ballooned in a rage. Then without warning, he swooped me into his Popeye arms, slinging me over his shoulder like a sack of potatoes.

"Put me down!" I screamed all the way down to my toes. My only hope of not being kidnapped was if he didn't heed maybe the neighbors would hear me. I screamed as we unceremoniously left the apartment and continued to scream all the way to his new 4-wheeler truck, but no one heard and not a soul came to my rescue.

As we approached his truck, I noticed that he had left the engine running while inside pleading his case. It was primed for a quick exit, as if he knew what my answer was going to be. Dumping me in the truck from the driver's side, he jumped in behind me and slammed on the accelerator, closing the door as we skid down the icy street. Fearing he was under the influence of multiple substances, I remained quiet. Only periodically did I ask where we were going and always in a subdued voice. All the while I was scared white as the snow of his actions, his speeding and his erratic driving. I didn't want "John the Soldier" to emerge while in a moving vehicle, so I tried to remain calm, as if I were in control of the situation instead of him. But each attempt at polite conversation and innocent inquiry as to destination was met with silence. Then just as I had given up on any coherent response from my kidnapper, I had my answer in 3D.

John pulled into a motel flashing NO VACANCY, and bypassing the motel office, he pulled straight into a room parking space. He *had* planned this in advance after all!

I said as forcibly as possible, "John, I want to go home, now. It's getting late, and I have school tomorrow." But his threatening eyes shot back at me not to challenge him, and for the first time in our relationship, I saw Dad II in him.

Warning number six.

I had no shoes and wondered briefly how deep the snow was going to be over my bare feet, but it was an irrelevant thought. No sooner had we slid to a halt than John grabbed me a little too hard and carried his conquest inside. Locking and bolting the door behind me, he commanded I sit on the bed. Instead I broke for the door, only to have him pull me back and sling me on the bed with him. As he made a move to forcibly pin me down, I grabbed the lamp beside the bed and in fit of panic, cold-cocked him on the side of his head. He fell back, and to add insult to injury, hit his head on the headboard. Dazed or dead, I wasn't sure which; he slumped in a pile on the bed.

I panicked as I watched the blood trickle from his head. What if I had killed him? I would rather die than take another person's life; even John's. I was too shook up to check his pulse – my hands were shaking so, but swore I thought I saw his chest move. Getting control of myself, I made my way to the bathroom and ran a cold towel to place on his bleeding temple.

In retrospect I should have run, but where to? I had no clothes, I had no shoes and I had no money. In the end, it didn't matter. I made the mistake of staying so why should I have been surprised when in the middle of offering aid; John came to and like an animal in heat, forced himself on me.

I lay there like a dead person with those wild bloodshot eyes bulging down on me. I couldn't believe this was happening again, only with the man I thought I had loved. Realizing this was a recurring event, I began to cry as I wondered what was wrong with me. It must be my fault this always happens to me! Then just as quickly as it had begun, John's wild thrashing ceased before he had gone too far. Evidently my frigid behavior had turned him off. Rolling off of me in contempt he got dressed and told me to do the same.

He drove me home without a word and deposited me like a discarded soda pop bottle at my doorstep. I watched him drive away peeking between the window curtains and thought, 'well, that is the end of it. John will never speak to me again.'

But John wasn't silent for long.

As if nothing happened that night, he upped his badgering at work from periodic to incessant; telling me he would change and that he would go to counseling, but *only* if I would go with him. It was as if John believed I was the problem more so than his own demons. I realized then that we probably had the wrong kind of love. In my eyes now, he was a human being that desperately needed help from many demons; most all likely stemming from the Vietnam War. In the end, I reasoned that I would do no less for a pet, so I agreed to go to counseling with him – but only as a support.

I researched and found the local Alcoholics Anonymous chapter. I set the time and date and John was to meet me there. It was appropriately enough, a church. I recall being extremely nervous as I paced up and down the street checking my watch every few seconds until after the meeting had started and still, no John.

Warning number seven.

I was quaking as I finally entered the meeting alone, but I was determined to get John help; even if I had to teach him myself. When I entered, I stood at the back to be as inconspicuous as possible and just listen. But at my entrance, the speaker stopped the meeting and motioned me to the front row where the only empty chairs were. How silly of me to think that I could go to a public meeting on alcoholism and remain hidden. So much for being inconspicuous.

The guest speaker was a businessman who spoke eloquently of losing everything he had to alcohol. His employer, his wife and his kids all abandoned him before he found the courage to become sober. I was caught up in the moment, moved by this grown man's tears as he told his story when to my shock, he looked straight at me.

"I bet you're here because of a boyfriend. Am I right? Hold up your left hand. I'll bet you have a ring on, don't you?" I slowly twirled the Sweetheart Dance promise ring as my hands burrowed deep into my lap in shame. The speaker continued, "I'll bet your father was an alcoholic and there has been some abuse in your family, hasn't there? You've come to this meeting to make a decision. You think you're in love, and you hope your love will change him. Well I'm here to tell you it will not. It didn't change me, and it won't change him."

Was I that transparent?

Of course he was right on all counts. I wasn't going to be able to leave this meeting and help John one iota! I left the meeting more resolved than ever to break it off. All I needed was an excuse.

All I needed was an excuse?

Who was I kidding? That thought was warning number eight. But I still hadn't reached my quota. It took one more....

We had planned dinner at John's folks after the A.A. meeting to give a show of solidarity in working on John's addictions. But when he showed up at my place to pick me up, he showed up stinking drunk. I almost threw him out after standing me up at the church, but this time something the speaker had said hit home. It was about well intended help that actually served as part of the disability. *My* well intended help in covering up or helping hide John's addictions. But this time it was going to be different. This time he was going to show up as the drunk he had become. I had decided to let John deal with his demons alone for the first time. And it will be in front of his parents, who I suspect were in denial themselves.

As we left, I had a sprig of hope in my heart that after tonight I would be able to get away from John for good. I also left with equal fear in my heart for my safety, considering the potentially dangerous and irrational state he was in. I watched the wintry landscape speed by, lost in my own self-serving thoughts. Then I made a near fatal mistake. I commented on how foul-smelling John was while driving.

It was as if Jekyll turned to Hyde. He slammed on the brakes as he jerked the wheel, turning the truck in a half spin before skidding to a halt. "Get out!" he hissed. His eyes were glassy and somewhere else.

We were in the middle of nowhere, so I frantically asked, "John, what do you mean 'get out'?"

I didn't have to wait for an explanation as he reached over and pushed me out of the passenger truck door and onto the damp gravel ground three feet below. Gasping for breath and unable to move for a second, I lay there and watched as John suddenly jumped out of the truck and to my amazement, started running bent over at the waist. He was bobbing and weaving as he made his way down a watery trench and headed for a thicket of hedges and trees behind me.

It was apparent to me that he was reliving Vietnam and his body motions revealed he believed he was actually dodging bullets! He hid behind a tree less than twenty feet from me popping his head up every few moments as if keeping watch of the enemy. I had heard of post traumatic stress disorder and now witnessed it in his screaming eyes. Being of oriental descent, I had no doubt by the disturbing way he looked at me he was making me out to be the Viet Cong. Immediately fearing for my life, I scrambled to my feet and ran for all I was worth in the opposite direction of John, but he was too fast.

Like a cat, he broke from his lair and pounced on me in seconds. He grabbed my jacket and spun me around, and for the first time ever, I could see Black Death in his eyes.

Beckoning him to reality, I shouted at him, "John, it's me, Amy!" I tugged against his clutches in an attempt to break free from him. Disoriented and off balance, John tumbled backward into a soggy ditch. Swimming with fear and sure I couldn't outrun him; I rounded the truck to hopefully a safe haven on the opposite side.

He was surprisingly swift as he circled around quicker than I could move, and then without warning I heard the whistle of death sing past my ear. The jagged edge of a hunting knife flew by me like an arrow, lodging itself into the thick tread of the truck tire just inches from my trembling body. Now it was my turn to have flashbacks as I saw Dad laughing at my fear of being target practice more than once, so many years ago. I froze immediately, confident if I moved I would die. I was still standing there gasping in fear with images of my throat being slit filling my head as John approached. I held my breath as he deliberately stalked me and then approached from behind. As he got close, I closed my eyes and waited for the end. But instead of killing me, he grabbed me by the hair, pulling me down on the ground like a Raggedy Ann doll, dragging me back around his truck.

Mud and gravel and dead grass plumed into the air as I fought to stand, but he was pulling me faster than my feet would work. The pain in my head was so intense I had to reach up and grab his massive forearm to relieve some of the pressure on my scalp. I screamed into the dead of the night as the sharp rocks in the gravel raked my back and legs. Every few yards I relinquished my grip and frantically grabbed at the air trying to right myself, but the searing pain from ripping hair in my head made me stop in a matter of seconds. I succumbed to going back to holding onto his Herculean forearms so I could retain consciousness as I was drug along like a bagged deer.

When we arrived at the passenger side of the truck, he picked up my limp body and threw me effortlessly inside, telling me to lie still and *not* get up. He spoke condescendingly, as if addressing a newly captured P.O.W. I tried to obey, but there was some loose gravel in the truck that was stabbing my knees as I laid front face down, afraid to look at John. I shifted my weight to better position my body from the sharp rocks and John immediately attacked, taking my movement as disobedience. His fists began to fly in a fit of rage, some landing and some not. I was somewhat protected by my heavy coat but every third blow or so landed full force, bruising my face and arms and knocking the air out of me. After a while I pretended to play dead, or as if I had blacked out. Only time and John's exhaustion made the beating end long after I stopped being able to feel it.

Apparently I was dazed to John's satisfaction, as he jumped in behind the wheel gunning the truck down the road, all the while spinning gravel. I groggily made my plans to take flight again as soon as we stopped. Surely if my legs still worked, I could now outrun an *exhausted* drunk.

Time slowed as the cold night air numbed my pain and cooled my bruises. I lost count of time and was only half aware of the slowing sensation of the truck after who knows how long. I slowly raised myself to all fours to peek out and try to see where we were stopping, but in the darkness of night and still dazed from the beating, I couldn't make anything out. I took a deep breath and sensing I had one last chance at escape, I sprang cat-like from the truck without looking back.

I landed with a thud, did one barrel roll and staggered to my feet. Gripped with fear, it didn't take long to get over the initial shock of leaping from the truck, and hit full stride before I even stood fully erect.

"I told you to stay in the truck!" John violently screamed in the background. As if hitting the ground cleared my vision, I saw immediately that we were at his parents' house and wasted no time making a beeline for their front door. Slamming on the brakes John jumped out and broke into full combat pursuit. He caught me on the porch, pounding and screaming for my life at his parents' door. I increased my screaming and started kicking to keep John away as he twirled me around to face him. Spittle ran down his chin with a rotting odor rising from deep inside his soured stomach. To silence me, he grabbed me by the neck and began squeezing with all his might, making my eyes feel as if they were grapes being squeezed out of their skin. He held me at arm's length and then tightened his death grip as he stretched up to raise me to my tippy-toes. My throat felt like a twig ready to snap and blackness closed in from lack of air when John's parents finally opened the front door to see what all the ruckus was about. Instantly frantic, they pried John's hands free and with some parental restraint, were able to convince him to leave me alone. My face was on fire from the rush of blood and my eyes felt like they needed help getting back in their sockets. I was in some of the worst pain in my life, and I had felt a lot of pain....

I was beaten and shaken as John's father disappeared into the house with John finally broken and in tow. Relieved to be free of him, I fell into a pile on the porch still gulping air when out of the corner of my eye I noticed John's mother standing over me.

"What did you do to my son to make him act like that?!" She accused hatefully. I couldn't believe my ears. It was as if she felt every bruise from John's fists and fingerprints on my neck were my fault. I slowly raised my head to meet my accuser but before I could answer, she turned in a huff, and walking into the house she slammed the door in my face.

John's little brother came out and volunteered to drive me home. He apologized for the actions of his older brother and begged me not to press charges as he walked me to my doorstep. He, maybe better than I, understood the pain the war had inflicted on John; indeed on a generation of young men. It was not his fault, but the aftermath was left unceremoniously for him to deal with. Beaten and wounded in spirit, I agreed not to press charges, but only as long as he gave John the message to leave me alone forever. My compassion had long since been wasted on my broken family life, and I could not afford another lifetime of attack on my spirit for fear of it being broken.

I had survived the excuse I was looking for... I had exhausted warning number nine – and like exhausting the nine lives of a cat, this last warning killed our relationship forever.

• • • •

I am living now with Mom.

She was very concerned for me, both mentally and physically. She feared every day I went to school or work that either John or Dad was going to lose it and come after me. She also has been very patient with me. Once I was free from Dad by moving in with Kathy and later moving out on my own and finding John, I thought I could tackle the world. Then after really, really breaking up with John, I thought I could handle anything in life.

But ironically, I had a fear of being alone that I didn't know I had. It was hard to admit that I felt I needed the protection of someone else, but I did. It was like admitting I couldn't survive on my own, and I found it degrading. But after John's ultimately two *harmless* attempts on my life, every noise startled me. The darkness of night was frightening and daily nightmares, terrifying. Those first few months after John (even though I was living with Mom), I was the loneliest and most terrified person on earth.

But with the passage of time and my submission to personal counseling, somewhere along the way I began to heal. I also began to feel that God had a plan for me. I had survived two violent, life threatening relationships. I could let it consume me, or I could turn my bad experiences to my advantage. But how?

I found solace and comfort from my best friend Clara. She had survived a teenage pregnancy and was making her way in the world as a single Mom. Her friendship and counsel were more than endearing. They were life saving. I always knew that I could go over to Clara's and blow off some steam or share my innermost feelings and fears. Over time she also helped me go out in public socially again. With her by my side, I began to lose my fear of abuse…and of men in general.

Two other things happened that helped guide my path back to one of hope instead of despair. I am now enrolled in college, and I prayed for a husband instead of a boyfriend – more than once. I needed to educate myself, and I needed to stop the "I gotta have a relationship" merry-go-round. Both are lifestyle changes and both are equally hard. School is a challenge, and giving up meaningless relationships is like giving up an addiction of sorts.

I have made progress in college but ever so slowly. With so much of junior high and high school a blank sheet of paper, I have to work twice as hard as the average student.

Thanks to Clara and the mystic healing power of time "Big, bad John" has melted from my life, breaking his addiction over me. It hasn't been easy, but as I came to realize that I could survive and be content alone the rest of my life, the bonds of addiction disappeared. When I knew I didn't need a man, I knew I was ready for one -

And then along came Rob…

Funny how Hidetoshi's teenage picture reminded me of my failed teenage relationship with John, and his strong presence beside me at the table now reminds me so much of Bob, the "love of my life..."

Chapter 18

do you believe in miracles...?

After lunch no one was ready to go to the cemetery…not just yet. Somehow we seemed to sense that this was the beginning of the end, and no one wanted it to end. Stalling for time, we decided instead to talk about what the week had meant to each of us.

The "talking" part worked for all of two seconds as we struggled to find the right words and still keep emotional control. Sensing the importance and the need to express ourselves, I suggested we write a letter to each other. Everyone thought that was a wonderful idea! After we were done, Maki would then transcribe them into our native languages.

The Suzakis expressed –

"You are a dream come true, so brave to make the journey. You are a free spirit that has brought new family to our old one. You show children that the world is nothing to fear. We must keep strength in family. You must come back and visit, and bring your family. We love you, Amy."

I hugged Hidetoshi for his kindness in inviting Rob and me into his home. I will never forget that he didn't have to; he could have insisted we stay at a hotel. Maybe he sensed the importance of our meeting as much as I did.

I needed to write two letters of thank you. I wanted to write one for the

Suzakis; Hidetoshi, Miyuki and Aunt Iseko - and then I wanted to write a separate letter for Maki. I wrote Maki's first. It was not difficult; all I had to do was look at her infectious smile, and I was moved to words.

"Dear sweet Maki, precious few are the moments we have been able to share. However, we are now of the same spirit; bonded together with the compassion of the tears we've shared. I promise I shall never forget you and take comfort in the assurance of our meeting again. Continue to grow in your knowledge, my wise friend. Consider seriously becoming a translator. You have served me well in language and in our newfound love. Amy."

I truly wished silently that she would visit me in America. We have so much in common, and I have so much more Christian love to share.

I looked around the apartment for something I could write about that would represent my feelings for the Suzaki family; something that could encompass the many overwhelming emotions that had been stirred by my visit. My eyes settled on Ai and the sweatshirt she had donned to brave the chill in the air on our visit to the cemetery this afternoon. It was pink in body with sleeves of blue and on the back it said, "Do you believe in miracles?" In English, no less! What are the odds? I truly felt like my trip across the vast blue ocean had been a miracle, and I needed to say it.

"My Hidetoshi, dear Miyuki and family, do you believe in miracles? Miracles surely happen. In the coming together as a family, this magic has occurred. As our love grows, we shall grow new wings just as the plant sprouts fresh green leaves. But we cannot fly with our newborn wings, without the continued growth of our love of each other. Your love will carry me home and back again someday. I promise. Love, Amy."

The analogy of the miracle is especially important to me. After two failed relationships as a daughter and a girlfriend, I needed a miracle. I've just never been able to decide which miracle was more important in my life.

Was it God bringing Rob to me, or Rob himself...?

I am a talker.

There, I've said it. I wanted two things in life after freedom from Dad and now John. A ten-speed bike and straight teeth. The bike because I never had one; the teeth partly for health, part vanity and partly because as I've said; *I'm a talker*. As I got older my teeth were so crooked I didn't want to smile a lot and besides, they had begun to inflict pain. Not good for conversation.

And one other minor detail - this time, I wanted a dentist to do it. You see the first time, my Dad did the dental work.

I recall in horror just starting junior high when vanity got a "push up" by my hormones on the list of adolescent needs. Or in my case it wasn't really vanity, I just wanted to look normal which I didn't; not by a long shot. All my teeth were crooked which was bad enough, but I had one tooth that was hideous. Mom said it must have been damaged when I fell down the stairs as a toddler, but I always thought it was an extra tooth that didn't belong. When it came in, it was shaped like a crooked stake, the kind you drove through a vampire's heart in the movies, only this was no movie. It was my life, and it was very real. To top it all off, the tooth was located just behind my front teeth. By the time I was twelve years old, it protruded *lower* than my front teeth making me look like a freak of nature. I was very self-conscious about it and tried everything I could to hide it in conversation. It also was becoming a physical pain, stabbing my tongue whenever I talked or ate.

I begged my Dad to take me to the dentist but he refused; money, or lack thereof. He didn't want to spend any money on me, so there was no way he was paying for braces to straighten out the rest of my worthless mouth – a certainty if I went to the dentist. He said he didn't need that kind of pressure from quacks. He kept his cigarettes and alcohol, but I had to lose my smile.

It got to the point where I couldn't bare to live with a witch's mouth anymore. To save the pain and humiliation, I quit the smiling and talked little; not an easy task since as I've explained, I'm a talker. And then it hit me; the perfect solution. I would challenge Dad to pull my tooth. Surely he would chicken out and take me to the dentist then...

Wrong.

He thought it was a fine idea. In fact, he loved it!

With no dentist in my future, I became resolved to let Dad go through with it. This tooth was coming out; I didn't care how much I bled. Without any planning and with no chance to back out, Dad immediately positioned me in a living room chair facing away from the dinner table so I had something to lean my head back against. He instructed me to sit tight as he went to get the pliers out of his tool box. While he was gone to the garage Kathy and Brock ran up to me and told me I was nuts! They tried their level best to talk some sense into me before Dad returned, but I refused to budge. Either Dad or me or the tooth was going to win; and I was *determined* it would be me.

Dad returned triumphantly wielding the pliers like a sword in the air. He was actually smiling as he tilted my head back onto the table and braced himself to do battle. Without even sterilizing the dirt stained pliers, Dad reached inside my mouth and grabbing a hold of the tooth, yanked with all his might. I could feel my neck muscles stretching as tears welled in my eyes. My hands in a death grip, dug into the arms of the chair. I groaned in pain, only to be matched by Dad's straining grunts and renewed pulling. I was shaken by a crunching sound as the pliers broke free and sent Dad reeling backward. The pain was like torture, and my neck felt like it was going to snap at any moment.

Dad paused to catch his breath as he tossed only a partial of the tooth onto the table, rattling in defeat. I leaned forward gagging on blood and spit into a dishtowel that Kathy sympathetically handed me. She then stood back beside Brock to watch from a distance, their mouths gaping open as if they were feeling my pain as well. I wiped the sweat off my brow and grabbing onto the arms of the chair, I braced for more torture. 'Dad, me or the tooth – and I'm going to win,' I repeated to myself.

Without regard for my well-being, Dad looked more determined than ever. He slowly wiped off the pliers, and then spreading my mouth wider, he dug in for round two. Again he pulled with all his might. I could feel the blood running out of my mouth and down my left cheek. My mind was shutting down from the pain when I felt Dad let go momentarily, and then gouge the pliers deeper into my gum in one last thrust. I thought I was going to pass out as my head echoed with the grinding of metal and the crunching enamel. I wasn't sure the tooth had broken free until I saw Dad sprawling back several steps. Balancing himself, he raised his arm in the air and proudly displayed the two pronged root in victory. I looked at the tooth through my bawling eyes, my body riveted in intense pain. The embarrassment it had caused me was long forgotten as Kathy handed me another dish rag; this one full of ice to put in the hole in my mouth where the tooth had been.

That pain has stayed fresh in my memory all these years as my crooked teeth continually caused discomfort. And that is why I so desperately wanted braces once I could pay for them as an adult; due both to my crooked teeth's discomfort and that little bit of junior high vanity creeping back into my soul again.

My braces came with only one slight complication. After many consultations and twice as many x-rays, it was decided that I would have to have both jaws broken and reset to correct my greatly exaggerated overbite.

Did I tell you I was a talker? Well it seems that after breaking the jaws, there is a minor inconvenience of wiring your mouth shut for six to nine weeks!

To this day, I cannot say whether Dad or the dentists hurt me worse.

When I came to after the jaw breaking surgery, my stomach was stirring from all the blood I had swallowed. I was in excruciating pain, even under heavy sedation. I managed to motion for a mirror, but the nurses refused to give me one. Not one to be denied, as soon as my determined legs could stop wobbling, I made a trip to the hospital room toilet.

I looked at the mirror and was horrified. Amy was not looking back in the reflection, but some kind of cruel joke. Instead of a face, I had a basketball with two black eyes! I crawled back in bed all alone in my hospital room and cried myself to sleep; literally afraid I had ruined my face.

Although the hospital stay was only a matter of days, I was in convalescence for nine weeks....NINE *long* weeks of drinking liquids through a straw and writing on a slate board. I doubted several times that I had done the right thing

And then I met Rob.

I had to go out to work for some insurance papers when another supervisor unexpectedly brought Rob into the break area to meet me. This supervisor and I had not seen *eye to eye* on several occasions, so Rob's introduction was totally unexpected by me and more than likely I suspected, a joke to embarrass me. The black and blue had disappeared, but my face was still swollen, and my mouth was still wired shut.

Rob came over and in a very classy way shook my hand and made me feel immediately comfortable. He encouraged me not to try and talk in my condition and commented on how brave I must have been to have this elective surgery.

I left with a tingle in my hand and a warning in my head saying, "you are not looking for a serious relationship, Amy!" But I don't think my heart was listening to my head at that moment.

Following my instincts and getting my butt off the couch to help with his two little boys when Rob was sick that first evening was "right on." The homemade soup had been a big hit with the kids. Rob, he could have cared less. He looked so sick and puny when I arrived, I didn't care if he didn't care about my homemade soup. He answered the door to his small cottage style house, pointed toward the kids and with a deep throated grunt, returned to bed. While Rob slept, I took care of Anthony (five years old) and Scott (three years old). Both were small in size and towheads to the end. Each had a loving smile, but different. Anthony's seemed open and outgoing and Scott's seemed more bashful, if not devilish.

I took care of Anthony more that first night simply because of Scott's shy ways. I gave Anthony a bubble bath, and then we played Candyland while Scott "the Bashful" peeked around the corner and watched us suspiciously. No amount of coaxing would get him to come join us. I didn't push it and soon Scott was curled up in the hallway, fast asleep on the carpet floor. Gently picking him up and tucking him in bed, I saw what Rob must have felt. The warmth of innocence in my arms made me warm all over as I laid him down between Snoopy and Charlie Brown sheets.

I returned to the living room and continued to play with Anthony. Anthony was extremely intelligent for his age. It was late November, and he was in a festive holiday mood so to impress me he recited the entire 'Twas the Night before Christmas. Being seventeen years his senior and not knowing the poem, I was indeed impressed.

In retrospect, both Scott and Anthony should have been wary of a total stranger. And I will forever be grateful that Rob had enough Christian faith to allow me the privilege of watching his children. He was very protective of them. His divorce had been pending for six months but was not yet final. He confided later that his biggest fear was that his ex-wife would come and steal them away when he was at work. He was so afraid of losing his children that he even worked out a coded conversation with his babysitter to alert him if she showed up.

When the bubble bath was done and Anthony safely tucked in bed in his Spiderman Underoos, I looked around the house for the first real measure of what life must be like for these three men before going home. The house was small but clean and organized. I could tell Rob ran a tight ship. Everything appeared to have a place, and everything was in its place. But I could also tell a woman's touch was lacking in decorating and in those little tell-tale lint balls in the carpet corners where men gloss over the vacuuming.

I gently knocked on Rob's bedroom door and asked if he needed anything else. His answer was "no," but the groan in his voice betrayed how he must have felt. After one last tuck-in of the boys, I quietly slipped out into the crisp fall air. I left feeling good about what I had done. I just wasn't sure if it was the act or who I had performed it for that gave me the warmest feeling inside.

As soon as Rob was feeling better, he called and asked me out; under the pretense of thanking me for the "inconvenience" of taking care of his kids while he was sick. I flattered myself by thinking it was something more.

And then while on the phone as he awaited my answer, I immediately found myself at an unexpected cross-road. My heart wanted to go, but my head said 'warning, warning, danger Will Robinson!' or something to that effect.

I risked everything and blurted into the phone a little too strongly, "No," then trying to recover as best I could, I quickly tried to explain that I would not go out with a married man, and then held my breath thinking I had pushed him too far.

Instead, Rob surprised me by saying he was really glad to hear that. He explained that after several months of separation he had tried dating a few times but the topic of his marriage status never came up... until now. "Refreshing and respectful" flowed off of his tongue in describing my moral stance, and he promised to not ask again until his divorce was final. He had taken my fear of refusal and put me completely on a pedestal. I was both impressed and on "cloud nine" when I gently hung up the phone.

When the divorce came through, true to his promise, Rob wasted no time in asking me out on a date. Well, if you can call a rousing day of raking leaves with him and the kids a date. He was committed to those boys! But the truth be known, we had a wonderful time!

My triumph of the day was getting Scott to open up to me shortly after arrival. I was so pleased with myself! We all wanted to go hit the leaves in the back yard but Scott was being his usual bashful self. We coaxed and coaxed with no success. That's when the maternal instinct in me kicked in. I produced a piece of fruity gum out of my coat pocket and the bashful melted away. He smiled, and I smiled back triumphantly as he reached around the hallway corner and took my offering. Our first real communication...and it was a bribe!

We raked the leaves into a mountain of color and jumping in, giggled and tickled wildly all the while. Then we would re-rake them into a pile and do it all over again. When our childish energy was spent, we whiled the rest of the day away with Rob and the boys proudly sharing old picture albums over steaming hot cocoa. When we got to pictures of the kids' natural mother, the room fell eerily silent. I studied Anthony as he gently touched one of him and her together.

Scott, at only age three, didn't seem disturbed by pictures of "Mom." Instead his eyes were radar on his brother. I could sense that he was tuned into Anthony's pain and not his own. Somewhere along the way, I found that maternal instinct I didn't even know existed, tugging deep inside my chest again.

Rob never once made a romantic move toward me all day. I really appreciated being treated as a friend and an adult, and not just a date or a conquest. He hugged me gently as he helped me on with my jacket at the end of the long day. We connected eyes and I found myself not wanting to pull away. The fact that he didn't kiss me that first night made me want him all the more. Closing the door to my car, I touched my mouth and imagined what his kiss would have been like.

I liked what I imagined. It was the best day of my life...until I got home. Then Mom started giving me a hard time.

"What you mean he wife gone? He must be baddddd! No mutter leave kids unless husband baddddd. You stay away! You hear?" She looked at me like I was crazy, sporting a crazed look of her own. By now Mom hated all men, so I pushed back.

"Why do you assume he did anything wrong? I've heard nothing but nice things about him at work. And he treats me like a lady, for the first time in my life like *a real lady!* What's so wrong with that?"

But Mom had a point, to a point. I had to find out what went wrong. I couldn't commit myself to even a friendship, if I had the least little doubt that he was an abusive man. The look of Anthony hovering over his mother's picture and the stone silence that had fallen on the room made me as curious as a cat. The next time, if there is a next time, I would have to find out what happened to Rob's marriage.

I didn't have to wait long. Rob called and made another Saturday date. I sensed that either the day would be wonderful, or it could end very badly, but I was determined to get all the answers to Mom's questions and I supposed, some of mine.

Rob greeted me with open arms and a playful hug and welcomed me into his home for the third time. He was dressed in blue jeans and a flannel shirt, apparently a holdover from his farmer childhood. This time Rob seemed to have planned some alone time, which was all right with me. He had the kids set up to play in their bedroom and shooed them off after short bouncy hugs from each of them.

While the kids played quietly, Rob spent time sharing his life with me. He pulled out some scribbling of poems he had written while suffering through the pains of divorce. It was very sad and romantic at the same time, and I found it touching that he felt comfortable enough to share his innermost feelings with me. I hoped silently I was the first.

When I felt the moment was right I cleared my throat, shifted my weight and tucking my legs under me on the couch, I asked, "I hope I'm not prying but I'm curious. Why did Jonnie leave? I mean, what could have gone so awfully wrong for her to leave her kids? Does she ever call or see them? Do you still see her?"

"Whoa. One question at a time," Rob pleaded. I guess I had gotten a little more curious than I had realized.

"First, Jonnie is several hundred miles away and has little contact, with any of us. And as you know, now that the divorce is final, I have custody of the children. As to what happened; that's a little more difficult. One, I spent too much time at work. I'm a supervisor on salary, so I have obligations that the normal hourly worker doesn't have. But that's not so unique in business today. What really didn't help was that I was on second shift. You should never leave a newlywed wife alone in the evenings...for five years...."

"So she found someone else?"

"Yesss," he responded hesitantly. "You could say that. She took a job working evenings as well, and somewhere along the way developed a close relationship with another co-worker; too close of a relationship. One thing led to another and as they say, the rest is history. However, over time I have come to realize that it takes two to end a marriage. I must not have been doing some things right to make her look the other way."

"What did your family say? I can tell by your pictures you have a close family."

"My family has been very supportive. The separation was a shock to them. They were about as close to Jonnie as to me. My Mom considered her another daughter. And it tears them up to be in another state while the boys and I are here in Indiana, pretty much alone and on our own."

Pausing for a moment of reflection, Rob shifted his weight on the couch and continued on, "There were few visible signs of her unhappiness, at least that I could tell – until it was too late. Maybe the biggest problem was that we didn't talk as intimately, and as often as we should have. She was excellent with the children. She made them clothes and planned intricate parties. She was active in school and church. Her leaving was the last thing on everyone's mind. We had dated four years and were married six. After ten years, I thought I knew her needs, when in reality I didn't. I assumed too much." Pausing, he finished by saying, "I won't make that mistake again."

Breaking the sober conversation, Rob asked if I wanted anything to eat or drink and then without waiting for my reply, disappeared into the kitchen. Meanwhile I sat and pondered his closing statement, which I found unsettling. I wasn't sure if he meant he learned from the mistakes and won't repeat them in a future relationship, or that he has already decided he would never marry again. A few minutes later he reappeared with an imitation sterling silver tray, ornately decorated with fruit, cheese and cracker snacks and placed it on the coffee table.

"Oh, I forgot the drinks!" Rob exclaimed as he jumped back up and pulled the disappearing act one more time.

After what seemed an inordinate amount of time, I hollered, "What are you doing in there?" I could hear the clicking and clattering of glasses in the kitchen, but had no idea what was taking so long. Then without warning, Rob came rushing around the corner and slid in next to me on the couch as if he was a baseball player sliding into home base. One moment I was alone and the next moment I had this grown man, with all of his man-size problems sliding his head on my lap, lying face up. Before I could catch my breath, he quickly pulled my head to his, and our lips met.

I did not resist. My entire body tingled from the chemistry flowing between us. Instantly I was aware that I was flushed from both embarrassment and not wanting the kiss to end.

"Holy cow. Where did that come from?" I said breathlessly as we pulled apart.

"Are you complaining?" he asked, as flushed as I was.

"Are you kidding? Did you feel what I felt? I have never felt that before!"

He gently pulled my head down and gave me a second longer kiss. It was a mystical magic I could not put into words.

And for the first time in my life, I was speechless.

• • • •

Rob and I have been dating almost six months now.

I had no idea why the summons to his house on this Sunday evening as I drove my Pontiac Sunbird into his driveway. He had said he wanted to show off his cooking skills and not just out of a can. All I knew was that the more I had learned about Rob and his family and got to know his children, the more I fell in love – with all of them. I was loving life for the first time. It was like I had never been alive before.

I knocked on the front door and with what had become my habit, let myself in. The air smelled of freshener and furniture polish as I entered. Inside I was startled to find the living room dark, save two glowing candles. There sitting in front of me was the coffee table, adorned with two white pillar candles burning brightly. The candles were flanked on three sides with dark red roses. It was a picture perfect setting but I had no idea *why*. As I slowly moved closer for a curious look, I noticed the something sitting on the fourth side of the burning candles facing me. The fourth side held a sparkling diamond ring with each cut facet reflecting the dancing candle light.

When I reached over and picked up the ring, my ears were greeted with tiny giggles. I looked over my shoulder to see three approaching men, one grown and two half-pints as they peeked around the corner of the hallway. They were all dressed in their Sunday suits, right down to neckties. Rob approached and placing his firm hands on my weak shoulders, he guided me to the couch.

All three of my men knelt in unison, and in turn each asked me to marry them, starting with Rob, "My kids go where I go, and I feel they should be a part of this marriage proposal."

For the second time in my life, I have no words. Sitting there and drinking it all in, I couldn't believe what I was seeing and hearing. Rob and Anthony were on bended knee while poor innocent Scott was struggling with his balance as he hunched down in a squat. I didn't realize I was crying until Scott catapulted onto my lap and started wiping my tears away.

"They're tears of happiness, Scottie," Rob said choking back his own emotions. Without my permission, Anthony picked up my left hand in his tiny palm and Rob slipped the ring on my finger. It was gold with one diamond in the middle flanked by two smaller ones.

"The smaller diamonds are from Scottie and me," Anthony announced triumphantly. I didn't feel the need to say "yes" as my tears shouted my answer. I just gathered them in my arms and gave them all the love my heart was feeling. I had to give some away because my spilling heart couldn't hold all of it.

I started making wedding arrangements the next day. Money was tight for the both of us with me still taking college classes and my leftover medical expenses from my jaw surgery. Rob was still recovering from the expense of the divorce, catching up past bills and such, and from providing for three mouths on one income.

But I didn't care about money. I took a second job waiting tables to help pay for the wedding. The job helped with the expenses but it didn't keep my mind off of what was fast becoming a problem for me.

Instead of feeling joy, withdrawal is more the order of each day. I knew deep down what was the matter, and I knew this day would come. I just hadn't thought it would come so fast. I was head over heels in love, but I couldn't continue a relationship built on omissions of truth. My past would come out eventually so *I knew Rob was going to hear it.* It was only right that he hear it from me, *and before we were married.*

My mind made up, I gave Rob a note at work to set up the evening.

"Dear Rob,
I tore this poem out of a magazine. I know it is not as good as some of yours but it explains my feelings right

now. Before I tell you what I have hidden inside me, I beg you to please have an open mind and hopefully afterward, you'll have an open heart. You have come from a wonderful nurturing family who has stood by you and the kids during your toughest challenges in life. I wasn't as lucky as you and quite frankly, I fear telling you some of my emotional baggage that comes with me.

Read the poem and then tonight, I have something to tell you.

"Ideals Are Like Stars"
by
Helen Steiner Rice

In this world of casual carelessness it's discouraging to try
To keep moral standards and our ideals high.
We are ridiculed and laughed at by the smart sophisticate,
Who proclaims in brittle banter that such things are out of date.
But no life is worth the living unless it's built on truth,
As we lay our life's foundation and eye the golden years of youth.
So allow no one to stop you or hinder you from laying,
A firm and strong foundation made in faith, love and praying.
And remember that ideals are like stars up in the sky,
You can never really read them hanging in the heavens high.
But unlike the mighty mariner who sailed the storm tossed sea,
And used the stars to chart his course with skill and certainty.
You too, can chart your course in life with high ideas and love,
For high ideals are like the stars which light the sky above.
You cannot ever reach them but lift your heart up high,
Your life will be as shining as the stars up in the sky.

I'll be over this evening after the children are in bed. Amy"

The house was dark when I approached, all except for the dim light of the television dully shining through the living room curtains. It was 9:00 PM, and I knew the kids would be in bed. More than likely I will find Rob folding laundry while watching television, as was his habit in an effort to keep up with his housework. The gravel crunched underneath my shoes as I stepped from the car and made my way toward the house.

It seems all my senses are heightened as I was fast doubting what I was about to do. I couldn't help but feel sheer dread as the black cloud of my past followed me into the house. Rob, so used to my upbeat attitude, could tell something was terribly wrong as soon as he set eyes upon me.

"What's the matter, Amy? You don't want to back out of getting married, do you? I've been on pins and needles ever since I found your note today."

"No, that's not it at all, Rob," I said as I closed the door and sat down on the opposite end of the couch. "I've got some things to tell you about me and my family. Some things that you may not think are very nice, but I want you to hear them from me instead of someone else later. I want our relationship to be based on truth. I would hate myself if you married me and then later on regretted it."

Shifting my weight and clearing my throat, I slowly began. But in time, my planned controlled cleansing built into a flood of emotion I couldn't stop. Every detail came out. Every sordid detail. Rob respectfully kept his distance as I told my tale. I could see Rob's jaw tighten part way through, but I plowed on. In the end, a single tear ran down his cheek as he slid the length of the couch to take a position next to me. I felt naked and completely exposed fearing his next move, his next word – his possible rejection…

It was as if history repeated itself as Rob surprised me once again.

"Oh honey, I had no idea," he cooed as he gathered me tenderly in his arms. All my fears were washed away as he held me like a fragile piece of glass. He allowed me to sob into his chest as if I were a waterfall he was patiently waiting to run dry. Periodically my sobs were broken with an "I am so sorry, Amy. I'm so sorry," and then Rob would let my sobs flow some more.

Toward the end, when I had spent all I had to offer, I asked with my face still buried, "Are you ashamed of me? Do you still want to marry me?"

Grabbing my face with his two strong hands, he forced me to look him in the eyes and said, "You don't have to hide your face, and neither will I. You've done nothing to be ashamed of. You *were* a victim of many things, but you *are not* a victim anymore." I felt the tension start to seep from my body as he stroked my hair. Continuing to console me he said, "I will never let anyone hurt you again. I promise."

He sealed his love by gently leaning over and kissing me on the forehead.

"I love you," I mumbled, as if they were the most natural words on earth. A year ago I wasn't sure I would ever surrender myself to another man. Now my prayer for a husband had been answered.

"I love you too, Amy. You are the strongest person I've ever met. You not only have survived horrible physical and mental abuse, but you found the courage to tell me about it. Anyone else would have kept that part of their lives hidden, locked in a dark secret; and it probably would have haunted us forever."

I wrapped myself around him. Totally drained he felt like a warm security blanket to me. He could have taken me right there, but we had made a vow to remain celibate until our wedding day. We both felt strongly that we wanted to start out our marriage with purity in our hearts. Instead of taking me, he remained chivalrous, resisting my silent offering. I think he sensed my vulnerability, and he refused to take advantage of it. Instead he gave me exactly what I needed; an open ear and an endless supply of hugs. I felt myself drifting off, eventually falling asleep as Rob relentlessly stroked my tear stained face.

He had succeeded where I could not. Rob had turned back the hands of time. I was no longer an abused child; I was a new woman.

A woman who was a virgin to the concept of love...It was a miracle.

*Unfortunately the mystery of death consumes
more of our energy than the miracle of life.*

Chapter 19

bury the dead and
not the past...

*As I stood inside the cemetery gates, the fresh air cleansed me from the inside
out and accomplished what four funerals had not done.*

*I had always wanted to bring closure in my mind concerning the deaths of
family members in the United States but couldn't. It is sad to say, but closure
was impossible in each and every death in my family up to this point. The
deaths of family members on the east side of the Pacific are the one side of the
family you think I could have reconciled. And of course up until now, family
death was impossible to reconcile in Japan. I was confident that visiting the
graves of my maternal line would help bring closure to the intimate deaths in
my life – bridging the spirit of both worlds if you will.*

*I could sense their presence from the past with me – Martin, Brock, Mom,
and yes, even Dad. Martin's because his death had been too easy to forget, until
now. I was too young in such experiences and had no recollection of his death.
But living through my hellish childhood, I had mixed emotions as I matured
about whether he was fortunate to have missed it, or if he would have made a
difference in how we were treated.*

*Closure on Brock's death is the one I have always struggled with the most,
and his presence is felt the strongest; Brock, the sickly one who suffered more*

than I could imagine and my protector when Kathy was gone. His hormone disorder left him gangly in appearance and unaccepted by many of his peers but I loved him dearly. I struggle standing in the cemetery in this encampment of death, because I was almost eight months pregnant when I stopped by his apartment after a doctor's appointment and he told me he was sick.

I had asked if he was taking his medicine, and he said, "Yes and no. When I need it." After several moments of chastising him, Brock had thrown me a curve. He responded that I didn't understand; that this was different – he was dying. But his response was so angelic, so matter of fact in his calm voice, that I chose to ignore his unspoken plea. I might as well have been the proverbial doctor saying 'take two aspirin and call me in the morning.' I told him his imagination was taking over again and that he should immediately take his medicine. Then I would call him in a couple of days to see how he was feeling. I never got the chance. He was found dead in his apartment two days later at the elderly age of 23; finally freed from his prison body.

I could not have closure on Mom's death because she died on the operating table. She was calm before she went into her heart bypass surgery. She, like Brock, tried to warn me she was dying. She didn't believe that she was coming back out of surgery alive.

I continued standing in silence in what the Suzakis must have thought was a trance as I recalled that fateful day. "God is calling me and my body is too frail to carry on," she whispered in her warning to me. Then she made me promise not to tell Kathy. Mom was afraid it would be too much worry for her. I didn't; in honor of Mom and in part because I was in denial ...again.

With such an empty life at times, Kathy, Rob and I were the only ones at the hospital when she was strolled into surgery. Somehow it seemed appropriate considering how she lived alone, yet it didn't seem fair considering the lives she had recently touched in the hospital. We couldn't visit a day without being told of her roaming the hospital hallways making friends and witnessing for God. As her gurney passed by us on the way into surgery we told her we would see her when she came out of recovery, but she would have none of it. Instead, she had the nurses stop the gurney and leave her for a moment with us.

When privacy with us was granted, she turned to Rob and said, "Please take care of my girls. They are your responsibility now." I didn't believe her.

Six hours later, we were pulled into a private waiting room and told of her passing. Rob was the only one there to prop us up. He gave Kathy and me each a shoulder to cry on and to this day, he has kept his promise to always watch over us. Mom was only 62 years young, so again, I never got to say good-bye.

I inhaled one more dose of fresh chilled air to clear my head and grabbed Hidetoshi's arm. Like the gentleman he was, he led me reverently through the gated entrance. The cemetery was not what I expected. In fact, I'm not sure what I expected. We were in the middle of a rural area that was tucked not too far from the inlet bay of Fukuoka City. The cemetery was nestled between the back yards of four adjacent houses so that you could not see it from the road at all.

The gate was actually an archway with ornate decorations bridging the top of the side pillars that bordered the fence. Immediately upon entering, I reined back on Hidetoshi's arm, stopping him as I took in the solemn view ahead. The cemetery was full of shrines, not markers as we know in the United States. Off to the right, not 30 feet away, was a family deep in the ceremony of burying a recently deceased member. In honor, we paused long enough to respectfully bow to the grieving family and then moved silently to the left.

Now with some distance between us, Hidetoshi whispered that we were standing in front of the patriarch of the Suzaki family – my great grandparents. It was a single shrine since they both were buried together. It was massive and one of the three largest in the cemetery. It stood six to eight feet tall and was twelve feet long by ten feet wide. There were three pillars cut out of slate gray marble granite that I could only surmise stood one for great-grandma, one for great-grandpa and the pillar in the middle for the Suzaki family. It was quite honestly breathtaking in beauty and reverence.

Hidetoshi then moved me further off to the left, stopping at a much smaller single pillared shrine that stood less than five feet tall. Hidetoshi paused with head bowed for a full minute. He broke the silence by pointing downward and said "grandparents and father." I wasn't sure I understood so I repeated his point and said, "Keiko's mother and father and Uncle Ilotta?' He nodded his head affirmatively.

It had never occurred to me that burial of a family could be a community affair. The singular column was decorated with Japanese Kanji that loosely translated, "may they rest in love for eternity." I moved forward a step clutching Hidetoshi's right elbow. I stood with great humility at the head of my maternal grandparents and my Uncle Ilotta's grave and reflected.

Grandpa Suzaki had passed away first – in his fifties. I don't know why. Uncle Ilotta died at the age of 56. He had suffered cruelly for two years at the hands of cancer. Grandma was the exception, passing away at the ripe age of 95. Now after almost 40 years of separation, all three were together again.

After some moments, in unison and respect, we got down on our knees. We were within an arm's length of the monument, so I reached out with my left hand and touched the stone. Subconsciously I wanted them to know I was there. After all these years, I felt I was there for Mom too.

"You want to see?" Hidetoshi asked. I reciprocated with another puzzled look, not understanding the question. Gathering that I hadn't a clue what he was talking about, he reached out and removed a square stone that jutted out in the front of the monument.

To my shock, there were three urns in a small cavern under the now exposed sanctum of the pillar. The urns were surprisingly plain; not decorative at all. In fact, two were gray-black almost sack-like, with a tie at the top. The other one was a snow white kettle, like something you would haul water or cook in.

"Grandma, Grandpa, Father," Hidetoshi counted off as he pointed at the urns from left to right. The he froze in silence again as he stared not at the urns this time but at the ground beneath his feet.

It was my turn to support Hidetoshi. I asked if he was close to his father. Not knowing if he would understand, I pointed to the snow white urn, then Hidetoshi and crossed my arms across my chest. Hidetoshi nodded sadly. Reaching down he pulled a weed out of the crawlspace where the urns sat, pruning his father's final resting place out of loving respect.

Going to cemeteries in America had never afforded me any peace. I believe the spirit that is the person is gone and all that remains is the dust of the body – the borrowed house of God's creation. Nothing had so elegantly driven home that point until I found myself looking down at the dust of my grandparents and my Uncle.

I suddenly realized I was crying. I wasn't sure when I had started or why.

Hidetoshi in turn asked me if I was all right and without waiting for my answer placed a strong left arm around my trembling shoulders. I felt calmness deep inside I had never found before.

It was a peace at the death of my brothers, my mother and yes, even my father that had eluded me for all these years…and I only had to come halfway around the world to find it…

―――――――

The closing of our house went quickly and quietly.

After twenty years in the same town, (the two oldest children now married and our youngest seventeen years of age), I had expected a little more fanfare. It had taken an arduous year to sell the house in Indiana after we had relocated to North Carolina. But now, we were on a short rope of time to close the old house and return to our new home, so I wasn't too disappointed when the town didn't break out in a parade at our final departure.

Rob, being the ever private person he is, was elated. The house selling at last was a huge financial burden lifted, since for the last year we had struggled to maintain two mortgages and a bridge loan. Deferring to his preference for a low key exodus, we had made the rounds to visit a few close friends for a final good-bye the previous day.

Having had supper with our closest of friends our last evening in town, only one chore remained.

The smell of fresh brewed coffee filled the air as we walked into Bob Evans; *the* agreed upon meeting place. I nodded to a few familiar faces, and as we made our way between tables and wondered silently if any of them after a year of being in North Carolina even knew we had moved.

As we were starting our second cup and reminiscing about what we were leaving behind forever, I heard a raspy voice say, "Hi, Amy. I couldn't find your table."

It had been 25 years since my last abuse at his hands, but I still cringe at the sound of Dad's voice. All throughout our marriage, Rob was tolerant for the sake of keeping the peace. Over the years contact with Dad has been sparse but civil and yet, I was still nervous at this last parting. I had never learned to trust Dad completely and to this day still expected anything to happen.

Dad slid in the booth with his current wife Carla sitting directly across from us. Carla was cheery, but hampered with a slight mental handicap; something she was aware of but never let it hold her back. The other notable trait to her otherwise common appearance was that she was years younger than Dad. As soon as she sat down, Carla began giggling at her stomach gas. I looked at her impish innocence, and it somehow made me a little more relaxed. I loved her immensely, so if she was all right, I should be too.

After only one year of absence, Dad's appearance was startling. His skin was greenish yellow and looked like leather that had gotten wet and then dried all wrinkly. He immediately lit a cigarette that further enhanced his nasty appearance. He had lost several pounds but still had a super-sized paunch for a belly. His bib overalls hung to one side with one shoulder strap undone, exposing that side of his belly. I was overcome with shame as he took his seat.

"Do you still have the birds?" I asked. The birds were always a safe place to start. After he remarried, Dad went into the exotic wholesale bird business. At least he called it a business. He had a large walk-in birdcage in what used to be a back porch. Loaded with exotic birds, he spent hours with them. He had them trained to sit on his shoulder or come with a whistle, or sit on an arm. The cockatoos would talk often, peppered with a cuss word or two as an attention getter. There were parrots, parakeets and how ironic, even lovebirds! Dad loved those birds. Locally he was dubbed "The Birdman." I think he liked the notoriety and the recognition – with his birds was the only time he was at peace with himself, which afforded us some peace as well.

"And the dogs, too!" Dad crowed proudly in response to my question. Then turning sour, "I got a bitch of a leg that is killing me. Not to worry though, the new medicine I'm taking is great." He bent over and gave his leg an imaginary rub under the table and his body odor rushed at me when he leaned closer.

Trying to be polite and keep up with the change in conversation, I asked, "What medicine are you taking?"

"It's to get more oxygen to my brain. I forget what it's called. It improves my circulation."

"Is it Cumadin?" I asked politely. "That's a blood thinner. Maybe that's it."

"Maybe. Hell, I don't know. It's a hallucinogenic drug though, or maybe that's caused by the horse pills I got for pain – I don't know; I think maybe it's the combination of the two together, but whatever it is, it's great."

"What kind of horse pill?" I asked assuming he meant 'big in size.'

"It's a 'for real' horse pill. You know, the kind they give horses. Got it from a veterinarian. He thinks I have a horse; ain't that grand! Kills the pain and man, when I take it with that other pill I see every memory of my life as if it were yesterday!"

"You're taking animal medicine?! You shouldn't be doing that and you shouldn't be mixing drugs, Dad. It's dangerous."

Ignoring my warnings, he babbled on suddenly in his own world, "I can recall things from the past that I couldn't recall before. I remember sitting in my high chair as a baby at nine months old," he announced triumphantly.

Rob and I looked at each other as if to say, 'You've got to be kidding.' I was beginning to feel uneasy. Either the waffle I ordered was getting too dry to swallow or my throat was tensing up from anxiety.

We stumbled for responses as Dad continued on about what he was wearing at nine months and what he ate while sitting in his high chair. We tried to be courteous as we listened. Thank God time was hastening us to leave. I looked at Carla who looked back and smiled. She was such an odd match for Dad. Their marriage reminded me of his and Mom's somewhat. He was as abrupt and rough around the edges as they were gentle and sweet. He was always in some type of depression, and Carla was always in a state of happiness. Dad had a short memory, whereas details that required observation such as dates or numbers showcased Carla's steel trap memory. If anyone would know if he is losing it, she would. And Mom, please! No one should doubt the mental ability of someone who taught something as complex as Buddhism or in mid-life learned a second language.

"Rob, I'm headed for the restroom before we take off…and we should be taking off soon," I coyly hinted as I stood up. "It's a long drive to the Indianapolis Airport, and we don't want to miss our flight."

"Wait, I'll go with you," Carla said, bouncing to her feet to tag along.

Hurriedly finishing my coffee and waffle upon returning, we said a hasty good-bye and left. I noticed Rob was in a sober mood as the miles flipped by on the highway. After twenty years of marriage, I could tell he was struggling with something.

"What is it, Rob?" I finally asked, breaking the silence.

"I was debating whether we did the right thing; leaving him like that with Carla."

"Meaning...what? Did he say something to you when we were in the restroom?"

At first hesitating and then finally opening up, Rob began. "Believe it or not your Dad said, 'Now that the ladies are gone, we men can talk. Did you know that if you want to you can make anything happen that you imagine; anything you want. All you have to do is close your eyes. Come on, do it with me. Do you see the colors? They should be there right before your eyes.'"

Rob said he was completely shocked. He had no idea where Dad's conversation was headed but he was about to find out.

"I was down at Jimmy's Restaurant the other day. They got the prettiest waitresses in town – all of them," Dad said to Rob. Then Rob said Dad closed his eyes and furrowed his brow in recollection. Slowly an evil smirk appeared encircling his yellowed teeth. "Now I see her. Do you see her Rob? All I have to do is order her to raise her skirt and she does it! Look at that! Now she's pulling her sweater up so I can see her perky breasts."

Rob said he held his breath not knowing what to expect next. But then just as quickly as his mind had checked out, Dad returned to reality and began drinking his coffee talking about the weather and generally how happy he was for Rob's career move that was leading us to North Carolina. Rob said he sat in silence not knowing what to do. He was concerned but when Dad seemed to snap out of it, he thought maybe he didn't really understand what Dad was doing – that he had lost something in translation. Or maybe it was just Dad's crude attempt at male bonding with his son-in-law.

Then it was my turn to confess. I told Rob I had been equally concerned after his baby flashbacks, so in the restroom I had asked Carla if she was all right. She replied as if sensing my real reason for asking, "Yea, it's the medicine. But the doctors think he's getting better. I'm okay, but thanks for asking."

In the next few miles of silence, I recalled giving Dad a hug for the first time in 25 years, and wondered why. I guess it just seemed like it would be a long time until we see him again and I think subconsciously, I was concerned for his health. He had bear-hugged me back and said that they would come and visit; not an appealing thought, and not a gesture that ranked high on my priority list. In fact I'm ashamed to admit it, but it wasn't on my list at all, unless only Carla came to visit.

We discussed Dad the rest of the way in the car to the airport. Was he dangerous? Did he present Carla with a risk living with him? Should he be committed? Were we doing the right thing leaving? To be honest, we were torn between just wanting to get away and if there was anything we should have done before leaving. Having lived through his abuse, Rob could tell I was nauseated even talking about Dad. In part, he probably hesitated telling me Dad's absurd fantasy *because* of my past. After all these years of marriage, he still possessed a sensitive side in wanting to protect me from painful memories.

I am not aware of Dad ever hurting anyone except family his entire life; not that he wouldn't have liked to at times. That ever volcanic anger seemed to put Carla the most at risk. But she didn't ask for help and showed no signs of fear or abuse. We finally decided that Dad was under doctor's care. They saw him more than we did and we had to confess, we were no doctors. We finally settled on the fact that maybe we were making too much out of it. But just the same, we agreed to call Carla when we returned home and keep in better contact with her just to monitor Dad. We knew that she was the wife and she had responsibility for him, but we wanted to point her in the right direction if she needed our advice.

We also wanted to make sure she told the doctors about his hallucinations and for Pete sakes, to tell them about the horse pills and have them taken away

...and then the unexpected happened.

• • • •

"Your father woke up last night and then collapsed on the bedroom floor!" Carla's childlike voice said on the other end of the phone line.

"He what? What's the matter, is he all right? Are you all right?" I responded stunned. It had been two years since I had seen my Dad at the Bob Evans Restaurant in Indiana. Yes, he had continued his typical weirdness, always had; but we didn't have a clue anything life threatening was wrong.

"The doctors think it was a blood clot. They think he's brain dead and have him on life support."

I felt my knees buckle and my head spin. "Did you say 'brain dead'?"

"Yup. I got the pastor here with me. He's helped a lot. I'm scared. They're running tests and in 24 hours we'll know." Although scared must have been an understatement, Carla seemed to keep her composure on the phone.

My mind turned to her welfare and what she must be going through. "Carla, we're here for you. You know that. You can get through this," I said as reassuring as possible. I sat down in a kitchen chair, not sure I believed my own words. "Have you called your family? Don't you have some sisters?"

"Yes, I already called and told them," she said, and then the phone went quiet.

"Amy, this is Pastor Thornburg. I asked Carla to let me talk to you. In 24 hours, Carla most likely will have to make the decision to 'pull the plug.' But I need your opinion; what you want to do? As the next to kin of a blood relative, it's only right...and Carla worries she will do something against your wishes and then you'll be upset with her. I also understand you have a sister. Maybe you need to consult with her too."

Without hesitation, I said, "Honor Carla's wishes. She is his wife, and we both will stand by her whatever she decides. If the roles were reversed I would never want anyone making that kind of decision about me but Rob. Carla deserves sanctity; the same marital courtesy."

"Well, he's a veteran and will have most of his medical bills covered," the pastor continued. "On the flipside he has no personal life insurance. If he should be allowed to die, I don't know how Carla's going to pay for the funeral expenses. Her immediate concern is for the health of Richard, but it's possible down the road she is going to need the support in both love and most likely, money."

The last comment hung in my ears. I became instantly angry wondering how even in death Dad was going to haunt me. He has been difficult and selfish in life, and he was going to go out the same way. I realized this wasn't a Christian attitude, but it seemed like my cup had reached its limit. Then without waiting for a commitment of our money, the pastor put Carla back on the phone.

Without even asking me the question, she said with resolve, "If he's brain dead, I want to turn him off. Is that okay? Do you think it's the right thing to do?"

My anger quickly subsided as I remembered at this moment in time she was a not a child but a woman and a wife. "Carla, only you can make that decision. But Rob and I will support you in whatever you decide." And then hanging up the phone, I braced myself for the next phone call... to Kathy.

Two days later I found myself and Rob on a plane to Indiana to attend Dad's funeral.

On the plane I wondered if God would be merciful. I shuddered to think what Dad would have to face if God was a truly just God. But even in spite of all the ill past, I hoped and prayed that he had found salvation and had asked for forgiveness before his last days on earth because I know in my heart God's justice is only surpassed by his grace. I had thought most of my early life I would one day dance on Dad's grave and celebrate this day; that I would relish in the burning hope that demons would haunt him for eternity much as he had haunted us.

But now – not so. I found I wanted mercy on Dad's soul so he could see what he had done wrong; what he had missed as a loving father and husband instead of what he had become. In some deep down corner of my heart, I discovered I still needed to love a father. I am sure that in heaven loving my father will be infinitely better than it had been on earth. And loving him in heaven now was the *only* chance I would ever get.

Rob was a pillar of strength, answering the call to be the patriarch of the family once again. He had settled the estates and handled all the funeral arrangements for Brock and Mom in the past. Mom's estate was particularly tough because she died in debt. She had a small life insurance policy; just enough to cover the funeral, but she had signed a home loan that adjusted to her income which was initially poor and then got worse on disability when she went legally blind her last torturous years on earth. Unfortunately, the added loan interest she couldn't pay was just piled on to the principal so at her death she owed more than what she had paid for the house ten years earlier. Rob worked tirelessly for over a year to get her assets closed; selling the house, the furniture and personal belongings just to break even so that my sister and I didn't have to bear the burden of her debt.

Brock had no real possessions, so after he died we just took tiny mementos; items to remind us of precious moments when he was with us. The rest of his belongings were donated to charity. The most disturbing aspect of Brock's funeral concerned Dad and his incessant selfishness, even at the expense of his own son's death.

At first Dad had been too shaken to handle the funeral arrangements. It was in part because Dad was the one that discovered Brock's body. He was so shook up he couldn't identify the body for the police when they were called to the scene, so they summoned Rob to do it. Brock had been dead a couple of days and to this day Rob is haunted by the memory of the awful sight and rank odor cast by my brother's body as he lay sprawled on his apartment floor.

Rob and Kathy's husband Don went to pick out the casket and make all the funeral arrangements. Like with Mom, Rob was careful to spend only what the small life insurance policy from Brock's employer would cover. But when we went to the visitation, Rob was appalled to find that the casket had been changed. Seeking out the funeral director, we discovered that Dad had gone to the funeral home later and had the casket changed to a cheaper rental model. It didn't take a genius to figure it out. Dad was the beneficiary of Brock's policy. Whatever didn't get spent on my brother was a windfall to him.

Kathy was far removed from her father emotionally; she has had virtually no contact in two decades, so the burden of Dad's funeral fell to me. But Rob knew I had mixed emotions about the past and compassionately assumed most of the burden for me. He has been working long distance from North Carolina with the funeral director to reduce costs at every opportunity and still have a respectful service. Rob knew it would be a regret later in life if we didn't.

We also agreed to quietly give money to the funeral director and the pastor to help cover some of the funeral expenses that Carla could not. The balance Rob had set up on a scheduled payment with the funeral home, who graciously underwrote the expense. Although it would have been a burden, we could have signed up to the total expense but we felt it was important for Carla to take some of the responsibility to continue her education into the adult world she was to face on her own.

Through it all, Pastor Thornburg has been the real Godsend. He's offered his church for the service and agreed to officiate the funeral. More importantly, he has offered to counsel with me concerning Dad, his last days on earth, and the state of his salvation.

We were familiar with the Nazarene Church, having lived in this small community most of our marriage. It is a big, modern facility, brick in foundation and as rock solid in faith. As we entered for our meeting with Pastor Thornburg, we found the office to be modest, comfortable, and private. With a heartfelt handshake from Rob and hug from me, we settled in to listen to what Pastor Thornburg would have to say in his effort to move us in Christian faith and charity toward my father.

Rob cleared his throat and searched for words to begin. Instead, it was me not being able to hold back my questions and fears that began.

"Pastor Thornburg, I want to be candid with you. Our household was dysfunctional growing up. We all suffered from immense mental, physical abuse and yes, sexual abuse. My sister despised Dad after her abuse, refusing to have anything to do with him since leaving home. Knowing what I know, I don't blame her. She has always felt contact would jeopardize her and her family's safety. Unless you've been there you have no idea what living in fear, and fear for your children is like.

"I have tried to be civil, praying he would come around someday, but it has been difficult. Many a time I thought I was crazy for holding onto a thought of salvation for Dad still, but hoping for a miracle, I gave him a Bible years ago. I wanted him to ask for forgiveness. I wanted him to amend our relationship; but honestly over all these years, I was never sure I could trust him. His approaches toward me over my entire life have not felt right, and at times have even caused me to panic. And through it all, I have never seen or felt any change in his spirituality that gave me one iota of faith in his salvation."

My voice slowed as it began to falter, until it finally deteriorated into a steady cry. And then I poured out what was really in my heart. "Over the years I begged for God's punishment on him. As a child I prayed for it. I damned him more times than I can count and demanded nothing less than to see him burn in hell. But, now that the moment of truth is here, I find I don't wish for him to suffer at all. Is it possible to get to heaven when he hasn't shown any remorse for his evil deeds?"

I couldn't help but notice the long silence as I tried to restrain my crying. Rob wrapped his arm around me and I leaned gratefully onto his shoulder, the same shoulder that comforted me at Mom's death in the hospital.

"Amy, I guess it's obvious it's been awhile since you have spoken to your father," the Pastor began, "or he simply never spoke to you about it. You see, I've been coaching him in Christianity." What a strange word to use, "coaching." But with Dad it somehow seemed appropriate. "He had taken baby steps toward learning about God and his own spirituality. He was very dedicated to weekly Bible lessons.

He always brought his own burgundy Bible with him every meeting, constantly writing in it."

I lost my breath. "Did you say a 'burgundy' Bible?" I sat up from my slump as my back became rigid with attention.

"Yes…"

"Was it a gold embossed American Standard Bible?"

Watching his eyes flitter back in memory, he said, "Yes, I believe it was. Why do you ask?"

I shook my head in disbelief as, in regards to my father, tears of joy flowed freely for the first time. "That's the Bible! That's the one! I gave him that Bible more than fifteen years ago. I had given up on the Bible ever moving him to repentance. I had totally given up, and now – who knew…" I sobbed as my shoulders lurched up and down with the gasp of each breath.

"The Lord knew… Amy, the Lord knew." Pastor Thornburg paused as if gathering his thoughts or pondering some great decision. Then as if his direction was clear, he plowed on. "Look, I don't mean to be cruel in saying this…but your father was not right in the head toward the end," the Pastor continued. "The doctors say he was suffering from dementia. With what I know and with what you've told me, I believe he was consumed by guilt and that guilt certainly contributed to his erratic actions. But Amy, I assure you," he said as he moved closer and gently took my hands, "I assure you; he was desperately reaching out for God's wisdom. Oh, at first he tried some tricks to abuse the church funds, but we were quickly onto him. The church was patient and we've been rewarded. He and his wife Carla have become active members of our congregation and are much loved. Richard will be missed."

I couldn't believe what I was hearing. Were we speaking of the same man?

"Thank you, Pastor Thornburg," was all I could offer as I moved now to place my hands over his. It was as if he had administered a healing touch. I was stunned that Dad found salvation. I had hoped my Bible would be put to use but I had long since perished the thought. "You and your church must have been so patient with him. I know, because most times I couldn't be. You've performed a miracle...I guess miracles do happen. I believe that now."

Rob hadn't said a word. But how could he? How could any of us top the miracle of such an evil man's salvation? I had finally found the answer I wanted and had hoped and prayed for; but had admittedly abandoned in *my* time, completely forgetting about *God's* time...

With nothing more to say, the meeting adjourned.

As I walked down the aisle at the beginning of the funeral service I noticed how beautifully arranged the church was. More flowers than I thought possible lined the sanctuary. Many of Dad's old classmates were in attendance and in their earlier greetings to me, they had spoken kindly of him in his childhood. Many church members were also there, as were our friends to support Kathy and me as we said our final good-byes. I passed Dad who was laid out in his only suit and for the first time I saw no tension in his forehead, no distrust in his eyes, no evil sneer curling his lips. It dawned on me how miserable he must have been, always angry, always fighting the world and always fighting his personal demons.

As the service concluded, I was the last to leave. With Rob by my side, I paused at the casket for several minutes but instead of emotional turmoil, I was at peace. Then I slowly turned my back on my father for the last time. But this time I was no longer running away as I had so many times before. This time I walked freely, and as I walked a poem I had written at the age of eighteen about *my life*, came to mind:

"Life's Experiences"

The golden leaves fall fluttering in the wind reaching the ground with barely a scratch. Like many floating feathers our friend the wind shoots them in a whirlwind, scattering them apart and smashing them one by one with rhythmic blows.

They are no longer soft, but coarse in texture from their sorry journey. With the last sweeping motion of the wind they find their final resting spot under the blades of grass.

The melody dies.

The shrill of the wind vanishes.
And all is quiet once more...

Then it occurred to me...Had I written the poem so many years ago about my life; or my *father's*?

Love is an invisible force. Therefore your time
would be better spent letting it find you.

Chapter 20

homeward bound, the circle complete

Ahhhhgggg! I could hardly take getting out of bed at 3 AM! Not wanting my visit to end we had stayed up until after midnight, sucking up every last memory so we can continually replay them until our next meeting. Thank God I had packed after our visit to the cemetery!

We arrived at the airport before sun up and killed our last fleeting hour pushing food around our breakfast plates, but consuming little. Ai and Uuto were as tired as I was and Hidetoshi and Miyuki as quiet. Shakespeare's definition of "sweet" is certainly different than mine when he penned "parting is such sweet sorrow."

At the airport security, everyone cried almost in agony as I ripped myself away from their clutches, amid a final solemn promise to return. As I passed through the metal detector I found myself wishing, "one week more; if I only had one week more..."

I am sure the Suzakis repeated the scene they had with Rob more than a week ago, watching from the airport balcony until my plane was in the air and out of sight. I suspect if they felt anything like I felt, they had a sad ride home because the first half of my flight to Tokyo was one of the saddest moments in my life. I had come so far that walking away seemed like an unnatural cruelty.

216

I have grown from the paternal family and Mom, Dad, Brock, Kathy and little Martin, to my family in marriage and children, to Rob's family and now finally the Suzakis. The journey begun 48 years ago in my mother's womb is now homeward bound, the circle complete.

I spent the two hours in flight reliving our time together and reflecting back on my journey to get there. I leaned my seat back and rested my head against the stiff headrest. Closing my eyes and opening my mind, I recalled Mom and her contact with her family after three decades of being stateside, to my unreturned letters after Mom's death and to my sweet friend Soshi and her improbable assistance finding the Suzaki family on her visit to Japan.

As I calmed my breathing and relaxed my soul, I drifted to my life woven in between. My husband, my dear sweet husband, who darn well had better be at Narita Airport to greet me; and his family, my children, and as improbable as it once seemed in my life – two grandsons.

My life has not been easy – even after Rob helped rescue me. The <u>tangible</u> fact was that after he rescued me, we were still beset with those financial woes which were little of our doing. It was just "the state of affairs": recovering from Rob's relocation (from my prayer that brought him to Indiana of course!), his divorce, and my medical and college bills. It didn't help that we started our journey together during high unemployment, high interest rates and before long found ourselves with five mouths to shelter, feed, clothe, doctor and provide for.

The <u>intangible</u> was my continued recovery from abuse and the fact that I found myself an instant Mom. My maternal instinct of "wanting" to care for the children was real but I was a tad short on "how" to care for the children. The first year was the toughest, having to adapt to tasks I had never been prepared for, tasks that embody what Moms are. In retrospect I had hardly enough time to consider matrimony, let alone 'mother-dom.'

But over time, my husband and my kids – I adopted Anthony and Scott and then we joyfully added Lee – became my world. Rob had success going back to school for Business Management and climbing to the middle rung of the corporate ladder. Much to my pleasure, he has continued his hobby of writing and has had modest success. Not the financial kind, just the rewarding kind. He has garnered a few poetry awards, been in several collections, one magazine, several newspapers and anthologies, and even added assistance on one Christian song for a dear friend. He has published his own collection of poetry,

<u>Shades of Living</u>, and the "International Library of Poetry" recently had my favorite poem of his, <u>Love's Masterpiece</u> issued on a CD collection. But if you ask him, his pride lies in the unpublished. He has made a habit of writing philosophical wisdoms, having authored approximately 500 of them that give me a headache to read, some are so deep in thought and insight.

The children were all active in Little League and soccer, and Scott in basketball and tennis in school. All nurtured their individual talents in theatre, music and art. Rob and I enjoyed endless nights of church and school performances, as well as Speech Team and Art Drawing competitions.

In school, academic grades came more naturally to Scott and Anthony, but were a struggle for Lee. Not so surprisingly, considering my dose of genes, he became the rebel of the bunch. Rob always kidded that all the kids looked like him but acted like me, and there was probably more truth to that than I care to admit. All have varying college education, with Anthony and Scott successful in the business world, and Lee, bless him, now a Paramedic, having passed his County, State and National certifications last year.

I have enjoyed modest success myself – Rob only having to remind me of that fact every couple of years. I have never completed a degree in college but have attended enough classes to earn one. I was one of the first in the state of Indiana to receive a Child Development Certification for my daycare. I had quit my job in the factory shortly after Rob and I were married to stay home with the children. To earn extra money, I started a daycare which I ran successfully for eight years. Since the daycare, my career moves have mirrored Rob's relocations in the form of retail and medical office jobs. I even earned another Certification, this time in Phlebotomy.

The thought of Phlebotomy and blood stimulated other distant memories.

Every ache, pain and childhood disease of our kids passed before my very eyes as I shifted positions and leaned to the right to stare out the plane window. Every car accident and major medical fears my kids experienced are burned forever in my brain.

Every birthday and Christmas, including the time I caught Rob in the closet at 1:30 AM playing with the kids' toys, are etched for eternity in family lore. I silently hugged the plane's "too small to be good for anything" pillow as I felt a sudden rush of warmth, recalling all those memories fondly.

But perhaps the day that I will remember above all the rest, is my wedding *day. It stands special because it was the happiest and, perhaps, the saddest day of my life.*

———————

"You're beautiful," Kathy assured for the tenth time as we put the finishing touches on my wedding dress. "You look so happy that even with an ugly dress, you would still look radiant."

"Thanks a lot! Are you calling my dress ugly?!" I exclaimed as I playfully smacked her on the shoulder.

I turned and looked in the mirror for the eleventh time. The back of the dress was daring. It was entirely cut out, held together with only spaghetti straps that criss-crossed from side to side. Glancing in my best Greta Garbo pose, I had to smile at my Jamaican hued tan I had worked so hard to get, just to be able to show it off. Turning to the front, I gave the white tiers of fabric that draped along my neckline one last scrutiny. Then I tilted my head back and forth to examine each side of my Lily of the Valley and Morning Glory flowered wreath my friend had designed as my wedding crown. Satisfied, I smiled and pretended that I was Athena, the Greek Goddess of… whatever…

In the meantime, Kathy as my Matron of Honor was flittering with her own last minute adjustments to her sleeveless dark purple dress. I glanced around and wished I could see Rob one more time. Maybe it would take away some of the jitters.

We had made several unique and sometimes hard decisions in preparation of this day. Since this was Rob's second wedding, he wanted a small affair. It was my first and I wanted to shout our love from the mountain top, but in the end we agreed to the smaller wedding. I did not need to start out my marriage with a soured husband.

The church was a modern cathedral with a thousand attendees in church every Sunday. But with the agreed upon small wedding we settled on getting married in a small chapel within the massive cathedral. It's quaint and delightful and almost like getting married in a small country church, only without the country. I actually had picked this chapel out about the time I had started praying for God to bring me a husband. After all, it never hurts to be prepared…

We decided to have both Rob's Dad and brother stand up for him. It was going to be like almost having two best men. Rob worships his Dad, and his younger brother (Rob is number 6 out of 7 kids) has been there for him and Anthony and Scott through every hardship of the last couple of years.

We also wanted Anthony and Scott in the wedding. After their sweet wedding proposal, I insisted! I smiled thinking about Rob having the chore of getting a six and four year old ready to be in the wedding. All three were going to wear white suits. I probably will need sunglasses so I won't go blind if I accidentally look at all three at the same time!

The boys also got the privilege of helping their father choose the wedding cake flavor. Rob chose chocolate, Anthony strawberry and Scott settled on lemon. I should have known... three guys, three flavors. It looks like a three layer Neapolitan Cake!

"Five minutes!" the Pastor's wife said as she stuck her head in the door. I jumped up and started my "are you sure you want to get married Amy" pace. But I was sure. It was my parents that were on my mind.

My parents still harbor much hatred for each other, resulting in both refusing to attend the wedding, simply because I wouldn't ban the other from coming. I sighed, remembering how nervous I was that such pettiness was going to drive Rob to change his mind about getting married. Instead he offered the solution – to have one coming to the wedding and the other to the reception. I shook my head thinking that I am soon going to be raising four kids including my parents, instead of just Rob's two boys. Dad let Mom choose first and she has chosen the wedding. Now I can't help but wonder if Dad will be a "no-show" at the reception.

The job of giving me away fell to my brother Brock. How could Kathy, Brock and I have been through so much and I not include him? He is truly honored to have the privilege; I can tell. He's usually a talker like me, but he is bashfully embarrassed about giving me away. With Brock, his silence is a true compliment.

"It's time," the Pastor's wife said, breaking my train of thought.

"It's time," I repeated in a whisper as I grabbed my sister by the arms. "Kathy, it's time!" I found myself squealing.

"May God bless this marriage," Kathy replied solemnly. Then breaking into a big grin, she planted a sincere kiss on my cheek, and then slipped past me to enter the church.

Peeking out the door, I watched the short procession of Maid and Matron precede me down the aisle, both in step with the organ music. And then... the Wedding March. It was my turn.

"My turn to live," I thought to myself as I emerged from my lair.

With all eyes looking at me, I steadied myself by looking dead ahead at my soon to be family; all my little men lining the altar; all in their sparkling white suits.

Brock was waiting to walk me down the aisle. I glanced at him gratefully and with no disrespect, I felt the twinge of tradition tugging at me. That tradition of a father giving away his daughter and honoring her with the first wedding dance afterward...

...and my father will approach and say, "Princess, would you like to dance?"
I will bow to him in deep respect as he directs my hand to his shoulder, and slips his hand onto my waist, as he smiles in "God's Presence" with a quiet confidence. I will feel safe in his arms as we waltz under soft billowy clouds together.
...I will no longer need to be afraid.
...I will no longer need to cry.
... I no longer need to dream of love, I will be experiencing it.

I slipped my arm into the crook of Brock's. I heard the door squeak as it closed behind me. I took my first step down the aisle and vowed never to look back.

And then I processed my final thought as a single woman – "Daddy still owes this little girl that dance...and someday, I hope to collect it."

EPILOGUE

My Dad told me a few years before he died that his life ended when he was fourteen.

He had survived verbal and physical abuse as a child; beatings so severe he could not walk immediately afterward. He survived child slave labor working in the fields and with the farm animals without proper food, clothing or hygiene. But during that era, hard work as "born" farmhands was expected of the children. So he received the "dawn to dusk" labor and the evening rebukes out of a sense of net worth – that it must be the only reason he was born. And he survived without one other important element in life - love.

That was until age fourteen –

He described the time of his "death" in graphic detail – for the first time in his life not to shock or disgust, but to relieve himself of a half century of burden and guilt.

He had just received a "mild" beating in the barn for not milking the cows on time. He was 30 minutes late. It was because he was "messin' with his 'damn' carrier pigeons" his lifeline to the sanity of the outside world. Grandpa finished the milking just as Dad arrived, failing in his assigned chores for the umpteenth time. After a severe tongue lashing and a slap by Grandpa, Dad was left to stomp away through the melee of cow droppings in solitude and full of hate for his father. His nostrils flared out in anger and were immediately rewarded with the pungent smell of manure and urine. He made his way up the ladder to the barn loft where he most liked it. It was his fortress of solitude, where he did most of his sulking.

The air was hot and muggy. You could see contrails of dust and debris in flight, suspended in the rays of sunlight shining through the cracked and gaping boards that made up the barn walls. Looking down as he walked across the sea of hay to prevent his foot from slipping in the crevices left between the bales, he did not see his seventeen year old sister Francine. She however, saw him. She was plump and unattractive. Her hair was dishwater brown and smelled worse. It was barely kept, Francine having no brush or makeup in sight. Her plight no better than her brother's; she had long succumbed to the desolate life of isolation within the family, a desolation that was already forming in the bowels of my father's mind.

As she watched Dad skulk over to a darkened corner and sit down on a bale of hay, she made no effort to close her blouse in the shadows of the loft. She often climbed in the barn to fondle herself while watching her brother tend the cows through a hole in the floorboard above the milking stalls. She was surprised he had not discovered her before now.

She also made no effort to silence her moans. Perhaps she had always wanted to be discovered. Clearing her throat, she made sure she deliberately announced her presence. Startled, Dad stared for the longest time, frozen on what to do as Francine slipped her hand down the loosened front of her jeans. This was taboo, but this stirred his youthful loins. With no self-confidence of ever having a normal life outside the world he knew, he rationalized "what harm could just watching do?" He became mesmerized by the sounds coming out of his sister's gaping mouth as she kept time with the rocking motion of her hands and hips. Then suddenly his sister stopped. She stood, staring a hole into his eyes and dropped her pants completely. She moved forward toward him, murmuring that she knew how to make his anger and hurt all better.

"Please don't fret," she said seductively. "You're going to like this." She would show him. Soon the pain would be all gone, replaced with the gratification of lust. His hands and mouth failed him as he could not speak or move. *His* spirit already broken, he didn't own the courage to resist as she loosened his belt buckle and started his jeans on a downward path.

To him, that began the end of his life.

Nothing had ever been the same since. He lived, putting up a facade to the public for the remaining years of childhood, but his introverted nature was screaming silently that something was wrong. He also knew it was not his sister's fault. She, like him, was a victim of the circumstances in which they lived and in how they were reared. In another year or two, he might full well have been the initiator if she had not approached him first.

He had resisted her further advances initially but then in time accepted them, and finally became possessed by them. In a valiant effort, he joined the military as soon as legally possible in an attempt to free himself from his home life.

It was alas, in vain – as unnatural desire gripped the rest of his life in a *stranglehold*. Every relationship had no emotional bond, and no consideration for others' feelings. *He only needed to complete "the act."* In the end, this lack of compassion and consideration doomed every business venture, instigated every improper discipline of wife and children, and drove him to every alcoholic drink. Ultimately his life, like his childhood, was awash with failure, until his conversion to Christianity.

I tried to forgive him in my adulthood. As I matured into my own life, I had my own set of problems. Unlike Dad however, I grounded them earlier in my Christian faith. But I never really understood how important both family and faith were, until I went to Japan. Dad never really had a family life... and I had searched all my life for mine –

The difference between Dad and me?

Dad sailed the "seas of his life," searching how to get back a family he never really had; his parents and sister, and later in life his own children and grandchildren. He died, I firmly believe, a Christian, landing fortuitously in heaven but never able to bridge the gap between him and family on earth.

I however am different.

I am striving every day to be rewarded with my eternal family in heaven by being more faithful and loving on earth. Do I profess to be perfect? If you think I am, you obviously haven't been reading too closely. I err and beg forgiveness daily with the lowliest of sinners. But by never letting my spirit be broken, I found on earth what Dad never could…. a Christian family to buoy me when the weight on my life appears unbearable. I am no longer that tiny ship being tossed in John's picture. I am at peace; may Dad be as well.

What may be even more important than finding my family, is the conscious effort I am making with this book. It is an effort to be true to myself. It has taken inner courage to face my pains, and tears have stained every page written. But finding my family has given me the trust in God to protect my yet unbroken spirit. My life has been filled with the two sides of love; darkened by twisted motives and pure as the new driven snow. Up until now I have always been careful to whom I tell my deepest thoughts, feelings, and my personal tragedies. I find that I am either judged or patronized by people who treat me as if I were broken beyond repair. People who have never fallen prey to physical or emotional abuse; who have never had attempts on their life, have a difficult time comprehending the experience and aftermath of such atrocities.

After Japan, I am driven to share my experiences - the good and the bad. My modest hope is that my experiences may swing someone's pendulum the other direction, or at least help them to make a decision to go look for their own peace, much as I have found mine. After Dad's funeral and now the improbable visit to the Suzaki family cemetery in Japan, I feel my past tragedies are truly dead. However since returning home, I am being very careful not to bury them.

Instead, I am moved to share how God has truly rewarded me in spite of my adversities and in spite of my shortcomings. When family abandoned me, God was always there. The times I have been alone were because I was too proud or afraid to trust Him. As usual, I find relief later coming to the thickheaded realization that hey, 'I still *need* Him.' And I *need* the past to continue learning from.

Since my travel to Japan, I have been born again for the third and last time in my life. My philosophy is now a simple one. Do not forget the past. Do not dwell on or bury it - but do learn from it, for as sure as the sun will rise tomorrow, you will have an opportunity to learn from it today.

With my spirit intact and family found, I will forever be a changed woman. But more importantly, I hope that I have started the change in two families that are now destined to be joined forever as one.

Do you believe in miracles? I have to – I'm living one.

Kathy – I love you.

Printed in the United States
124871LV00001B/205/P

9 781592 99933